MANDARIN CHINESE

An Introduction

To my mother Jiang Yuanrong
And father Gao Renfa
Whose lives were like humble Chinese oil lamps
That were burnt out
To give light for their children

MANDARIN CHINESE
An Introduction

MOBO C. F. GAO

OXFORD
UNIVERSITY PRESS

OXFORD
UNIVERSITY PRESS

253 Normanby Road, South Melbourne, Victoria 3205, Australia

Oxford University Press is a department of the University of Oxford.
It furthers the University's objective of excellence in research, scholarship,
and education by publishing worldwide in

Oxford New York

Auckland Bangkok Buenos Aires Cape Town Chennai
Dar es Salaam Delhi Hong Kong Istanbul Karachi Kolkata
Kuala Lumpur Madrid Melbourne Mexico City Mumbai Nairobi
São Paulo Shanghai Taipei Tokyo Toronto

OXFORD is a trade mark of Oxford University Press
in the UK and in certain other countries

Copyright © Mobo C.F. Gao 2000

First published 2000
Reprinted 2002, 2004, 2005, 2006

National Library of Australia
Cataloguing-in-Publication data:

Gao, Mobo C.F., 1952–.
   Mandarin Chinese: an introduction.

   ISBN 0 19 554002 6.

   1. Chinese language—Textbooks for foreign speakers—English.
   I. Title

   495.182421

Typeset by Desktop Concepts P/L, Melbourne
Printed through Bookpac Production Services, Singapore

Contents

Tables

Figures

Preface

This book, like the successful *Introduction to Japanese Language* by Backhouse, also published by Oxford University Press, aims to provide an overview of the Chinese language from the perspective of the undergraduate English-speaking learner of Mandarin Chinese. The common practice in tertiary education is that different textbooks on Chinese are used by different institutions at different times. This book, therefore, is not intended to be a textbook for any particular year of study or any particular course but aims to complement other textbooks used in the classroom.

There is, therefore, a need to single out two points related to the issue of audience. One point is about presentation, and the other is about the content of the book. First, because the intended audience is English-speaking learners, a comparative approach is taken in which many grammatical features and other issues related to the Chinese language are presented, whenever appropriate, in a way where they contrast with relevant issues in English.

Second, there is the question of which chapter or chapters should be read at what time during the period of undergraduate study. A beginner may read the whole book initially for a general orientation and then come back to specific chapters for more detailed information. In this sense the book may serve as a companion for a couple of years in the course of undergraduate study. The chapter on language and its setting can be read at any time during undergraduate study. The chapter on language and politics may be read in later years, while the chapter dealing with sounds and tones may be read at the very beginning. Once a student has established a foundation in the sounds and tones of

Chinese, say, after the first eight weeks, the chapter on writing can be read, or it can be left until the student starts to embark on mastering the technique of writing Chinese characters. By the time the course approaches the three-quarters point in an academic year, some sections of the grammar chapter can be read in conjunction with other textbooks. The grammar chapter can be turned to again for detailed reference whenever a specific grammatical feature comes up in classroom instruction. The chapter on vocabulary can be approached even later, perhaps when the student is involved in the second year of the undergraduate course. Finally, the chapters on politics and discourse can be read later as well.

As I will discuss in detail in the book, currently several terms are used to refer to the Chinese language and to select one is not a simple matter. The title of this book refers to the subject of discussion as *Mandarin Chinese,* and the term 'Mandarin' serves the purpose as a general, but non-technical, term. However, a more precise and technical term may be 'Modern Standard Chinese'[1].

An acknowledgment has to be made that this book closely follows the book on Japanese by Backhouse with regard to its structure and the contents covered. There are many differences, however; one, for instance, is that more examples are given in this book as illustration. Another important difference is that I have added a chapter on Chinese politics and its influence on Chinese language. I have done this because it is my belief that without such a discussion the book would be inadequate in its very conception. Modern Chinese politics has played a very important role in the development of Mandarin.

This book is a product of my experience of being a learner of English and linguistics (my doctorate thesis was in linguistics), a student of Chinese politics, and then a teacher and researcher on the Chinese language and Chinese politics. Therefore the book may, to some extent, reflect my personal views and interests in the way some issues are analysed and presented, and in the way certain issues are focused on while others are dealt with only briefly.

The book covers a wide range of topics. Chapter 1 provides a general overview of the geographical, historical, and social context of Mandarin. The issues of what Chinese is, what Chinese dialects are, and what the relationship between Chinese dialects and Mandarin is are dealt with briefly in this chapter as well. This is followed by a chapter on Chinese politics and its influence on the development of Mandarin. In this connection the origin, content, and consequences of language reform are discussed at length.

Chapter 3 deals with the sounds and tones of Mandarin. This chapter is not intended as an instruction manual for learning the sounds or tones. As any practising teacher knows, no written description or pictorial illustration is good enough for teaching the sounds of a language. Sounds and tones have to be taught face-to-face and through a lot of monitored practice. This chapter, therefore, can only serve as a general overview of the sound system and related issues. In other words, it is a big picture rather than a substitute for tutoring and practice. In order to help the learner, however, Chinese sounds are compared with English sounds wherever appropriate.

In most teaching institutions and increasingly in written materials, *pinyin*, a Romanised script to help with the pronunciation of Chinese and which is used in mainland China, is used. *Pinyin* is, therefore, employed in this book also. However, the student may also find the Wade-Giles system of Romanisation useful since it is still used in some written materials and library cataloguing. Therefore, an appendix (Appendix I) is attached at the end of this book to show the similarities and differences between the *pinyin* and Wade-Giles systems.

Chapter 4 focuses exclusively on the Chinese script, and in particular the writing of characters. Issues dealt with in this chapter include stroke order, radicals, whether character writing is phonetic, origin and structure of characters, simplification of character writing, and characters used in the written languages of countries other than China. Throughout the book simplified characters are used as the standard.

Chapter 5 deals with the topic of vocabulary. It includes discussion on parts of speech, the relationship between a syllable and a word in Chinese, compound words, loan words and translation, the issue of affixes and names, and naming and reference.

Chapter 6 provides a general discussion on some main issues of grammar. These include word order and phrasal structures, lack of inflection, grammatical particles, quantifiers, and finally, sentence patterns. The last chapter attempts to provide some background knowledge for language in use in China. Issues such as regional accents, gender, conversational fillers and phraseology, formal and informal styles, and the politics and sociology of addressing each other are discussed briefly.

Some critics may argue that the topics and issues covered in this book are dealt with in greater depth elsewhere in separate volumes and that all the student needs is to turn to existing sources. While this may be true there are two points to be considered in fending off such criticism. One is that this book aims to bring these topics and issues together in one volume and, therefore, not only makes it convenient for the student but also presents a coherent big picture. The other point is that specific topics such as discourse or Chinese politics dealt with in separate volumes or monographs may be too specialised for an undergraduate student of Chinese.

In order to engage the student, study questions are provided at the end of each chapter. Finally, for the benefit of those students who may be interested in pursuing further any of the topics or issues covered in the book, a reference reading list is provided at the end of each chapter.

I have attempted to make discussions on grammar approachable for the student by giving examples; nevertheless, a minimum number of technical terms have been used. For those people who are not familiar with certain grammatical terms an appendix (Appendix II) is attached in which a number of these essential terms are explained in the simplest language possible.

Apart from the works cited in notes and reference reading, the authors of which I owe my gratitude to, I would also like to thank those who have helped directly with the production of this book. First of all I thank three anonymous reviewers commissioned by Oxford University Press whose valuable comments and suggestions are appreciated and most of which are incorporated in the final version. I would also like to single out Chen Ping, Phillip Lee, Maria Flutsch, Camellia Cseko,

Adrienne Petty, and Eric Zhang for their comments, suggestions and corrections.

Finally I would like to take this opportunity to thank my publisher, Jill Henry of Oxford University Press, without whose patience and encouragement the book in the present form would not have been possible, and my editor, Kate Ritchie, whose meticulous work and professionalism have improved the final product. Any errors, of course, are entirely my own.

ENDNOTE

1 By convention, we will use the term 'Mandarin' in this book. However, it needs to be pointed out that what is described in this book as Mandarin is only a variety of Mandarin, albeit the standard form. The people in Henan speak a different Mandarin to the Beijingers, who speak a different version to people in Yunnan, and so on. It may be likened to Received Standard English, the version of English which has won general acceptance in England and certain other places as the correct or standard version.

CHAPTER 1
Language and Setting

This book is about the Chinese language. Much can be said about its formal properties such as phonology (sound system), morphology (word formation), syntax (sentence structure), and semantics (meaning). These formal properties, which can be studied in isolation from social environment, are of great interest to scholars and linguists. However, as a means of communication, language exists in a community. Languages arise from the need to communicate, and develop as a result of social evolution. Therefore, for a student of a language who wants to learn it as a means of communication, an understanding of the language cannot be separated from an understanding of the society in which the language is used.

By and large, the use of a language is part and parcel of social behaviour, and it takes place when members of a society interact. Therefore, behind the formal properties of any language there are behavioural assumptions based on historical, geographical, cultural, and social factors. This is what we call the setting. The aim of this chapter is to present, in brief, the Chinese language in the context of setting. In order to provide a sense of the big picture, we will also discuss, again very briefly, different versions of the Chinese language, ethnic minorities in China and their languages, and the relationship of Chinese to other languages.

Most speakers of Chinese live in China, but not all Chinese nationals speak Chinese. There are more than fifty different languages spoken in this vast and diverse country. By Chinese we may simply be referring to the Han ethnic group which is the majority in China. However, officially there are fifty-five ethnic groups in China which are not Han Chinese. They are called national minorities in China and most of them have their own languages.

GEOGRAPHY

Land

China has a varied, but in a sense straightforward, topography, with terrain that is high in the west and low in the east. It has the world's highest peak—Mount Qomolangma (Mt. Everest) on the China–Nepal border, and the world's lowest basin—at Turpan—in the Xinjiang Uighur Autonomous Region, which is 154 metres below sea level. While there are vast deserts in the northwest, there is a long fertile coast in the east and south, washed by the Pacific Ocean and irrigated by mighty rivers such as the Yangtze, Yellow, and Pearl. China's climate varies from desert to tropics. In general, it is temperate and humid in the southeast and central south, and dry in the north and west.

The total land area of China is 9 600 000 square kilometres, slightly larger than that of the USA, and almost as large as the whole of Europe. The country can be roughly divided into seven major geographic regions: central, east, north, northeast, northwest, south, and southwest. There are twenty-two provinces (excluding Taiwan), five autonomous regions, and four municipalities—Beijing, Shanghai, Tianjin, and Chongqing.

Population density

China is not only large in land area but also in population. According to official statistics, the population in China in 1994 was 1 198 million[1], easily the largest in the world. In spite of the current government policy of one child per family, imposed most strictly on the urban Han Chinese, the annual increase in population is about fifteen million.

A city of several million people is not considered to be large in China. A distinctive feature of China for any visitor from the West is that there are enormous crowds of people everywhere. However, the vast areas of west and northwest China are sparsely inhabited because of the hostile physical environment—

deserts and mountains. China possesses only about 12% of the arable land on earth[2] but it has to feed more than one-fifth of the world's population.

In China, as in Australia, a large proportion of the population lives along the east and southeast coasts. There is also a large number of people located in the central part of China in provinces such as Hunan, Hubei, Anhui, and Sichuan. In Sichuan alone, there are more than one hundred million people scattered across the fertile Sichuan Basin[3]. Along the east coast, the average population density is about 235 people per square kilometre, whereas in the northwest it is only ten people per square kilometre. Apart from the northeast plain where wheat and other dry land crops are grown, most of the central and southeast coastal areas cultivate rice. In China, as is the case in Japan and other parts of Southeast Asia, rice is a staple food and is valued very highly.

Rivers

Not surprisingly, the river plains of the three mighty rivers Yangtze, Yellow, and Pearl are densely populated. These rivers have not only created fertile land, but also provide water for paddy field irrigation. The *Changjiang* (Yangtze) is 5 800 kilometres long; starting in the southern part of Qinghai province it enters the East China Sea near Shanghai. Its river basin covers Tibet, Sichuan, Yunnan, Hubei, Hunan, Jiangxi, Anhui, and Jiangsu provinces. The second longest river, *Huanghe* (Yellow River), is 4 845 kilometres long and starts from the south of Qinghai, entering the Bohai Gulf through Shandong province. Its river basin takes in Sichuan, Gansu, Ningxia, Inner Mongolia, Shaanxi, Shanxi, Henan, and Shandong provinces. Further south is the *Zhujiang* (Pearl River) which has its source in Yunnan. Its river basin covers Guizhou, Guangxi, and Guangdong provinces; it is more than 2 000 kilometres long, finally entering the South China Sea. All three rivers have one thing in common: they rise in the western mountain ranges and descend to the lowlands through rocky gorges and mountain plateaus, and eventually reach the sea in the east after traversing vast alluvial plains.

Regional differences

Although urbanisation has been taking place at great speed, especially since the economic reforms of the 1980s, China is still predominantly an agricultural country with more than 70% of its population living in the countryside. In recent years, the economic development along the southeast coast has attracted a large number of rural people. According to one estimate, since the early 1990s there have been one hundred million people on the move at any given time, either seeking jobs or performing itinerant work.[4] The economic integration and migration from the hinterland to coastal areas has great linguistic implications. On the one hand, there are increasing numbers of people from the north and northwest of China who are trying to learn southern dialects because of work; on the other hand, rural people of all ethnic and linguistic backgrounds have to speak Mandarin as the lingua franca.

HISTORY

National boundaries

The country called China on modern maps has never been a static geographical entity. For some periods in China's history, the northern boundary was the mountain range which forms the southern boundary of the grass steppes of Mongolia—the range along which the Chinese built the Great Wall; at other times Chinese influence penetrated further north beyond these limits. Historically, the southern boundary of China has had an even less precise limit. At times some parts of what is called Indochina were incorporated into the Chinese Empire.

The concept of a nation-state was not something that the Chinese were much occupied with until modern times. They used to think that China (*zhongguo*—literally meaning the Middle Kingdom) was the centre of civilisation and that people at the peripheries should naturally become part of a cultural China. Over the centuries, the frontiers of the political state have fluctuated while the area of Chinese civilisation has steadily increased—from a tiny state covering parts of what are now called Gansu, Henan, Hebei, Shanxi, Shandong, and Shaanxi in about the ninth to eleventh centuries BC—to a vast empire when the Yuan Dynasty expanded the territory of China to its greatest extent.

Ironically, the two largest empires in Chinese history were not ruled by ethnic Han Chinese from whom Chinese culture is supposed to have originated: the largest empire, the Yuan Dynasty (1279–1367) was ruled by Mongols; and the second largest empire, the Qing Dynasty (1644–1911) was ruled by Manchus. Both ethnic peoples invaded China from the north and became absorbed into the Chinese cultural world. In the case of the Manchus, the assimilation seems complete and final: they even lost their language.

Therefore the history of China is characterised by the fluidity of frontiers and the expansion of cultural influence. The fluidity of frontiers is explained by the fact that the Chinese are less a nation than a fusion of peoples united by a common culture, and the history of China is the record of an expanding culture, more than that of a conquering empire.[5]

Chinese civilisation
The Han Chinese and Chinese culture

The origin of the Han Chinese is not very clear. Archaeological records show that by the fifth millennium BC Neolithic cultures flourished in several parts of the country; however, the origin of these cultures cannot be definitely determined. With the advent of the Shang Dynasty (circa 1600 BC – circa 1050 BC), historical and archaeological records begin to coincide; the Chinese accounts of the Shang rulers match the diviners' inscriptions on animal bones and tortoise shells found during the last century at the city of Anyang in the Yellow River valley.[6]

What is also certain is that the diviners' inscriptions on animal bones and tortoise shells were early forms of Chinese characters. Therefore it can be established that Chinese writing has a continuous history of more than three thousand years. That is why it is often claimed in Chinese history textbooks that the Yellow River is the cradle of Chinese civilisation. As in the valleys of the Nile in Egypt and the Tigress and Euphrates in Mesopotamia, the Yellow River provided abundant water and fertile yellow earth (loess) for farming. Neolithic farmers, the first Han Chinese, hunted, fished, and settled along the Yellow River by the fifth millennium BC.

Subsequently, two distinct cultures developed: the Painted Pottery of the Yangshao Culture, and the Black Pottery of the Longshan Culture. The Painted Pottery people grew millet and made red pottery painted with geometric designs. The Black Pottery people cultivated millet, rice, and possibly wheat, and made fine black ware using a potter's wheel. Both cultures had much in common with the first historical Chinese culture—the Shang.

Ancient Chinese culture was at its highest point during the sixth century BC. The most important ancient thinkers whose thoughts influenced subsequent Chinese history established themselves during the Spring and Autumn Period and Warring States Period, from around 700[7] to 221 BC. The founders of Confucianism, Confucius and Mencius; the founder of Mohism, Mozi; the alleged founders of Daoism, Laozi and Zhuangzi[8]; the founder of Chinese military thinking, Sunzi; and the founders of Chinese Legalist thought, Han Feizi and Xunzi all emerged in this period. It is interesting to note that important Greek thinkers such as Socrates, Plato, and Aristotle also came to prominence at about this time in history.

Chinese culture has made a great contribution to human civilisation. Foremost among this contribution are the inventions of paper, printing, gunpowder, and the compass. Chinese tea, silk, and porcelain are just a few examples of the richness of Chinese culture and civilisation, and the splendid cultural heritage of China. The American economic historian Albert Feuerwerker, who is known for his aversion towards hyperbole, sums it up in this way: 'From 1000 to 1500 AD, no comparison of agricultural productivity, industrial skills, commercial complexity, urban wealth or standard of living (not to mention bureaucratic sophistication and cultural achievement) would place Europe on a par with the Chinese Empire'.[9]

Modern developments
Economic and technological developments in China started to stagnate at the time when there were dynamic developments occurring in the West. Beginning from the sixteenth century,

China started to feel the impact of Western civilisation. Western missionaries brought Christianity, and with it Western science and technology, to the Middle Kingdom. However, Western influence was strongly resisted and restricted until the door of the ancient empire was blasted wide open by the powerful Western gunships, symbolically manifested in the defeat of China by the British in the notorious Opium War in 1840. During the second half of the nineteenth century, China lost every war that it fought with foreign powers—Great Britain, Russia, Japan, and France.

China was divided and gradually carved up by foreign powers, with Russia and Japan occupying the north and other powers claiming territory on the southeast coast. China was the victim of aggression and yet had to pay enormous war indemnities to the victorious foreign invaders. As industrial goods from foreign powers gradually penetrated the Chinese market, traditional Chinese handicraft industries started to crumble, a process that pushed ordinary Chinese—who had already been living on a fragile and subsistence economy—further into misery.

Finally, the Qing Empire collapsed in 1911 when the dynasty was overthrown in a bloodless revolution (by the standard of modern Chinese history) and a republic was declared. However, the President of the Republic, Sun Yat-sen (Sun Zhongshan[10]), was very weak and soon gave away the Republic to the warlord Yuan Shikai. During this time of great change, warlords sprang up everywhere and China was plagued by civil wars, bandits, and poverty. Chief among these wars was the one fought between the Communist Red Army headed by Mao Zedong and the Nationalist government of Chiang Kai-shek (Jiang Jieshi).

Precisely because of the weaknesses and internal divisions within China, Japan launched a full-scale invasion of China in 1936. Under the pressure of Japanese aggression, the Communists and the Nationalists formed a half-hearted front against the Japanese; however, as soon as the Japanese surrendered in 1945 the Communist and Nationalist forces resumed their civil war.

Mainland China and Taiwan

The final civil war between the Communists and the Nationalists lasted three years until 1949 when the Nationalists were defeated and fled to Taiwan. As the Communists took power in 1949, there were two Chinese governments: one in Taiwan in the name of the Republic of China, under the rule of the Nationalists headed by Chiang Kai-shek; and one in Beijing in the name of the People's Republic of China (PRC) under the rule of the Communists headed by Mao Zedong.

Taiwan, supported by the USA and its allies, held the seat for China in the United Nations until 1971. When the PRC was accepted as the government representing China, the Republic of China in Taiwan was driven out of the United Nations. After President Nixon's visit to China in 1972 the USA started to engage in diplomacy with the PRC, but it did not officially recognise the PRC as the sole representative of China until 1979 when embassies were set up in each country. Australia established diplomatic relations with the PRC in 1972.

Under the leadership of Mao, the PRC first tried to form an alliance with the Soviet Union for economic aid to build up the new nation. However, relations between China and the Soviet Union finally broke down in the late 1950s. Isolated and surrounded by a very hostile environment, the PRC began to embark on a self-reliance policy to build up its economy. For a complex set of ideological and economic reasons, and chiefly pushed by the powerful Mao, the PRC launched a number of political and economic campaigns. Chief among these were the Great Leap Forward in 1958 and the Great Cultural Revolution in 1966, both of which had disastrous consequences.

Although the Chinese, under the rule of the Communist Party of China led by Mao, endured tremendous hardship—and some of them even unspeakable suffering—it is also fair to say that China in the same period had gone quite a long way towards modernisation. Although at the end of 1976, when Mao died, the living standard in China was still very low, in terms of education, women's liberation, health care, and life expectancy China had progressed enormously under the leadership of Mao.

After the death of Mao, China, under the rule of Deng Xiaoping, started to carry out the Open-Door Policy and economic reforms. Since the late 1970s, these reforms have attracted huge foreign business investments, and the Chinese economy has remained the fastest growing economy in the world.

When Chiang Ching-kuo (Jiang Jingguo), who took power from his father to rule Taiwan, died in 1988, the Taiwanese economy was already very well developed. Since then President Lee Teng-hui (Li Denghui) has pushed Taiwan along the path of democracy. In 1996, the first democratic presidential elections were held in Taiwan and Lee Teng-hui was elected President of the Republic of China. Currently around thirty nations recognise Taiwan as the sole representative of China while the rest of the nations in the world recognise the PRC as the sole representative of China. China maintains that Taiwan is a province of China; but Taiwan, in the late 1990s, took the bold step of suggesting that it is time for independence, creating huge tensions across the Taiwan Strait.

SOCIETY

Given that this is a brief introduction, only some salient features of Chinese society can be mentioned here. It must be stressed that contemporary Chinese society is not only diverse, but also dynamic and continues to change very quickly.

Hierarchy

Chinese society traditionally was, and still is, highly structured and hierarchical, although change is rapidly under way. One is immediately impressed by the absence of pluralism both in terms of civic organisations and personal opinions.

This apparently is a continuity of the Chinese patriarchal tradition. In traditional China, the father held absolute authority in the family; the head of the clan possessed absolute authority over its clan members; at county level the magistrate was a *fumu guan* (parent official); and the whole country was under the despotic rule of the emperor. When the hierarchy broke down, for instance during peasant rebellions or through palace coups, the country fell into chaos until order was restored.

The Communist revolution in 1949, radical as it was, did not sweep away this tradition. The Communist bureaucracy is extremely hierarchical. For example, Mao ruled like an emperor; so did Deng Xiaoping to a lesser extent. Patriarchal tradition is particularly salient in rural China. In many counties and rural towns traditions die hard. The number one party official is an authoritarian figure who may rule like a small emperor.[11]

Absence of a middle class

Because Chinese society is hierarchical there is not one dominating class. What is called the middle class, in the sense that we know it in the West, never figured prominently as a social force in Chinese society. Even today, after two decades of reform when many individuals have become rich and, therefore, increasingly sharp social differences with respect to material possessions exist, a distinctive middle class has yet to appear.

The mass media is very powerful but there is no distinct class of people which controls or influences it. At every level: the central, provincial, or county, the control of the mass media is in the hands of bosses who are responsible only to those above them. Of course, this is part and parcel of public ownership and of communist authoritarianism. It has to be pointed out, however, that commercialism and market forces have now begun to have an effect on how the mass media operates.

Regional but no class accent

Linguistically, the absence of horizontal class dominance means that there is no dialect or accent that is considered to be prestigious; there is no clear-cut linguistic divide reflecting different classes. Indeed, the Chinese are not class conscious about their manner of speech. Mandarin is the official language, but many of those who are in power cannot speak it very well. This is particularly true of the old generations of government officials. Communist leaders such as Mao Zedong, Zhou Enlai, Deng Xiaoping, and Nationalist leader Chiang Kai-shek all spoke the dialects of their hometowns, or Mandarin with strong accents.

Not only are there many versions of Chinese, but also these versions can be further divided and subdivided because of local peculiarities. People have accents not because they belong to different classes in society but because they live and work in a particular cellular region. For instance, people throughout Jiangxi province are supposed to speak a distinctive dialect called Gan, which is one of the eight major dialects of China. However, the Gan dialect itself is not undifferentiated: the people in Boyang County speak Gan with one accent; those in Duchang County speak with another accent; the residents of Boyang County Township speak a version of Gan that a farmer from a nearby village finds hard to understand; and a villager who goes to Boyang County Town is looked down upon as an uneducated peasant simply because he or she cannot speak the dialect of the town. In fact, people in the major cities of Jiangxi province such as Nanchang, Jiujiang, and Jingdezhen all speak distinctive varieties of Gan. Wherever you come from, once you speak you betray your identity as an 'outsider' of a particular area.

Gender and the issue of equality

With the impact of Western civilisation and Communist ideology, women in China have made great progress in their struggle for equality. In traditional, patriarchal China, women were placed at the very bottom of society. Although footbinding had been abolished long before 1949, traditional ways of suppressing women were still prevalent when the communists took power in China. The Communist revolution brought with it many policies in favour of the liberation of women. The fruits of these policies can be seen across such areas as education, work, and health; in equal pay, the marriage law, and even through political leadership positions.

Inequality

Considering that Chinese women were still completely subjugated fifty years ago, they have raised their social status considerably. However, it remains far from ideal. In politics, with few exceptions, men still hold power in Chinese society. In rural areas, poor families would still prefer to send male children to school while keeping female children at home to help with family chores. The harsh family planning policy hits the female sex hardest, although this is true only in rural China. In urban China there is generally less discrimination against the female sex. In rural China, if and when there is infanticide, the victim will be a girl. This is the case mainly because in the countryside there is no social security system. If the only child in the family is a girl, there will be no one to look after the elderly family members when she marries and moves to live with the family of her husband.

Gender discrimination in characters

Sexual discrimination against women is clearly expressed in some Chinese characters. The original script for 'female' was a person in a kneeling position. The character for 'wife' consists of a female person and a broom (妇). The characters meaning slave (奴), monster (妖), and jealous (妒) all have the script denoting female on the left. One version of the character for 'rape' consists of three females, one on the top and two at the bottom, although it is the man who commits the crime. Some other characters may be interpreted ambiguously; for instance, the character for good is female plus children (好), the character for peace is female under a roof (安), and that for wonderful is female plus young (妙).

In much of the discourse in classical Chinese literature, when a wife spoke to her husband she would say something like, 'I, your humble slave …' To what extent this was true in real life is not clear. In a very educated gentry family this might well be the rule of behaviour in the household; however, for the uneducated, i.e. those who were not indoctrinated by the discourse, there might not be such a rule. In some parts of rural China even today, the husband may simply refer to his wife as *nei ren* (the person inside the house).

Absence of discrimination in grammar

Considering the fact that in traditional China women were looked down upon, it is surprising that there are few discriminatory elements in modern spoken Chinese. Characters which contain discriminatory connotations with regard to women remain unchanged; however, in terms of the manner of speech and sentence reference in Chinese language it is not necessary to avoid sexually discriminatory language as is necessary in English. There is no Chinese equivalent of the male third person singular 'he'—in Chinese *ta* is used to refer to both sexes; similarly, the male reference in '*man*kind' to refer to all humanity is absent in the Chinese 'people' category. The equivalent word for 'chair*man*' in Chinese is gender neutral because *zhu xi* means the main chair. According to a Chinese legend, it was a woman, *Nüwa*, who used yellow earth as her raw material and made man and woman and later scattered them all over the world.

GROUP IDENTITY

In-group and out-group

In a highly hierarchical society everyone needs to find a place to belong. In China, people have a very strong sense of group identity. In most situations a line between an outsider and an insider is drawn either explicitly or implicitly. When a Chinese wants to have a conversation with a stranger, one of the first questions is *na ge danwei de?* (which work unit do you belong to?). There are many terms like *tongxue* (schoolmate), and *laoxiang* (people who share the same place of origin) which imply group identity and mutual obligations.

Group identity in context

Group identity can be scaled according to the situation. A schoolmate from the same class is identified with more than a schoolmate from the same school but a different class. Thus, schoolmates of the same class even after not meeting each other for many years will feel a strong sense of intimacy when they come across each other once again.

Laoxiang can mean people born in the same province—a province of say fifty million people. This identity changes in different situations. Chinese people in the province where they were born use counties or towns as their affiliation; when meeting up in another province, for example Jiangxi people in Guangdong province, they will feel that they are part of an in-group. People may be perfect strangers, but once the same place of origin is established and they speak the same dialect, a friendship is immediately established. Simply because people are from the same place of origin, gestures of friendship such as lending a hand or even lending money after the first time they meet are not uncommon.

The tendency to affiliate so as to establish group identity is also reflected in other social behaviour. A child or a teenager is always taught to call any unfamiliar woman *ayi* (aunty), and any unfamiliar man *shushu* (uncle). A young person is expected to greet an elderly man as *lao daye* (grandpa) and an elderly woman *lao daniang* (grandma). Children are never allowed to address adults by individual names.

This tendency for the Chinese to identify themselves in terms of a group but not as an individual is also shown in the way they refer to non-Chinese nationals as *waiguo ren* (foreign country people), or *yang ren* (ocean people). This usage sometimes leads to absurdities: many who were born and raised in China but live in Australia as Australian citizens still refer to other Australians as *waiguo ren*.

Group identity and discrimination

Language which discriminates against the female gender is also demonstrated in group identity. For instance, grandpa and grandma on the maternal side are called *wai gong* (outside grandpa), and *wai po* (outside grandma).

In rural China there are many clan villages in the sense that all the villagers belong to the same clan and have the same surname. In these villages discrimination against the female gender is shown by how children are named. According to this system, when a male child is given a name, the first name must be the clan name, and the second name must be the generation name. Every male child of the same generation in a clan village will therefore have two names in common. Only the third name of a male child is his own name. However, for a female child, only the clan name is required as the first name; no generation name is given (though in some areas of Taiwan, girls are given generation names too). She is not considered to be a member of the clan after she marries and, furthermore, she is not entitled to any inheritance from her parents.

TWO CHINAS

Even when we talk only about mainland China we always have to remember that there is no such thing as a single entity. Apart from the fifty-five national minorities who may have different religions and different cultural heritages from the Han Chinese, there is also a world of difference between urban and rural China.

Rural versus urban China

Generally speaking, the urban population is more educated, more Westernised, and enjoys a higher standard of living than those living in rural areas.

In the era of Mao, because of the *hukou* (household registration) system,[12] barriers between the urban and rural populations were strongly maintained. There was little migration either way. Although more than seventeen million educated youths were sent to the countryside to 'learn' a practical way of life from the farmers in the late 1960s and early 1970s, most of them returned to cities after Mao's death. Some young rural people were recruited as workers in certain industrial sectors. People in China at this time were not able to migrate freely from place to place.

Urban residents enjoyed a range of welfare benefits until the late 1980s. These included virtually free housing, free health care, free education, lifetime employment, and retirement pensions. On top of these they received guaranteed food supplies at government subsidised prices.

On the other hand, farmers, who were the majority, had none of these benefits. Proportionally speaking, the government spent very little of its budget on rural education and health. Rural people were not allowed to sell their produce at the market; they were forced to sell grain to the state at state-designated prices. The prices for agricultural produce were kept low to squeeze the rural population so as to accumulate capital for rapid industrialisation.

In post-Mao China, economic reforms and the Open-Door Policy have brought about great changes. To start with, the *hukou* system is beginning to break down and rural people are now allowed to travel, mostly to the cities along the east coast, as migrant workers. In some rural areas such as Jiangxi, Hunan, Anhui, and Sichuan provinces, a quarter of the population, consisting mostly of teenagers, has left. This huge migration from rural to urban areas has placed an enormous infrastructure burden on the urban sector. The crime rate is increasing rapidly in cities like Beijing, Shanghai, and Guangzhou. On the other hand, a whole range of guaranteed welfare benefits provided for the urban sector—what is referred to as *tie fan wan* (iron rice bowl)—are under threat as the government tries to further its economic reforms.

CHINESE: THE LANGUAGE

Mandarin Chinese

As mentioned previously and as the following paragraphs will make clear, there is no such thing as a single Chinese language. There are a number of dialects which are subcategories of Chinese and this book is about one dialect which is often referred to as Mandarin Chinese. The word 'Mandarin' itself originally meant 'official of the imperial court' in traditional China. Therefore, the original meaning of 'Mandarin Chinese' was 'language of the officials' and it was these officials who spoke this northern dialect. Since the establishment of the People's Republic of China, Mandarin has been designated as the official language of China, no longer the language of the officials. It is used throughout China and it is designated as the standard language by the government.

Nowadays, this dialect is used, for instance, as the medium in classrooms, on radio, and on television. It is also the official language of Taiwan, and one of the official languages of Singapore, and it is one of the five designated official languages in the United Nations. It is also spoken by many of the millions of ethnic Chinese all over the world.[13] In Taiwan this language is officially called *guo yu* (national language). In overseas Chinese communities it is called *hua yu* (Chinese language). In mainland China it is normally referred to as *putonghua*, literally meaning 'the common language'. Therefore, technically speaking, an accurate term might be 'Modern Standard Chinese'.

Language and dialects

One definition of language is: 'the whole body of words and of methods of combining them used by a nation, people, or race'[14], whereas a dialect is often understood as 'a manner of speaking peculiar to an individual or class, or as a variety of a language arising from local peculiarities, or a provincial method of speech'.[15]

By these definitions, different dialects may just be varieties of one language which are understood by the speakers of all the dialects. English, for instance, is the national language of a number of different nations, and there are varieties of English arising from local peculiarities; however, even though the speakers of English in the USA, Australia, and the United Kingdom do understand each other, the English speakers of the USA, or of Australia, for that matter, may not like the idea of their English being referred to as a dialect of English.

The example of English shows that what is taken to be a language or a dialect can be a political issue as much as a linguistic one. This is more evident in the Chinese situation. Yue (Cantonese), or Minnan (a variety of Min spoken in Fujian and Taiwan), are often referred to as dialects, or varieties of Chinese. However, these main dialects in almost all linguistic senses are separate languages because they are spoken in definable places by identifiable populations and are mutually unintelligible.[16] The differences between Yue and Minnan, or Mandarin, are as great as those between, say, Spanish and Italian in the sense that a speaker of Spanish can understand as much Italian as a speaker of Yue can understand Mandarin.[17] We often say that Yue and Mandarin are two dialects of Chinese, but we do not say that Spanish and Italian are two dialects of one language. One of the reasons is that those who speak Yue and Mandarin belong to one nation whereas those who speak Spanish and Italian do not.

Recently, those pushing for Taiwan's independence from China have been advocating the use of their own language. They argue that their language is not Chinese, but Taiwanese. During the 1996 Taiwan presidential elections, the ruling party, the KMT, and the New Party candidates who did not advocate independence spoke Mandarin to the voters while the Democratic Progressive Party, which was advocating independence, insisted throughout the election campaign on speaking what they called Taiwanese. As a matter of fact, what is called Taiwanese is

Minnan, the language spoken in Fujian province in mainland China. In other words, whether Yue or Minnan are considered to be different languages or varieties of the Chinese language may depend on political and historical circumstances. If Hong Kong, where Yue is spoken, or Taiwan were independent nations, Yue and Minnan would be called different languages.

Language: Speaking and writing

The linguistic situation in China is further complicated by the fact that the written form of the language is very much detached from the spoken form. Although the sound systems of Mandarin, Minnan, and Yue are different they all have the same written script. This is perhaps another reason why they are considered to belong to one language of Chinese. The speakers of Mandarin, Yue, and Minnan speak differently and therefore cannot understand each other when speaking, but they can understand each other in writing. They all write Chinese characters.

Non-alphabetic language

That this is possible is derived from the fact that Chinese, indeed any variety of Chinese, is not an alphabetic language. In an alphabetic language we can more or less spell the way we speak. In other words, in an alphabetic language the way we write corresponds to the way we speak. English is an alphabetic language. For instance, we say [spel] and we write 'spell'. We say [spi:k] and we write 'speak'. So long as we learn the alphabet and a number of rules, we can more or less spell out the sounds we speak. Of course there are exceptions; for instance, in the word 'fish' *f* is pronounced as [f]; and the writing and speaking correspond perfectly; but in the word 'enough', *gh* is pronounced [f]. In order to spell 'enough', guess work is not enough. A classic example is shown in the sentence 'Did h*e* bel*ie*ve that C*ae*sar could s*ee* the p*eo*ple s*ei*zed the s*ea*'. In this sentence *e, ie, ae, ee, eo, ei,* and *ea* all represent the same sound.[18] However, even in the case of 'enough' we spell out the word using the alphabet. It is an entirely different story for Chinese. The word for 'speak', for instance, may be pronounced differently in various dialects, but it is the same character in writing, i.e. 说

Chinese script: Characters

For political and historical reasons as well as the fact that all these dialects or languages have characters (*hanzi*) as their common written form, it is accepted that there is such a thing as a common entity. We need a term to refer to the existence of such an entity. For this purpose the term *hanyu* (meaning languages of Han Chinese, which all use *hanzi* as the script) is adopted in this book. Thus *hanyu* refers to different spoken languages and one common written language.[19]

Finally, it is worth pointing out that due to the influence of their own dialects, the majority of Mandarin speakers speak Mandarin with an accent. Some southerners, for instance, do not differentiate between the sound *l* and that of *n* when they speak Mandarin. A foreigner who has learned Mandarin may hear a Chinese say: 'You speak better Chinese than I do'. This, in a sense, is a compliment but it also reflects the fact that a learner of the second language is often taught the standard pronunciation.

Language variety

So there are many varieties of *hanyu*, a term used in this book to refer to different spoken languages but one written language. Apart from *hanyu*, there are also languages spoken by ethnic groups other than the Han Chinese. These ethnic groups are referred to as national minorities in China.

There are fifty-five officially recognised national minorities in China. The largest of these is the Zhuang nationality with a population of more than thirteen million and the least populous is the Hezhe nationality with about fifteen hundred members.[20] Fifty-three of the fifty-five national minorities have their own spoken languages and twenty-one of them have their own written languages. Of these the most prominent are Tibetan, Mongolian, Uighur, Kazakh, Korean, and Miao. Some are still developing their own written languages. The script for the Yi (Nuosu) language[21] did not became standardised until the late 1970s.[22]

The linguistic situation in China is extremely complex. For instance, while some national minority members speak nothing but a version of *hanyu* as their language, there are groups of ethnic Han Chinese who do not speak *hanyu* at all. Most of the

Hui, Manchu, and She national minorities speak a version of *hanyu*. On the other hand, on Hainan Island more than half a million Han Chinese speak Be and Cun languages.[23] Moreover, among the national minorities themselves, some do not speak their own ethnic languages; for instance, some Mongolians speak Tibetan instead of Mongolian.

The question of how many versions there are of *hanyu* is a matter of definition. Mandarin, Min, Yue, Wu, and Hakka are the five obvious dialects that have been recognised as such for a long time. In 1934, the distinguished linguist Y. R. Chao divided the Mandarin group into Northern China Mandarin and Southern China Mandarin.[24] In 1939, Chao further revised his classifications and subsequently Xiang and Gan began to be recognised as different dialects. The 1987 version of the *Language Atlas of China* further classified Jin as another dialect. According to this atlas, there are eight major dialects of *hanyu*: Mandarin, Wu, Min, Yue, Hakka, Gan, Xiang, and Jin.

Mandarin: Modern Standard Chinese
The narrow but loose definition of Mandarin now is: a sound system based on the Beijing accent, a vocabulary stock based on the Northern dialect, and a grammar system regulated by contemporary textbooks.[25] Currently, 65% of China's population speaks *hanyu*, and of these 68% speak Mandarin.[26] Because Mandarin is the official medium for classroom instruction (although in some places this applies only in theory), and for central radio and television broadcasting, most educated people in China understand Mandarin even if they may find it difficult to speak.

Most people to the north of the Changjiang (Yangtze River) and in Northwest regions speak Mandarin. All over China— from Nanjing to Urumqi, from Kunming to Harbin—most educated Han Chinese speak Mandarin although they may speak another version, or versions, of *hanyu* as well. Many members of the fifty-five national minorities also speak Mandarin. As previously discussed, there are many groups and subgroups of Mandarin, therefore, it is hardly surprising that we will find all kinds of accents speaking Mandarin across China. These accents are, in a real sense, also different dialects of Mandarin, and they arise from local peculiarities, not from class or social status.

Hakka

Hakka, which means guest family, is a language spoken by people from the north of China who migrated to the south a long time ago. Because they arrived after the early settlers they were *guests* as opposed to the hosts who had preceded them. Hence, their language has been referred to as a guest language. The speakers of Hakka amount to more than thirty-five million, mostly scattered over Guangdong, Fujian, Jiangxi, Hunan, and Guangxi provinces. A large number of them have migrated overseas to Southeast Asia and other parts of the world.

Jin

More than forty-five million people in 175 cities and counties speak Jin. The Jin speakers are mostly located in Shanxi, Hebei, north of the Huanghe (Yellow River) in Henan, in the central and western parts of Inner Mongolia, and in the northern part of Shaanxi. There are eight subgroups which can be considered dialects of Jin.

Wu

The total number of Wu speakers is more than seventy million; they live in the areas of southern Jiangsu and Zhejiang provinces, the municipality of Shanghai, northeast Jiangxi province, northern Pucheng in Fujian province, and southern Anhui province. Wu can be divided into six subgroups because of the different accents spoken in different areas.

Min

Min speakers number more than fifty-five million. Some Min speakers are found in Guangdong and Hainan provinces. Min is another name for Fujian province, and therefore most Min speakers are located in Fujian and Taiwan, where the majority of the early settlers were from Fujian. Min can be divided into four major groups which are Minnan (Southern Min), Minbei (Northern Min), Mindong (Eastern Min), and Minzhong (Central Min).

Minnan is the largest of the four groups with more than thirty-four million speakers, mostly located in southern Fujian and Taiwan.

Yue
More than forty million people speak Yue, which is often referred to as Cantonese in English because the language is spoken in the capital of Guangdong province—Guangzhou—which used to be called Canton. Apart from Guangdong province, Yue is also spoken in Hong Kong and Macau.

Gan
The total number of Gan speakers exceeds thirty-one million; they are located along the Fuhe River, the Ganjiang River, and the Poyang Lake in Jiangxi province. There are also speakers of Gan in eastern and southwestern Hunan, southeastern Hubei, southern Anhui, and northwestern Fujian.

Xiang
Speakers of Xiang are mainly found along the Xiangjiang, Yuan-shui, and Zishui rivers in Hunan province. The number of its speakers is about thirty-one million.

Mandarin and dialects: A two-way influence
As we have seen, although Mandarin is the official language of China, a vast number of Chinese are brought up with their own dialects which can be considered different languages. They then learn Mandarin at schools or through the mass media. These dialects are different not only in terms of sound systems such as syllables and tones, but also in terms of vocabulary. In other words, there are words in these dialects which do not exist in Mandarin, and vice versa. Ever since Mandarin was assigned as the official language for the whole nation, there has been a two-way influence. For instance, when the Chinese Communist government encouraged writers to learn from and write about the masses, the result was a body of literature in Mandarin which includes sayings and vocabulary from different dialects. Equally, some new terms in Mandarin have been absorbed into different dialects.

LANGUAGE RELATIONS AND TYPES

Some languages may be related genetically to others in that they have developed historically from a common parent language. We may give this genetic relationship the term 'family of languages'.

The Sino-Tibetan family

The Indo-European family is the biggest of all language families. It includes the Germanic, Slavic, and Romance languages, various languages in India, as well as some languages in the Middle East such as Persian. The language family that *hanyu* belongs to is Sino-Tibetan, which includes Tibetan, various versions of *hanyu*, various languages spoken in Thailand and Burma, some languages in east India, and the Miao-Yao language in China. In terms of the number of speakers, Sino-Tibetan is the second largest language family.

There is no ready-made record to tell us which language belongs to which language family. Language family trees are drawn as a result of painstaking research by scholars and linguists who classify different languages into types after analysing and comparing various linguistic features.

Family features

Languages belonging to the Sino-Tibetan family, for instance, have certain features in common, namely, a tendency to be monosyllabic, tones, and the use of what are often called measure words or classifiers as a part of speech.

Ignoring the complicated issue of what can be defined as a word, and in spite of the fact that in Mandarin many words are composed of more than one syllable, Mandarin is still held by some scholars to be monosyllabic in that every syllable has at least one meaning. For instance the Chinese equivalent of 'proletariat' is *wuchanjieji*. The four Chinese syllables can be isolated to mean: without, property, rank, and grade respectively. By putting them together it means 'those belonging to the rank and file (social class) who are without property', i.e. the proletariat.

Mandarin is a tonal language in that the production of the same sound with different pitches will make different words. A classic example is the sound *ma* which means 'mother' when said in the first tone, 'hemp' in the second tone, 'horse'—third tone, and 'curse' or 'call someone names' in the fourth.

In English the production of the same sound with different pitches renders different meanings only when the sound is used as a one word sentence. The word yes can either mean a real 'yes' or a question depending on the tone.

There are other features that languages such as English have which are absent in Mandarin. For instance, English has inflections such as singular versus plural, and vowel changes in words such as s*i*ng s*a*ng and s*u*ng. English also requires person and number agreement in sentence construction. Thus, we have to say 'She work*s*', not 'She work', and 'They work', but not 'They work*s*'. For a native speaker of Mandarin these are very alien concepts.

Connections between unrelated languages

On the other hand, there are features that genetically non-related languages have in common. For instance, both English and Mandarin are SVO languages (subject + verb + object). Thus, in 'The mouse ate the cheese', *the mouse* is the subject, *ate* is the verb and *the cheese* is the object. The same word order applies to the Chinese sentence *laoshu chi le nailao* (mouse ate cheesé). A native speaker of English, or Mandarin, may take this word order for granted. However, other patterns of word order are not only possible but quite common. Japanese, for instance, is a SOV language. To express the meaning in 'The mouse ate the cheese' a Japanese will say *Nezumi ga tiizu o tabeta* (mouse cheese ate).

Some languages may not be genetically related to each other, but nevertheless have a close relationship as a result of historical accidents. Such is the relationship between Chinese and Japanese. Because of direct cultural contact dating back some 1 500 years, *hanyu* has provided a rich source of lexical borrowing for the Japanese language. Most importantly, Chinese characters were borrowed as part of the Japanese writing system. *Hanyu* also influenced Korean and Vietnamese in the same way. Today, the Japanese still use Chinese characters as do the South Koreans to a lesser extent, while the Vietnamese have abandoned character writing altogether.

Of course borrowing is not just a one-way process. For instance, many Sino-Japanese terms coined in Japan during the Meiji Reform Period were subsequently reborrowed into Chinese when the Chinese were trying to translate some Western concepts such as 'democracy'.

STUDY QUESTIONS

1. Who are the Chinese? Does the term 'Chinese' refer to ethnicity or nationality? What is the difference?
2. Where do most Han Chinese live in China?
3. Who speaks Mandarin in China?
4. Is Cantonese a dialect of Chinese or a different language? Why?
5. What images come to your mind when you think of Chinese culture?
6. When was the People's Republic of China founded and by whom?
7. In what way do you think Chinese society is still hierarchical?
8. How does the Chinese language reflect the idea of group identity?
9. How is gender discrimination reflected in Chinese writing?
10. What language family does Chinese belong to? Why?

REFERENCE READING

Benedict, Paul K., *Sino-Tibetan: a Conspectus*, Cambridge University Press, Cambridge, 1972.

Bodman, Nicholas C., 'Proto-Chinese and Proto-Tibetan: Data towards Establishing the Nature of the Relationship', in Frans Van Coetsam and Linda R. Waugh (eds), *Contributions to Historical Linguistics, Issues and Materials*, E. J. Brill, Leiden, 1980.

Buoye, Thomas M., *A Study Guide for the Chinese Adopting the Past Facing the Future*, Center for Chinese Studies, University of Michigan, Ann Arbor, Michigan, 1992.

Chao, Y. R. et al., 'yuyan quyu tu' (Language Distribution Map), *zhonghua minguo xin ditu* (the New Atlas of China), map 5-b, Shenbaoguan, Shanghai, 1934.

Chao, Y. R., *Aspects of Chinese Linguistics*, Stanford University Press, Stanford, 1976.

Ebrey, Patricia Buckley (ed.), *Chinese Civilisation: A Sourcebook*, second edition, the Free Press, New York, 1993.

Elvin, Mark, *The Patterns of Chinese Past*, University of California Press, Stanford, 1973.

Erbaugh, M. S., 'Southern Chinese Dialects as a Medium for Reconciliation within Greater China', *Language and Society* 24, (1) March 1995, pp. 79–94.

Fairbank, John King and Reischauer, Edwin, *Tradition and Transformation*, Allen & Unwin, Sydney, 1989.

Fairbank, John King, *China—A New History*, Harvard University Press, Cambridge, Mass., and London, 1992.

Fitzgerald, C. P., *China, A Shorter Cultural History*, Century Hutchison Publishing Group, Melbourne, first published in 1935, revised edition, 1987.

Forrest, R. A. D., *The Chinese Language*, 2nd edition, Faber and Faber Ltd, London, 1965.

Gray, Jack, 'Rebellions and Revolutions, China from the 1800s to the 1980s', in J.M. Roberts (ed.) *The Short Oxford History of the Modern World Series*, Oxford University Press, Oxford, New York, Toronto, 1990.

Hansen, Chad, *Language and Logic in Ancient China*, University of Michigan Press, Ann Arbor, 1983.

Light, Timothy, 'Bilingualism and Standard Language in the People's Republic of China', in James E. Alatis (ed.), *Current Issues in Bilingual Education*, Georgetown University Press, Washington DC, 1980.

Needham, Joseph, *The Grand Titration, Science and Society in East and West*, George Allen & Unwin, London, second impression, 1979.

——, 1954 onwards, *Science and Civilisation in China*, Cambridge University Press, 1954.

Norman, Jerry, *Chinese*, Cambridge University Press, Cambridge, 1988.

Qian, Nairong (ed.), *hanyu yuyanxue* (Chinese Linguistics), Beijing yuyan xueyuan chubanshe, Beijing, 1995.

Rodman, Fromkin, *An Introduction to Language*, second edition, Holt, Rinehart and Winston, New York, 1978.

Spence, Jonathan, D. *The Search for Modern China*, Norton, New York, 1990.

Wang, Gungwu, *The Chineseness of China, Selected Essays*, Oxford University Press, Hong Kong, 1991.

Wang, Li, Wang Guzhang et al., *xiandai hanyu jiangzuo* (Lectures on Modern Chinese), Zhishi chubanshe, Beijing, 1983.

Wurm, S. A., Li Rong et al. (eds), *Language Atlas of China*, Longman, Hong Kong, 1987.

Xiao, Shiling et al. (ed.), *China's Cultural Heritage: Rediscovering a Past of 7 000 Years*, Morning Glory Publishers, Beijing, 1995.

Zhou, Fagao, *lun zhonguo yuyanxue* (On Chinese Linguistics), Chinese University Press, Hong Kong 1980.

ENDNOTES

1   *China Statistical Yearbook, 1995*, China Statistical Publishing House, Beijing, 1995, p. 59, table 3–1.
2   According to a Central Chinese Television official news broadcast in June 1996, 12% of the world's arable land was an underestimate. Instead, the Chinese government claims it is 17%.
3   Recently Chongqing, the former capital of Sichuan province, was granted the status of a municipality, on a par with Beijing, Tianjin, and Shanghai, under the direct control of the central government. This, in effect, removed about 30 million people (Chongqing and surrounding areas) from the population of Sichuan, even though geographically Chongqing still lies within the boundaries of the province. The largest province in terms of population now, therefore, is no longer Sichuan, but Henan.
4   There is no accurate figure available for this. According to some reports the number could be as high as two hundred million.
5   C. P. Fitzgerald, *China, A Shorter Cultural History*, Century Hutchison Publishing Group, Melbourne, first published in 1935, revised edition, 1987, p. 1.
6   Patricia Buckley Ebrey (ed.), *Chinese Civilisation: A Sourcebook*, second edition, the Free Press, New York, 1993, p. 1.
7   A precise date is not given here because different scholars put forward different dates.
8   As will be discussed in chapter 3, there are several methods of Romanising Chinese words, or spelling conventions. Daoism, for example, used to be spelt Taoism. You will sometimes see Laozi spelt Laotzu, and Zhuangzi as Chuangtzu.
9   Quoted in John King Fairbank, *China—A New History*, Harvard University Press, Cambridge, Mass., and London, 1992. For the history of Chinese civilisation: Joseph Needham, *The Grand Titration, Science and Society in East and West*, George Allen & Unwin, London, second impression, 1979 and his monumental volume *Science and Civilisation in China*, Cambridge University Press, 1954 onwards; and Mark Elvin, *The Patterns of Chinese Past*, University of California Press, Stanford, California, 1973.
10 Following on from the explanation about spelling conventions above, Sun Yat-sen is one such historical figure. The spelling in brackets is occasionally used.
11 As stated previously, China changes fast. Many towns have held genuine elections in recent years.
12 The system was more rigid than the name suggests. It was a system that placed barriers between urban and rural in a very strict sense. For instance, any person registered with a rural household could not move to live or work in an urban area without official approval.
13 Qian Nairong (ed.), *hanyu yuyanxue* (Chinese Linguistics), Beijing yuyan xueyuan chubanshe, Beijing, 1995, p. 1.
14 William Little and C. T. Onions et al., *The Shorter Oxford English Dictionary on Historical Principles*, vol. 1, third edition, Guild Publishing, London, 1987, p. 1174.
15 *The Shorter Oxford English Dictionary*, p. 539.

16   Timothy Light, Bilingualism and Standard Language in the People's Republic of China, in James E. Alatis (ed.), *Current Issues in Bilingual Education*, Georgetown University Press, Washington DC, 1980.

17   Jerry Norman, *Chinese*, Cambridge University Press, Cambridge, 1988, p. 187; Y. R. Chao, *Aspects of Chinese Linguistics*, Stanford University Press, Stanford, 1976, p. 87.

18   Quoted in Fromkin Rodman, *An Introduction to Language*, second edition, Holt, Rinehart and Winston, New York, 1978, p. 57.

19   For many, *hanyu* may simply be another term for Mandarin.

20   S. A. Wurm, Li Rong et al. (eds), *Language Atlas of China*, Longman, Hong Kong, 1987, p. A–1.

21   There are many Yi languages. The Government, in fact, selected one of the written languages as the standard, see S. Robert Ramsey, *The Languages of China*, 1989, Princeton University Press, pp. 250–61

22   Stevan Harrell and Bamo Ayi, Combining Ethnic Heritage and National Unity: A Paradox of Nuosu (Yi) Language Textbooks in China, *Bulletin of Concerned Asian Scholars*, vol. 30 no. 2, 1998, pp. 62–71.

23   Wurm, Li et al.

24   Y. R. Chao et al., 'yu yan quyu tu' *Language Distribution Map*, 'zhonghua minguo xin ditu' *The New Atlas of China*, map 5–6, shenbao guan, Shanghai, 1934.

25   Wang Li, Wang Guzhang et al., *xiandai hanyu jiangzuo* (Lectures on Modern Chinese), Zhishi chubanshe, Beijing, 1983, p. 20.

26   Wurm, Li et al.

CHAPTER 2
Language and Politics

The history of contemporary China is a turbulent one, full of rapid political and social change. Intrusion and invasion by foreign powers, deterioration and the final collapse of the Qing dynasty, rebellions by the peasantry, civil wars, and revolutions—these events occurred one after another. Because of the intensity and scale of these changes, contemporary China has been seen as very violent.

Such political and social changes have, of course, affected the development of the Chinese language. This chapter briefly discusses the relationship between political and social change in China and the development of the Chinese language. I will focus on some political issues which are related to the differences between written and spoken Mandarin. In particular, I will discuss how the cry for political change led to language reforms, and finally how political events influenced everyday linguistic usage.

THE DIFFERENCES BETWEEN SPOKEN AND WRITTEN CHINESE

Before we actually discuss how Chinese politics has affected the Chinese language, we need to talk briefly about the language and therefore show what the problems were. A foremost problem was that there were very great differences between spoken and written Chinese.

In any language there are differences between the spoken and written forms. Written language is normally more precise and more coherent than speech where there is always hesitation and redundancy. In fact, if one speaks too precisely and too succinctly the speaker places extra burdens on the listener.

In Mandarin, the difference between speaking and writing is reflected by the fact that there may be more words consisting of two syllables used in speaking than in writing. Very often, each syllable of a two-syllable word means the same thing. This repetition, however, does not sound repetitive because information redundancy is necessary to lessen the comprehension burden for the listener. In writing, however, redundancy may not be required since the reader can have control of the speed at which they read and can go back if necessary.

In Mandarin, the written style is called *shumian yu* (language of the books), and the spoken or the colloquial is called *koutou yu* (language of the mouth). The degree of difference between them varies from person to person and from occasion to occasion.

However, in pre-modern China up to the end of the nineteenth century, the difference was not a matter of style; they were different languages: the literary language and the spoken language.

This is not to say that either the literary language or the spoken language have always been the same. Throughout Chinese history there were different kinds of literary and spoken languages. For instance, in what is broadly called the literary language there were the archaic inscriptions on oracle bones, the literary language of the Zhou Dynasty sages, the language of Tang and Song poetry, and the vernacular languages of classical novels as well as modern literature. The so-called spoken language has also evolved greatly and therefore differs not only from one geographical area to another, but also from one period of history to another.

The written language consequently does not only refer to the classical literary Chinese based on the prose of the late Zhou and Han periods, but also to the vernacular literary language which first arose during the Tang Dynasty. A general term referring to this category of literary Chinese is *wen yan* (literally 'cultural language').

Wen yan the cultural language

Wen yan was the monopoly of the educated, the gentry, and the scholars. In *wen yan* texts, characters were written from right to left and from top to bottom. Every word consisted of one syllable and there were no punctuation marks. It was not until the early twentieth century that the format of writing from left to right and punctuation marks were systematically adopted for the first time in a monthly journal called *Science*.

Wen yan was so detached from the community at large that eventually it did not correspond to any form of spoken language. It was a purely written language, just like Latin is today. For the vast majority of the people who could not afford to spend years at school, it was not their language. They did not possess any written language.

At this point it may be worthwhile recapping some points about the linguistic situation in China that we have discussed so far. First, as discussed in chapter 1, there are many different versions of Chinese such as Min, Yue, and Wu. Second, although these so-called dialects can be as different from each other as different languages, they have the same written script. Third, and this is related to point two, Chinese is not an alphabetic language and the written language is not spelt according to the sound system of any version of the language. Fourth, there is a great difference between written texts and the spoken language in terms of, say, grammar and vocabulary.

Linguistic unification

The diversity of the Chinese language long ago was recognised as a problem. During the Qin Dynasty (221–207 BC), Qin Shihuang, the first emperor who unified China by ending the Warring States Period, imposed a standard way of writing characters that was implemented throughout the nation as a means to further consolidate the power of the central government.

By the time of the Ming Dynasty (AD 1368–1644), the northern dialect had already started to become the language of the Mandarins (hence the name for the language—'Mandarin'). Later the Manchu rulers of the Qing Dynasty tried to promote Mandarin as the national language. In 1728, for instance, the Qing government set up *zheng yin shuyuan* (Academy for Standard Pronunciation) in Fujian and Guangdong, the two provinces where Min and Yue speakers were mostly located, to teach Mandarin. The Qing imperial court even decreed that those who could not understand Mandarin were not allowed to take part in the imperial examinations (civil service entry examinations). However, no government in pre-modern China (modern China is taken to mean since 1840 when the Opium War broke out) tried to narrow the gap between the official texts written in *wen yan* and the language spoken in ordinary life.

Plain speech movement

Around the beginning of this century efforts were made to narrow this gap and a movement called *bai hua* (plain speech) started in China. The aim of the movement was to promote a form of written language as a standard language for the nation which was closer to the spoken language. By the 1940s the battle was won and the monopoly of *wen yan* over the production of written texts was thus broken.

The *bai hua* style of writing did exist before pre-modern China. The precise time of origin is not clear, however it is quite likely that the rise of *bai hua* had something to do with the spread of Buddhism in China because the monks had to make the textbooks accessible to the general populace.[1] *Bai hua* writings were later used in the written texts of folk operas.

By AD 1200, in the Northern Song period, *bai hua* literature in the form of novels was already in existence. However, these writings were considered unorthodox by the imperial rulers as well as the scholar–gentry. Outstanding novels in the *bai hua* form of language appeared during the Ming and Qing periods, such as *san guo yanyi* (The Romance of Three Kingdoms), *shuihu zhuan* (The Water Margin), *xiyou ji* (The Pilgrimage to the West), *rulin waishi* (The Scholars), and *honglou meng* (A Dream of Red Mansions). These novels are regarded as classics now, but at that time they were considered low class by the government and in official discourse and were not allowed to be taught in schools.

THE CRY FOR CHANGE: FROM POLITICS TO LANGUAGE

By the mid nineteenth century linguistic change as a consequence of the impact of Western civilisation was inevitable. However, it was nationalism that brought the issue of language reform to the forefront.

Nationalism and political change

In order to meet the challenge of Western science and technology, the power of which shook the very foundations of the Chinese empire, the Qing government launched what was called *yangwu yundong*, which is often translated as 'Westernisation Movement' (West here includes Japan) or 'Self-Strengthening Movement'.

This ambitious, but somewhat ambivalent, approach by which the purpose of learning things Western was to outperform the West itself is succinctly summarised in the main slogan of the movement *zhongxue wei ti xixue wei yong* (preserve Chinese learning as a system while adopting Western learning for technical use). Students were sent to Western countries to study science and technology. Modern industrial enterprises were set up and warships and guns were purchased from Western countries. It was thought that by using Western technology to fight off foreign powers the traditional Chinese political, ideological, and social systems could be kept intact.

However, the Chinese political system was impotent; the official ideology looked increasingly outdated and society was on the brink of collapse. China lost every battle fought against foreign powers. These include the Sino-British War in 1840, the war between China and Anglo-French forces in 1856, the Sino-French War in 1884, the Sino-Japanese War in 1894, and the war between China and the Eight-Nation Alliance in 1900. The result of China's two military encounters with Russia in 1858 and 1860 was that China lost to Russia territory the size of Germany and France put together. China was considered to be 'the sick man of Asia', and appeared to be a giant whose feet were made of clay. After repeated defeats by foreign powers the Chinese began to doubt their political, ideological, and social systems. Those Chinese who were politically active wanted change.

After the failure of imperial reforms initiated by Kang Youwei and Liang Qichao in 1898, Republican revolution activities went on for some time until 1911 when the Qing Dynasty officially came to an end. Not long afterwards, the imperial court of the Qing Dynasty was forced out of the Forbidden City palaces in Beijing. However, the abolition of the dynasty and the establishment of a republic did not lead to any improvement in the political and social situation in China. China was plagued by warlordism, corruption, violence, famine, and starvation.

From nationalism to language reform

Being desperate in seeking a solution and true to their tradition of emphasis on moral and cultural imperatives, the educated Chinese began to think that the Chinese nation could be saved only by raising the spirit of the people. It was thought that political change—such as republicanism—was a change only in form, not substance. In order to achieve fundamental change the educated Chinese believed that China required both cultural and moral change.

Lu Xun, who was arguably the greatest modern Chinese writer, is a celebrated example of the educated Chinese at that time. When Lu Xun was young, his father died after many years of illness which had been treated with traditional Chinese medicine. Disillusioned with Chinese medicine, Lu Xun decided to go to Japan to study Western medicine. However, Lu Xun soon changed his mind. He came to believe that Western medicine was not much good even if it could make the Chinese physically healthy while the nation continued to be spiritually sick. Consequently Lu Xun chose to become a writer instead. He wanted to awaken the Chinese people from their spiritual weakness through writing. To write about them so as to awaken the Chinese populace required a language that was accessible to them. Hence the language needed to be reformed.

It was, therefore, Chinese nationalism that spurred the movement of modern language reform. It was not just an attempt to make the written language more accessible to the people so as to educate them. The *bai hua* movement was also a way to unify different linguistic groups to build a modern nation. In other words, the problem facing Chinese nationalism was not just a problem of societal division maintained by the gap between *wen yan* and *bai hua*, but also a problem of regionalism by different dialects. By propagating Mandarin based on *bai hua* the edu-cated Chinese were trying to build up a common language to serve nationalism. That was why Mandarin, which was first called *guo yu* (the national language), is still used today in Taiwan and some other overseas communities.

In order to educate the Chinese populace—that is the major-ity of Chinese who did not know how to read and write—the issue of language reform became a priority. Learning Chinese characters is a formidable task and requires years of hard work. Moreover, the *wen yan* written language was so different from the spoken language that it made reading and writing even more difficult; consequently language reform became a political issue.

Thus, the challenge of nationalism spurred a language reform movement. In order to build the nation politically the educated Chinese believed that a change in culture was necessary. In order to change the Chinese culture they had to start with the lan-guage. By translating Western books into Chinese, translators like Yan Fu and many others who translated Japanese books into Chinese had already introduced many Western ideas and concepts to the educated Chinese. The next requirement was to introduce these ideas to the majority of Chinese who were not educated. To make this task easier, the first step was to make the written language more accessible. Hence language reform was the first step of a new culture movement.

LANGUAGE REFORM AND THE NEW CULTURE MOVEMENT

Lu Xun was not alone in this movement of nation building. The anti-Qing revolutionary Tan Sitong had argued for phonetic spelling to replace characters decades earlier in the nineteenth century. The American-educated scholar Hu Shi, the British-educated translator Yan Fu, the Japanese-educated Chen Duxiu who was one of the founders of the Communist Party of China, as well as the Japanese-educated versatile writer and poet Guo Moruo were foremost among the educated Chinese who thought, like Lu Xun, that the Chinese had to be taught the modern spirit.

Many attempts were made in this direction. For instance, a plain language newspaper, *bai hua bao*, appeared in Hangzhou in 1903. Another one called *zhongguo bai hua bao* (the Chinese Plain Language Newspaper) appeared in Shanghai in the same year, and in 1904, *yangzijiang bai hua bao* (the Yangtze River Plain Language Newspaper) also appeared. In 1906, even the Qing government issued some decrees and documents in plain language.

LANGUAGE REFORM AND ANTI-TRADITION

It should not come as a surprise that in this new cultural movement many Chinese intellectuals became radical and opposed to tradition. In September 1915, for instance, the first issue of a radical journal *xin qingnian* (the New Youth), edited by Chen Duxiu (who later became the first General Secretary of the Chinese Communist Party established in Shanghai in 1921) appeared. *Xin qingnian* influenced many young Chinese intellectuals with its scathing criticisms of Confucian traditions. In 1917, another influential reformer, Hu Shi, published his reform plans for language and literature, followed by his article on the literary revolution in 1918.

The Chinese script, *hanzi*, was a particular target of anti-traditionalist attacks. Together with footbinding, and pigtails worn by men, they were categorised as the three evils of tradition which had to be eliminated. Lu Xun likened the so-called *fangkuai zi* (Chinese characters) to tuberculosis germs in the body of the Chinese labouring people which if not killed would cause the latter to die.[2]

In the same year when Hu Shi proclaimed his famous plans for the reform of language and literature, Lu Xun published *kuangren riji* (A Mad Man's Diary) which shook the intelligentsia and marked the first victory of the literary revolution. This short story was written in plain language, the first in modern literature. It was, both in content and style, a political manifesto of a new culture aimed at the destruction of the Confucian cultural order. In 1921 Lu Xun published the influential *Ah Q zhengzhuan* (The True Story of Ah Q), arguably the best and certainly the most well-known of his works. In the same year Guo

Moruo published a collection of poems *nüshen* (The Goddess), which were not only of high artistic quality but also were written in plain language.

Poetry written in plain language was considered revolutionary because it sounded so unpoetic. Classical Chinese poetry is accessible only to the highly trained because it must be composed according to complicated rules which stipulate rigid tonal patterns and rhyme schemes as well as fixed numbers of lines and words. The efforts by the Western-inspired Chinese intellectuals, who wanted to transform Chinese culture and language in order to save the nation, had advanced the revolution in literature and language so far that it could never be reversed.

ROMANISATION: ABOLITION OF THE CHINESE SCRIPT?

The new style of writing abolished the huge gulf between *wen yan* and *bai hua*. The new cultural revolution had achieved its aim of bringing spoken Chinese closer to written texts. In other words, written texts, from this time, started to correspond more or less to spoken language in terms of grammar and vocabulary. However, reform of a non-alphabetic Chinese script, that is a script consisting of characters, proved to be an entirely different matter.

Just as a native speaker of English acquires the English sound system, a Chinese can acquire the sound and tone systems without much effort. However, the Chinese cannot acquire Chinese characters by just growing up in China. They have to be learned one by one, just like a second language learner. A huge effort is required to learn to read and write the thousands of characters.

The reformers of Chinese language naturally recognised this problem straight away. Some recommended the abolition of the Chinese script altogether. Instead of writing characters, they suggested, Chinese should be written alphabetically. This was called the debate of Latinisation or Romanisation. Even Mao Zedong, who was not Western-educated, said in 1951 that the written language must be reformed and that China must proceed in a phonetic direction similar to the paths followed by all languages of the world.[3]

Arguments against the abolition of characters

The argument for Romanisation, although taken very seriously by some, never took root in China. It was too radical even for the radicals. Some argued that the abolition of characters would spell political disaster for the nation. Character writing had held China and Chinese civilisation together for thousands of years because it had the function of unifying all dialects. Once abolished, all dialects would become different languages, so the argument went.

There was also the artistic argument: the beauty and richness of the Chinese language lies precisely in its script, which is the foundation of the art of calligraphy. What could one do with alphabets to transform them into poetic calligraphy?

There are also inherent linguistic properties in Chinese that argue against the abolition of characters. To start with, there is an economy in the sound system in Mandarin, for instance. There are only about four hundred syllables consisting of more than twenty consonants and approximately half a dozen vowels. Apart from the nasals *n* and *ng*, and *r* there are no consonants at the end of any syllable. The paucity of sounds is, of course, compensated by the tones. However, although tones can be spelt out graphically, they cannot be spelt phonetically. Moreover, the same sound with the same tone can mean a number of different words.

Written alphabetically, these monosyllabic words are all the same while written in characters each one is different. Of course, in everyday conversation words of the same sound and same tone seldom, if at all, occur in one sequence. Therefore the ambiguity caused by some sounds disappears in context. However, the point is a valid one. In order to emphasise this point, the well-known linguist Y. R. Chao composed a poem of thirteen lines. The poem has ninety-three words and they are all pronounced *shi*. Written alphabetically, the whole poem consists of nothing but ninety-three occurrences of *shi*! It is totally incomprehensible. However, it makes perfect sense when written in characters.

Simplification of characters

Nowadays, few people take the idea of abolishing the Chinese script seriously. Still the controversy around reforming the script is very much alive. The debate focuses on whether characters should be simplified, and, if so, to what extent.

Some argue that characters not only take time to remember but also take too much time to write. For instance, one of the characters for 'Tibet' is 藏, involving sixteen strokes and the character for 'dance' is 舞 with fifteen strokes. Writing these characters can be very time-consuming.

In fact, in informal writing or private correspondence, many people invent their own script which is simplified and time-saving. For instance, many people, instead of writing 舞, just write 午 which has the same tone and sound as 舞 but means 'noon'. Hence 'to dance' in Mandarin is not written as 跳舞 (jump dance) as it should be, but as 跳午 (jump noon). Because of the context, confusion does not occur.

The above example illustrates the rationale as well as the nature of the controversy. For some people, to simplify characters for the purpose of efficiency is to destroy the language. However, simplification of characters is not as radical as it appears. The process of simplifying writing has been an undercurrent throughout the evolution of the Chinese script. When the first Chinese emperor, Qin Shihuang, issued imperial decrees to standardise the written script in the third century BC, the simplest form of writing was selected as the standard. The trend towards simplification continued with the development of *li shu* (official script) as an alternative to the official *xiao zhuan* (small seal script).

Li shu greatly reduced the number of strokes and made writing faster and easier. The development of *kǎi shū* (regular script) in the later Han Dynasty (AD 25 to 220) made characters even easier to write. Throughout Chinese history merchants, artists, shopkeepers, and popular writers of plays, novels, and folk songs continued to simplify characters against official sanctions. The situation was getting so serious for the imperial court that in the Qing period the government took steps to admonish scholars who imitated vulgar characters from base people.

Systematic attempts to simplify the writing so as to make it more accessible to the population at large came in response to the political changes arising from the impact of Western civilisation. From 1909 to 1921 Lu Feikui developed a groundbreaking plan to simplify characters, which reduced the number of characters in common use to two thousand. Qian Xuantong, in 1922, presented another plan for simplification and called for eventual phoneticisation.[4]

The momentum was such that in 1935, the then Nationalist government, which wanted to appeal to the common people, issued an official Table of Simplified Characters. However, the Nationalist government became more and more conservative and it subsequently neglected to promote the reform for political reasons. In order to strengthen unity under its leadership the Nationalist government put aside all language reform other than the unification of the national spoken language (*guo yu*).

The Communists, on the other hand, continued the course of language reform. Simplified characters were used in a number of materials published in Communist-controlled border regions during the 1930s and 1940s. In 1955, six years after taking power over all of China, the Committee for Chinese Writing Reform was established by the government, which, together with the Minister of Culture, published the Table Regulating the First Group of Variant Characters.

In this document, thirty-nine simplified characters which had been in use for centuries were officially sanctioned. In 1956 the Chinese government published a Plan for Chinese Character Simplification which abolished twenty-nine characters because they were hardly ever used, and simplified 515 others. In 1964 the Chinese government issued a document which stipulated that 132 *pianpang*s (*pianpang* is translated as 'radical' in English which is part of a character) were to be simplified.

As a consequence, 1 754 characters which contained these radicals were simplified. In the same year, another 352 simplified characters were listed. In 1977 another plan for simplifying characters was promulgated by the Chinese State Council, in which 245 characters were simplified in ways which were already in use.

Simplified versus traditional script: Regional differences
Thus, by central planning, and by collecting and systematising characters that had already become simplified in popular usage

in various parts of the country, the government accomplished the simplification of Chinese characters in the People's Republic of China. On the other hand, in the British colony of Hong Kong, the Portuguese colony of Macau, and in Taiwan under the rule of the Nationalist government, no official simplification of characters has taken place. Although some people in these areas write some simplified characters unofficially, traditional characters have been kept intact. Some conservatives argue that the simplification of characters by the Communists might well be their attempt to obliterate the Chinese past.[5]

A point worth noting in this respect is that in Singapore, where Mandarin is one of the official languages, simplified characters have been officially adopted. However, among overseas Chinese communities most publications adopt the traditional writing system. Even overseas newspapers and publications sponsored or influenced by the mainland Chinese government adopt traditional character writing in order to cater for an audience which consists predominantly of Hong Kong and Taiwanese migrants. It is only in recent years that a number of overseas publications, including electronic journals such as the influential *huaxia wenzhai* (Chinese News Digest), have adopted both the simplified and traditional characters because of the large group of students migrating from mainland China since the 1980s. A Chinese daily newspaper in the USA, the *US China Tribune* has recently started using some simplified characters.

The situation is further complicated by recent economic exchanges between China and Hong Kong, and Taiwan. The pen is perhaps mightier than the sword, but money is certainly mightier than the pen. With increasing economic investment from Hong Kong and Taiwan in China, the language used in Hong Kong and Taiwan has become prestigious. Many northern and inland Chinese have started learning the Yue and Min languages which they used to despise. Some of them even try to imitate Yue and Min accents when they speak Mandarin.

This influence from Hong Kong and Taiwan has also manifested itself in the written language. It is now popular for mainland Chinese to write advertisements, signboards, and brand names in traditional characters because that is how they are written in Hong Kong and Taiwan. This increasing trend has alarmed some people in mainland China to the point where warnings of linguistic colonisation are voiced in the Chinese mass media from time to time. In 1993, a department of the central government, the National Language Committee, issued a circular instructing all the provincial and municipal language committees to inspect all publications and signboards for the writing of traditional characters.[6]

POPULARISATION OF PHONETIC SPELLING

Chinese language reform generally involves three problems. The first is how to narrow the gap between spoken and written language; the second is whether to adopt an alphabetic or phonetic spelling; and the third is, if phonetic spelling is not to replace the characters, how to make characters easier to write. The first problem was substantially solved by the new cultural movement at the beginning of the twentieth century. *Wen yan*, the extremely traditional version of written Chinese is now considered to be like something in a museum, studied either as an academic pursuit, or by experts. Written Chinese nowadays generally reflects and corresponds to the spoken language.

We have already discussed the attempts made to solve the third problem, particularly in mainland China. However, the issue is far from being solved. In fact students of Chinese now face the task of learning both versions of characters. In order to read materials published in mainland China they have to learn the simplified characters, while they need to learn traditional characters in order to read materials published in Taiwan and Hong Kong as well as old writings.

As for the second problem, the issue of whether to adopt phonetic spelling is still not settled. However, consensus generally has been reached on at least two points. One is that phonetic spelling is not to be used to replace characters. Some people actually argue that the discipline of learning to write characters helps increase intelligence; the classic difficulty of typing Chinese characters is no longer a big problem either with the advance of computer technology. The second point of consensus is that a form of phonetic spelling should be adopted as a tool for learning the sounds of the language.

Different systems of phonetic spelling

The need for a phonetic spelling system is illustrated by a very simple question: How does a child or any learner know which sound is associated with which character? A simple but very clumsy way is to be taught orally, character by character.

The Chinese had long thought about the problem, without inventing a phonetic spelling system until the nineteenth century. They invented a system called *fan qie* (contrast spelling) as a tool for learning the pronunciation of characters. In this system, two characters, usually commonly used and easy ones, are put together to indicate the sound of a given character. The consonant of the first character is taken as the consonant of the target character and the vowel and tone of the second character are taken to be the vowel and tone of the target character. Thus the pronunciation of the target character is the combination of the consonant of the first character, and the vowel and tone of the second character. The obvious problem with this approach is that a learner has to know the pronunciation of the two characters employed as tools first.

The Italian Jesuit Matteo Ricci first used the Latin alphabet to indicate pronunciation of Chinese characters in 1605. Following the defeat of China in the Opium War in 1840, a great number of missionaries went to China and sought better means of communication to spread the gospel. By the end of the nineteenth century, all of the major dialects had been reproduced in Romanised orthography, and many Romanised versions of the Bible were produced also. The most influential phonetic spelling system invented by Westerners was the one first devised by a British diplomat, Thomas F. Wade, which was later modified by H. A. Giles for his *Chinese–English Dictionary* published in 1912. This system, which has since been referred to as the Wade-Giles system, is still in use today.

The Chinese themselves since the late nineteenth century have tried a number of phonetic spelling systems in their efforts at reforming the language. By 1911, at the end of the imperial era, there were twenty different phonetic plans in existence. A set of symbols for pronouncing Mandarin known as *zhuyin fuhao* (phonetic symbols) was promulgated in 1918 by the then Republican government and introduced into primary schools in 1920. These symbols were not meant to replace characters, but to aid in character pronunciation.

In 1928 a national Romanisation system invented by Y. R. Chao, Qian Xuantong, Li Jingxi, and several others was officially promulgated by the Ministry of Education. This system was not only a true writing system that could be used to replace characters but also incorporated the tones of the spoken language. However, the complexity of the tonal system was one of the reasons why this system of Romanisation did not become popular.

In 1933, the Communists, and most notably Qu Qiubai, worked with a Russian Soviet, A. A. Dragunov, and designed a Romanised system called Latinised New Script, which did not indicate tones and was not limited to a single dialect.[7] The Latinised New Script proved to be more popular because it was easier to learn. In 1956, a Draft Plan for the Phonetic Spelling of Chinese was published by the Chinese Communist government. This system, a modified version of the Latinised New Script, was designed to phoneticise only the northern dialect in accordance with a government decision to promote a standard vernacular *putonghua* throughout the country. This is what is now called *pinyin* (spell sound).

Pinyin: The system used in mainland China
Pinyin was promulgated as the official system in 1958 and since then has been used in China to teach character pronunciation and spread the use of Mandarin. There are still two outstanding problems with the *pinyin* system. The first is that *pinyin* itself does not indicate tones. The solution currently adopted is to use diacritical marks above the vowels of each syllable. The other problem is whether syllables should be spelt separately or joined up when they form one word. It can be argued, for instance, that the words *pinyin* and *putonghua* should be spelt separately as *pin yin* and *pu tong hua* since each syllable has at least one separate meaning as well as one character associated with it. After all,

pinyin is not intended as a writing system to replace the characters, instead, it is used as a tool to help learn the pronunciation.

Currently both word-spelling and syllable-spelling are practised for different purposes. For instance, in a standard Chinese language textbook, each syllable is spelt separately so as to correspond to each character. The practice adopted in this book is that sometimes syllables are spelt separately and sometimes they are joined up, for different purposes. For example, when there is a need to translate the meaning of each morpheme[8] into English each syllable is spelt separately.

THE POLITICISATION OF LANGUAGE: NAMES AND TERMS

As Chinese culture and society became more and more exposed to Western civilisation, many educated Chinese of all political persuasions were convinced that traditional Chinese ways were inadequate, if not downright bankrupt, for coping with the modern world. As China moved into the twentieth century, often amid violence and bloodshed, piecemeal reform was insufficient to arrest the deteriorating situation. The continuous worsening of China's social and economic conditions led to the rise and eventually the victory of the Communist revolution in 1949.

The success of the Communist revolution brought unity to China and a sense of pride to the people. In believing that it owed its victory to Communist politics, the Communist Party of China, led by Mao Zedong, thought it could build not only a strong and prosperous but also a classless nation by launching political campaigns and by further politicising the nation. Therefore, radical politics penetrated every sphere of life from the 1950s to the mid 1970s.

Politicised terms in everyday language

The politicisation of every sphere of life is evident in the everyday usage of the Chinese language. The success of the Communist revolution in 1949 was thought to be a watershed in Chinese history, and history before 1949 was and still is referred to simply as *jiefang qian* (before Liberation) and after 1949 as *jiefang hou* (after Liberation). Other political terms became part of everyday speech because they were used by Mao Zedong in his writings or in political campaigns during his lifetime.

As the clouds of the Cold War (between the capitalist world headed by the US, and the Communist countries, chiefly the Soviet Union) became heavier and heavier, Communist China first sought help from the Soviet Union. The Soviets were then referred to as *lao dage* (big brother). When China broke away from the Soviet Union in the late 1950s, China became very isolated and had to be self-reliant in the path to modernisation. The political slogan of Mao Zedong, *zili gengsheng* (self-reliance) became a psychological weapon for the Chinese to meet the challenge of isolation.

Political slogans

No country in the world has more political set phrases and slogans than China to describe contemporary development. There was *da yue jin* (Great Leap Forward) in the 1950s, *wen ge* (Cultural Revolution) in the 1960s, *zhi laohu* (paper tiger) referring to the Western imperial powers, *si ren bang* (Gang of Four) to refer to the radical group of Jiang Qing (widow of Mao) and her radical colleagues, *gao gan* (high-ranking official) for the Communist power holders, *zhi qing* (educated youth) for the young people sent to the countryside in the 1960s and 1970s, *shangshan xiaxiang* (up the mountain and down to the countryside) for the rustication movement during the Mao era, and *chijiao yisheng* (barefoot doctors) for rural health workers. Every phase of political and economic development in China since 1949 can be encapsulated in some sort of slogan.

An interpretation of the Hegelian-Marxist dialecticism by Mao was termed *yi fen wei er* (one divided into two which means that everything has good points and bad points); the emphasis on political qualifications, *you hong you zhuan* (both red and an expert meaning socialist-minded and professionally competent). The involvement of China in the Korean War in the early 1950s was *kangmei yuanchao* (resistance against the USA and aid to Korea); the conflict of China with the Soviet Union was *fanxiu fangxiu* (combat and prevent revisionism). A work place is called *danwei* (single place, meaning 'unit'). It was a single place because until recently once you were assigned to a work unit by the authorities you were tied to it for your entire life.

Each of these highly politicised terms embraces a whole range of ideological, institutional, and practical assumptions. Everyday use of the Chinese language was so politicised and many terms and slogans were so charged with political assumptions that students of contemporary China have had to master them in their basic course work.[9]

Since the 1980s China has become less politicised. However, there remain many highly political terms. For instance, post-Mao China is simply referred to as the period of *gaige kaifang* (reform and opening-up to the outside world); the Cultural Revolution is simply *shi nian haojie* (ten years of holocaust); the 1989 Beijing events and the Tiananmen Massacre are given two words *liu si* (six four, meaning June 4, 1989). The policy to encourage people to get rich is termed derogatively *xiang qian kan* (looking towards money); and for the intellectuals and government office workers to give up their meagre but secure incomes and opt for business is called *xia hai* (jump into the sea) meaning to plunge into the sea to swim into uncertainty.

Politicised personal names

Traditionally the Chinese are great believers in the power of names: if it is repeated often enough, it will come true. They wish their daughters to be pretty and good, so they often give them the names of flowers, colours, or precious stones; terms of elegance and beauty, or of feminine virtue.[10] If they want their next baby to be a boy, they may call their baby daughter *zhao di* (beckoning for a little brother). They tend to give boys names that indicate qualities of heroism, brightness, bravery, strength, intelligence; or invoke powerful natural objects such as rivers, or mountains.

During the time when Maoism dominated China, personal names also became very politicised. In the late 1940s, *jian hua* (build China), and *jian guo* (build the country) were popular names because in 1949 a new China was believed to have been established. In the early 1950s, many babies were given names such as *tu gai* (land reform), or *yuan chao* (aid Korea). There must be hundreds of people who were given the name of *yue jin* (leap forward) in the period of the Great Leap Forward. During the Cultural Revolution, names such as *hong wei* (defend the red), *yong hong* (forever red), and *wei dong* (*wei* means 'defend' and *dong* is the word for both 'East' and the last given name of Mao—Mao Ze*dong*) were very popular. The last of the three—*wei dong*—means both 'to defend the East' (as opposed to the West) and 'Defend Mao'.

In post-Mao China, parents no longer feel embarrassed about giving their babies names to express their desire for wealth and prosperity.[11] Thus many babies are given names with connotations of *cai* (wealth) and *fu* (riches).

CONCLUDING REMARKS

In conclusion, contemporary political and social events in China led to systematic and conscientious language reforms by the Chinese elite. These reforms included narrowing the gap between written and spoken language and thus the development of plain language writing; the simplification of the script; and the invention and practice of phonetic writing systems.

As for the non-elite population in China, contemporary political and social changes and events not only affected their way of life but also their everyday usage of language. Political terms have become daily life phenomena and even the personal names of many reflect the ups and downs of political and social change in China.

STUDY QUESTIONS

1. What was the nature of the difference between spoken and written Chinese before the language reforms took place?
2. Why do you think the Chinese launched the so-called 'plain speech' movement?
3. What do you think is the connection between Chinese nationalism and language reform?
4. What aspects of the language did the Chinese seek to reform?

5. In what areas and to what extent was language reform successful?
6. Why do you think the Nationalist government in Taiwan is opposed to the simplification of characters?
7. Why do you think there are so many political slogans in mainland China?
8. Why do you think many Chinese parents name their children after political events?

REFERENCE READING

Barnes, Dayle, 'Language Planning in Mainland China: Standardisation', in Joshua A. Fishman (ed.), *Advances in Language Planning*, The Hague, Mouton, 1974.

Befu, Harumi (ed.), *Cultural Nationalism in East Asia, Representation and Identity*, Institute of East Asian Studies, University of California, Berkeley, California, Summer 1964.

Chuang, H. C., *The Great Proletarian Cultural Revolution A Terminological Study*, Studies in Chinese Communist Terminology no. 12, Center for Chinese Studies, Institute of International Studies, University of California, Berkeley, California, August 1967.

——, August 1968, *The Little Red Book and Current Chinese Language*, Studies in Chinese Communist Terminology no. 13, Center for Chinese Studies, Institute of International Studies, University of California, Berkeley.

Defrancis, John, *Nationalism and Language Reform in China*, Princeton University Press, Princeton, 1953.

Dittmer, Lowell and Chen Ruoxi, *Ethics and Rhetoric of the Chinese Cultural Revolution*, The Center for Chinese Studies, Institute of East Asian Studies, University of California, 1981.

Hisa, T. A., *A Terminological Study of the Hia-Fang Movement*, Studies in Chinese Communist Terminology no. 10, Center for Chinese Studies, Institute of International Studies, University of California, Berkeley, California, February 1962.

——, 1964, *The Commune in Retreat as Evidenced in Terminology and Semantics*, Studies in Chinese Communist Terminology no. 11, Center for Chinese Studies, Institute of International Studies, University of California, Berkeley.

Hodge, Robert and Kam Louie, *The Politics of the Chinese language: The Art of Reading the Dragon*, Routledge, London, 1998.

Li Chi, *General Trends of Chinese Linguistic Changes under Communist Rule*, Studies in Chinese Communist Terminology no. 1, East Asia Studies, Institute of International Studies, University of California, Berkeley, California, July 1956.

——, July 1956b, *Preliminary Study of Selected Terms*, Studies in Chinese Communist Terminology no. 2, East Asia Studies, Institute of International Studies, University of California, Berkeley, California.

——, December 1958, *The Use of Figurative Language in Communist China*, Studies in Chinese Communist Terminology no. 5, East Asia Studies, Institute of International Studies, University of California, Berkeley, California.

——, April 1957, *Part I, Literary and Colloquial Terms in New Usage, Part II, Terms Topped by Numbers*, Studies in Chinese Communist Terminology, no. 3, East Asia Studies, Institute of International Studies, University of California, Berkeley, California.

——, December 1957, *Part I, The Communist Term The Common Language and Related Terms, Part II, Dialectal Terms in Common Usage, Part III, Literary and Colloquial Terms in New Usage*, Studies in Chinese Communist Terminology no. 4, East Asia Studies, Institute of International Studies, University of California, Berkeley, California.

——, June 1960, *A Provisional System of Grammar for Teaching Chinese* with Introduction and Commentary, Studies in Chinese Communist Terminology no. 6–7, Center for Chinese Studies, Institute of International Studies, University of California, Berkeley, California.

Li, Lincoln, *Student Nationalism in China, 1924–1949*, State University of New York Press, Albany, 1994.

Li Xingjian (ed.), *zhongguo yuyanxue nianjian* (Chinese Linguistics Yearbook), Yuwen chubanshe, Beijing, 1993.

Lu Shuxiang, *yuwen changtan* (Talk about Language), Sanlian shudian, Beijing, 1980.

Meisner, Maurice, *Mao's China and After Mao, A History of the People's Republic*, The Free Press, New York, and Collier MacMillan Publishers, London, revised edition, 1986.

Pickowicz, Paul, *Marxist Literary Thought and China: A Conceptual Framework*, Studies in Chinese Communist Terminology no. 18, Center for Chinese Studies, Institute of International Studies, University of California, Berkeley, California, 1980.

Shao Jingmin and Shi Youwei (eds), *wenhua yuyan zhongguo chao* (the Tide of Cultural Linguistics in China), Yuwen chubanshe, Beijing, 1995.

Serbolt, Peter J. and Gregory Kuei-ke Chiang, *Language Reforms in China, Documents and Commentary*, M. E. Sharpe, Inc., University Microfilms International, Michigan, 1978.

Serruys, Paul L. M., *Survey of the Chinese Language Reform and the Anti-Illiteracy Movement in Communist China*, Studies in Chinese Communist Terminology no. 8, Center for Chinese Studies, Institute of International Studies, University of California, Berkeley, California, February 1962.

Spence, Jonathan D., *The Gate of Heavenly Peace: the Chinese and Their Revolution*, Penguin Books, New York, 1982.

Wang, Zhigang and Micklin Michael, 'The Transformation of Naming Practices in Chinese Families: Some Linguistic Clues to Social Change', *International Sociology*, June 1996, vol. 11 (2), pp. 187–212.

ENDNOTES

1   Lü Shuxiang, *yuwen changtan* (Talk about Language), Sanlian shudian, Beijing, 1980.

2 Shao Jingmin and Shi Youwei (eds), *wenhua yuyan zhonguo chao* (the Tide of Cultural Linguistics in China), Yuwen chubanshe, Beijing, 1995, pp. 121–2.

3 Quoted in Peter J. Serbolt and Gregory Kuei-ke Chiang, *Language Reforms in China, Documents and Commentary*, M. E. Sharpe, Inc., University Microfilms International, Michigan, 1978, p.1.

4 Peter L. Serbolt and Gregory Kuei-ke Chiang, *Language Reforms in China*, p. 9.

5 For the arguments on both sides of this controversy see Peter J. Serbolt and Gregory Kuei-ke Chiang, *Language Reforms in China*.

6 Li Xingjian (ed.), *zhongguo yuyanxue nianjian* (Chinese Linguistics Yearbook), Yuwen chubanshe, Beijing, 1993, pp. 63–4.

7 Wang Li, Wang Guzhang et al., *xiandai hanyu jiangzuo* (Lectures on Modern Chinese), Zhishi chubanshe, Beijing, 1983, p. 52.

8 For the sake of brevity I will give a loose definition of the concept of a morpheme here. A morpheme is the smallest meaningful unit in a language. In English, for instance, the word 'boys' has two morphemes, *boy* and *s*, the latter of which indicates the plural number in the language.

9 The Center for Chinese Studies at the Institute of East Asian Studies, University of California, carried out a series of projects called *Studies in Chinese Terminology*. For the Cultural Revolution alone, Lowell Dittmer and Chen Ruoxi compiled a booklet *Ethics and Rhetoric of the Chinese Cultural Revolution*. However, the booklet contains only some of the terms.

10 Although we witness similar practices (naming females after flowers, for instance) in English, the scale and intensity is far greater in Chinese.

11 For a discussion of names associated with political events see Wang Zhigang and Michael Micklin, 'The Transformation of Naming Practices in Chinese Families: Some Linguistic Clues to Social Change', *International Sociology*, June 1996, vol. 11 (2), pp.187–212.

CHAPTER 3
Sounds and Tones

SPEAKING A LANGUAGE

With the exception perhaps of Latin, nowadays few people would want to learn a language just for the purpose of reading it. We want to speak and understand a foreign language for the purpose of communication. Natural language originated from the desire of humans to speak to each other. Writing systems came into being only as offshoots of the spoken language. In fact there are many natural languages in the world that have no script at all. In China, more than thirty of the fifty or so national ethnic minority languages do not have a script. We may invent a writing system just for the purpose of written communication; but that kind of system is not a natural language in the technical sense of the word.

Speaking a language involves a thorough mastery of its sound system. A native speaker of any language acquires its sound system without special effort. Learning a second language, however, involves conscientious effort. A learner has to learn the sound system as a complex set of habits so that it becomes second nature to them. In order to achieve this, a learner has to imitate the sound patterns and be exposed continuously and repeatedly to the sound system.

Very often, the sound patterns of our first language will play their part in the process of our learning the sound system of a second language. This is demonstrated by the fact that people who are not brought up speaking English may speak English with accents. By the same token, we may find it easier to learn those sounds in a second language that have equivalents, or are similar to sounds in our first language. The aim of this chapter is to highlight some similarities and differences between sound patterns in Mandarin and English.

PINYIN: THE SPELLING OF CHINESE SOUNDS

The phonetic spelling that is commonly used to represent sounds in Mandarin is called *pinyin*. It is important to reiterate that *pinyin* was invented only in the twentieth century and it is now used as an aid for speaking Mandarin. The *pinyin* spelling for 'I am now studying Chinese' is *wo xianzai zai xuexi hanyu* (ignoring the tones which are discussed later in the chapter). However, no Chinese person writes *pinyin* except for specific purposes such as teaching and learning. Instead, they write characters:

我现在在学习汉语

Still, *pinyin* is a very useful tool for all the reasons discussed in relation to language reform in chapter 2. Therefore, our discussion of the sound system of Mandarin will be based on *pinyin*.

Consonants and initials

As a convention in the *pinyin* system, any consonant which begins a syllable is called an initial and whatever follows the consonant is called a final. Therefore, if a syllable (more discussion on syllables shortly) consists of a consonant followed by a vowel then the consonant is the initial and the vowel the final of the syllable.

There are altogether twenty-three consonants, all of which except *ng* and *r* [ʁ] can function as initials in a syllable. Following are the initials. The first letter in italics represents the *pinyin*; the square brackets contain the pronunciation in international phonetic script.

1   *b* [p] *p* [p'] *m* [m] *f* [f]
2   *d* [t] *t* [t'] *n* [n] *l* [l]
3   *ng* [ŋ]
4   *z* [ts] *c* [ts'] *s* [s]
5   *j* [tɕ] *q* [tɕ'] *x* [ɕ]
6   *zh* [tʂ] *ch* [tʂ'] *sh* [ʂ] *r* [ɻ]
7   *g* [k] *k* [k'] *h* [x] *r* [ʁ]

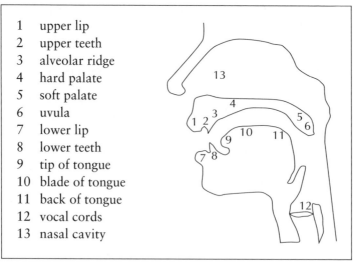

1	upper lip
2	upper teeth
3	alveolar ridge
4	hard palate
5	soft palate
6	uvula
7	lower lip
8	lower teeth
9	tip of tongue
10	blade of tongue
11	back of tongue
12	vocal cords
13	nasal cavity

Figure 3.1   Places of atriculation

The consonants are organised into groups as above because of their place of articulation. Figure 3.1 shows the various places of articulation.

Note that there are two versions of *r* in *pinyin*, an *r* pronounced as [ɹ], and an *r* pronounced as [ʁ]. Apart from *r* [ʁ], and *ng* [ŋ], all the consonants listed on page 53 can function as initials in a syllable in Mandarin. However, only *n*, *ng*, and *r* [ʁ] can appear as part of the final in a syllable. In other words, these are the only three consonants which appear at the end of a syllable in Mandarin.

The consonant *b* is similar to *b* in English except *b* in English is voiced. When we produce a voiced sound like *b* in English the vocal cord vibrates. The pronunciation of *b* in the *pinyin* system is the same as *p* in the English word 'speak'. The first three consonants of group one (*b, p, m*) are bilabials because they are pronounced with the lips. The last in the group (*f*), however, is a labiodental.

The difference between *d* in *pinyin* and *d* in English is the same as for *b*—*d* in English is voiced. The pronunciation for the sound *d* in *pinyin* is the same as that for *t* in 'study'. All the sounds in the second group (*d, t, n, l*) are produced with the tip of the tongue touching the alveolar ridge.

With the exception of *s*, the consonants *z, c, s, j, q, x, zh, ch, sh*, and *r* [ɹ] do not have any equivalents in English. The three sounds in group four are produced with the tip of the tongue touching the front of the hard palate. The three sounds in group five are produced with the front two sides of the tongue touching the front of the hard palate. The four sounds in group six are produced with the tip of the tongue touching the middle of the hard palate; and finally, the first three in group seven are pronounced the same as in English, whereas the last will be dealt with in detail later.

Vowels and finals

According to the convention in *pinyin*, a syllable consists of an initial and a final if and when the syllable has a consonant followed by a vowel. In this system all finals must have a vowel; but not all syllables have an initial and a vowel as final. For instance, there are syllables which are formed simply by vowels. Vowels can be a syllable on their own. Only when a vowel follows a consonant in a syllable is it called the final of that syllable. When a vowel following a consonant is itself followed by a consonant, then the vowel and the final consonant together form the final of the syllable.

Vowels

There are seven basic vowels in Mandarin which are:

a [a], like *a* in *father*

o [o], like *o* in *lot*, but the *o* in English is shorter

e [ɣ], there is no English equivalent. It is somewhere between the English *a* and *er* in the word *fatter*

i [i], like *ee* in *Lee*

u [u], like *oo* in *look*

ü [y], there is no English equivalent. The way to pronounce it is to start with [i] and move quickly rounding the lips to finish off the sound. This sound is close to the French *u*, e.g. in *sucre*

-i [ɨ], has no English equivalent either. It is something between the Chinese [i] and *er* in the English word *letter*

In Mandarin *ü* does not appear anywhere else except after *l*, *n*, *j*, *q*, and *x* whereas *u* never appears after *j*, *q*, and *x*. Therefore, *u* and *ü* contrast in meaning only when they appear after *l* and *n*, and because they both can appear after *l* and *n*, in these cases the meanings are different, for example *nü* and *nu* mean female and slave respectively.

As a convention, the two dots above *ü* are not written when they appear after *j*, *q*, and *x*. In other words, *ju*, *qu*, and *xu* in *pinyin* must be pronounced as *jü*, *qü* and *xü*, though in spelling the two dots are not included as a convention. This convention is stipulated precisely because the two vowels have complementary distribution; that is, they do not contrast in meaning in these contexts. However, when *ü* appears after *l* and *n*, it must be spelt as *lü* and *nü*.

When two contrasting sounds in a sound system never appear in the same context and therefore confusion does not occur, we call this phenomenon complementary distribution. Complementary distribution applies to another pair of sounds in Mandarin. The pair is *i* and *-i*. Due to the fact that *i* never appears after *zh*, *ch*, *sh*, *r* [ɿ], *z*, *c*, and *s* while *-i* never appears anywhere else in the language except after these consonants, *-i* is never spelt out as a convention. Instead, it is spelt as *i* when it appears after *zh*, *ch*, *sh*, *r* [ɿ], *z*, *c* and *s*. In other words, *i* in *zh*, *ch*, *sh*, *r* [ɿ], *z*, *c*, and *s* should be pronounced as *-i* though it is not spelt as *-i*.

All of the seven basic vowels on page 55 can be the finals of a syllable.

More finals

Each of the above basic vowels may be combined with another basic vowel to form a diphthong or triphthong as a final. They may also be combined with a nasal to form a final. Let us examine the following combinations first:

ai, pronounced as the *i* in *like* in English

ei, pronounced as the *a* in *lake* in English

ao, pronounced as the *ow* in *gown* in English

ou, pronounced as the *ow* in *low* in English

ia, pronounced as the *yar* in *yard* in English

ie, pronounced as the *ye* in *yes* in English

iao, this in fact is a combination of *ie* and *ao*. By saying *ie* and *ao* together quickly we will get the pronunciation of *iao*

iou (-iu[1]), this is a combination of *ie* and *ou*. By saying *ie* and *ou* together quickly we will be able to pronounce *iou*

ua, this is a combination of *u* and *a*. The pronunciation of *wa* in the English loan word *walla* or *wallah* is the nearest in sound

uo, this is a combination of *u* and *o*, similar to the *wa* in *wash* in English

uai, combination of *u* and *ai*, the pronunciation is the same as that of *why* in English

uei (-ui), combination of *u* and *ei*, like the *wa* in the English word *wane*

u:e, a combination of *ü* and *e*. By saying *ü* and *e* together quickly, the sound of *üe* is produced

Finals with nasals

In Mandarin a syllable does not end with a consonant except for the two nasals, *n* and *ng*, and *r* [ʁ]. In other words, all the finals in Mandarin are vowels except when these three consonants appear. The following are the possible finals:

an, a combination of *a* and *n*, similar to *an* in a loan word *annatto* in English

en, a combination of *e* and *n*, similar to the pronunciation of the letter *n* in English

ang, a combination of *a* and *ng*, similar to the pronunciation of the French word *ancien*, or *hung* in English

eng, a combination of *e* and *ng* with *ng* pronounced [ŋ] in English *ong*, a combination of *o* and *ng*, similar to the pronunciation of *ong* in *Mongolia*

ian, a combination of *ia* and *n*; there is no English equivalent. The way to pronounce it is to move from *i* to the pronunciation of *Anne*

in, a combination of *i* and *n*

iang, a combination of *ia* and *ng*

ing, a combination of *i* and *ng*, like the *ing* in English

iong, a combination of *i* and *ong*

uan, a combination of *ua* and *n*

uen (-un), a combination of *ue* and *n*, similar to the pronunciation of *when* in English

uang, a combination of *ua* and *ng*

ueng, a combination of *u* and *eng*

üan, a combination of *u:* and *an*

ün, a combination of *u:* and *n*

The *r* [ʁ] sound

The sound *r* [ʁ] needs some special attention. It is similar to the *r* in English in terms of articulation. However, this sound never appears as an initial in Mandarin. Instead, it only appears at the end of a word and it always appears after a vowel, or a nasal. When it appears after an *n*, the *n* disappears in pronunciation. For instance, when *r* appears in *yidianr*, it is pronounced as *yidiar*, though it may be spelt as *yidianr*. The disappearance of *n* is only natural because it is easier to say *r* without *n*.

Another important point about this sound is that in many but not all cases *r* [ʁ] is not semantically significant (see the section on affixes on page 114 for a discussion on suffixes). In other words, although one can add *r* [ʁ] at the end of many words, whether one adds it may not make a difference to the meaning. In the south of China, speakers of Mandarin hardly use this *r* in their speech.

However, *r* does have semantic significance when it appears in certain contexts. For instance, when it appears after *e*, it is semantically significant. The sound *e* means one word and the sound *er* means another word. For more discussion see chapter 5.

SYLLABLES

In Mandarin there are a number of salient features in terms of syllables. The most striking one (as mentioned a moment ago) is that with two exceptions a syllable never ends with a consonant. One exception is *r*. The other exception involves the two nasals, *n*, and *ng*, which do appear at the end of syllables.

Another feature is that Mandarin, in contrast to English, has no clusters of consonants in one syllable.[2] In English, for instance there are strings like *pl* as in *please*, *br* as in *break*, and *spl* and *nt* in *splint*. For the word *sprints* in English there are six consonants, three before the vowel and three after. Such strings, either as an initial or as a final of a syllable, do not exist in Mandarin. Although in the *pinyin* spelling *zh*, *ch*, *sh*, and *ng* look like strings of two consonants, they are not pronounced one by one, but represent single sounds.

Vowels as syllables
There are only six vowels that form syllables by themselves. They are:

a   ai   ao   e   o   ou

Vowel followed by a consonant as a syllable
Apart from two nasals which are categorised in a different group in this book, there is only one syllable in Chinese that is formed by a vowel followed by a consonant. It is *er*.

A consonant plus a vowel plus a nasal as a syllable
There are three nasals in Mandarin, *m*, *n*, and *ng*. However, *m* never appears as part of a final. Therefore only two nasals

appear after a vowel in a syllable. Examples are *long*, *leng*, *nan*, and *shen*.

Semi-vowels

There are two semi-vowels in Mandarin. They are *y* and *w*.

Syllable tables

In Mandarin, the number of syllables having nasals *n* and *ng* at the end is the largest.

In appendix I of this book the first four tables show all the syllables of Mandarin in *pinyin*. The four tables not only show how complementary distribution works in the sound system of *pinyin*, but also what combines with what to form a syllable. The tables also show the spelling conventions and the rationale behind them. Notice that there are altogether not many more than four hundred syllables in Mandarin. Many cells have been left blank in the tables because syllables resulting from these combinations do not exist in the language.

Thousands of words in the language are, of course, made up by the variation in tones in the approximately four hundred syllables. Even when the tone variations are added there are only about one thousand, three hundred syllables.[3] Therefore there are many words in Chinese that not only sound the same but also have the same tone.

PHONETIC SYMBOLS IN TAIWAN

Pinyin is only one possible way to spell the sound patterns in Mandarin. A system that is used in Taiwan is called *zhuyin fuhao* (phonetic symbols). In this system there are twenty-one symbols representing the consonants (initials) and sixteen symbols representing the vowels (finals). The system was first invented in 1913 and made official in 1918 by the then Republican government. The system is not phonetic in the alphabetic sense of the word because the symbols are not alphabet letters, such as *p*, *b*, or *m*. They are symbols that have to be memorised.

Because this system is not alphabetic it is considered harder to learn. The system is, therefore, under pressure to change. In 1999, in fact, Taiwan decided to give up *zhuyin fuhao* and adopt something like *pinyin* instead.

OTHER ROMANISATION SYSTEMS

Apart from *pinyin* and the phonetic symbols used in Taiwan there are two Romanisation systems which are worth mentioning here. One is the Yale system which is still used in some libraries and you will still find certain materials citing Chinese text using this system. As the use of the Yale system is very limited we will not spend any more time on it. Interested readers may refer to Dennis Yee in the reference reading list at the end of chapter 3 to compare the Yale system with *pinyin*.

The other is the Wade-Giles system which is widely used in written materials and in libraries. In appendix I there are four tables showing syllables using the Wade-Giles system; interested readers can make a comparison between *pinyin* and the Wade-Giles system.

TONES

A language is like a huge, complex structure consisting of levels of building blocks. The smallest building material consists of individual sounds such as consonants *p*, *t*, *d*, and *l*; and vowels such as *a*, *o*, *ai*, and *e*. The next layer comprises words formed by sounds put together such as *pet* and *dog*. At a higher level still are words put together to form sentences.

In this complex process we can also place different stresses on different words to convey our intentions. We can also produce the sounds with different pitches, sometimes high and sometimes low. We may also use different intonations in a sentence to indicate different meanings. In English, for instance, we may raise the intonation to ask a question. Thus, instead of making a statement by saying 'You do not like it', we might say 'You do not like it?' with rising intonation to make it into a question.

Tones versus intonation
The most salient difference between Mandarin and, indeed, other varieties of the Chinese language, and English is that Mandarin and other versions of Chinese are tonal languages while English is an intonation language. In an intonation language, different pitches applied to a single syllable do not make different words, although different pitches used in a sentence do

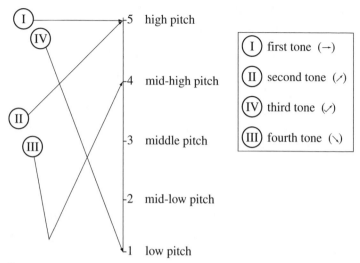

Figure 3.2 Pitch scales of the four tones

render different meanings. In a tonal language, however, different pitches applied to the same syllable form different words.

Let us look at pitch at the syllable level first. For a common personal name pronounced [li:] it is spelt *Lee* in English but *Li* in *pinyin*. With any tone, or pitch, the sound [li:] means *Lee* in English. However, when we say [li:] with four different pitches more than forty different words are derived in classical written Chinese, although in Mandarin not every one of them is a word by itself.

How do we know which word is meant from a group of homophones? Ambiguity disappears in context. In natural speech we seldom use just one sound. When we produce a sentence, the context—the words around it or the situation—will make clear which word is meant when one says [li:] with a given tone.

Mandarin does not use intonation to express meaning. Unlike English, in Mandarin one does not raise the intonation at the end of a sentence to create a question. Many native speakers of English learning Mandarin tend to use rising intonation at the end of a sentence when they ask a question in Chinese. As a matter of fact, to raise the intonation in Chinese when asking a question can easily lead to a mistake in tone.

When we raise the intonation we actually change the tone of the word on which the raised intonation is placed, and this, then, changes the word.

Tones in Mandarin

Different tones are made by different degrees of pitch. There are five tones in Mandarin, four marked tones and one neutral tone. Figure 3.2, along the lines developed by Y. R. Chao[4], is an illustration of pitch scales of the four marked tones in Mandarin.

The first tone is produced with high pitch and is kept level. To produce the second tone, the pitch starts at the middle between scale three and scale four and then it rises until it gets to scale five. To produce the third tone, the pitch starts at about the middle and then goes down to scale one before it rises to scale four. To produce the fourth tone, the pitch starts at scale five and then goes down to scale one sharply. Finally, the neutral tone is produced without a marked pitch.

As a convention, diacritical marks are used to indicate the four tones whereas the neutral tone is unmarked. The diacritical marks are placed on the vowel of a syllable. Thus, *Lī* for the first tone, *Lí* for the second tone, *Lǐ* for the third tone, and *Lì* for the fourth tone. For a syllable with a diphthong or triphthong, the diacritic is placed on the main vowel. As tone marks have been introduced, from now on words in *pīnyīn* in this book will be spelt with tones.

SOUNDS OF LOAN WORDS

It is perhaps easier to borrow words from languages of the same family. There are, for instance, a lot of loan words in English borrowed from languages such as German and French. Even some languages in different families have extensive loan words borrowed from each other. The most striking example is Japanese, which borrows freely and extensively from Chinese as well as from English.[5]

Chinese language, from the past to the present, has also borrowed foreign elements. A number of terms which have been identified by such scholars as Friedrich Hirth[6] and Berthold Laufer[7] as having originated from Iranian languages are associated with items of material culture, the names of which were borrowed along with the product.[8] These include, for instance, pútao (grape) and *mòli* (jasmine).

Early in the twentieth century, many terms of modern technology and Western political and economic concepts were reborrowed from the Japanese in the form of characters. However, Mandarin is very resistant to borrowing foreign terms outright. Most modern terms are native creations or what are called calques.[9] There are, however, a small number of loan words from English which are accepted as everyday words. The examples cited by Norman[10] include *mǎdá* (motor), *léidá* (radar), *mótèr* (model—as in fashion), *bàng* (pound of weight) and *xiūkè* (shock).

From the latter half of the nineteenth century, the Chinese started to borrow many terms from Western sources and thus they came across the problem of whether to translate them by meaning or through simple transliteration. For instance, the word for 'cement' was first translated as *shìmǐntǔ* by Cantonese speakers, a transliteration of *ce-men-t*. Then a Shanghai translation *shuǐméntīng* appeared—another transliteration of *ce-men-t*. Then the term *yánghuī* (foreign dust) was used for some time until, finally, *shuǐní* (water mud) became the accepted term.

Transliteration and proper names

Cantonese speakers in Hong Kong are more open to transliterations. The story of a gentleman with a stick who takes a taxi to go to a store to have some toast illustrates the point. The Cantonese transliteration for 'stick' is *si-di*, that for 'taxi' is *di-si*, for 'store' is *si-duo* and 'toast' is *duo-si*. Thus, the gentleman with a *sidi* takes a *disi* and goes to a *siduo* to have some *duosi*! [11]

For proper names, i.e. names of people and places, from European languages, transliteration is the normal solution. The way to do it usually is to break the names into different syllables and find a sound in Mandarin that sounds similar to the syllable. For instance, the name 'David' is transliterated as *dàwèi*, which literally means 'great defence'. 'England' is transliterated as *yīnggélán*, which sounds very near to the English pronunciation. 'The USA' is translated as *měiguó*; apparently *měi*, which means 'beautiful', is derived from the sound of *me* in 'America', whereas *guó* means 'country' or 'nation'. There are no ready-made rules for transliterating names into Chinese. Whoever first comes across a name from a European language will coin the transliteration which may or may not be accepted by the community. Once accepted it becomes common parlance.

Translation

Very often, when translating, the Chinese will forget about the sound of a word from a foreign language. They will translate the meaning. For instance, 'bus' is translated as *gōnggòngqìchē* which means 'public shared automobile', and 'taxi' as *chūzūqìchē* which means 'rent out automobile'. 'Telephone' is translated as *diànhuà* (electric speech), and 'movie' is *diànyǐng* (electric shadow). 'World Wide Web (www)' is translated as *wànwéiwǎng*. The three written characters are, 万 which means 'ten thousand', 维 which means 'connect', and 网 which means 'net', or 'web'. The beauty about this translation is that each of the three words has *w* as its initial.

In some words for objects the Chinese may translate both their sound and meaning. For instance, 'vitamin' is translated as *wéitāmìng*. The sound is similar to the English word, and the meaning of the three syllables is 'maintain his life'. Still some Chinese are not happy with the sound transliteration. So 'vitamin' is also translated as *wéishēngsù*, meaning 'maintain life's elements'.

Some transliteration of both sounds and meanings of this kind can work very well. For instance 'Coca Cola' is translated into *kěkǒu kělè*, meaning 'good taste, and happy'! The famous German-made car Mercedes-Benz is translated as *bēnchí*. The sound of *bēnchí* is very similar to the sound of 'Benz' and the meaning of the two characters are 'speedy' and 'gallop'. Another example is the translation of 'Internet' which is *yīntèwǎng* or *yīngtèwǎng*. *Yīntè* or *yīngtè* is the transliteration of *inter* whereas *wǎng* means 'net'.

The people in Hong Kong are good at accepting new things. They do not translate 'bus' as 'public shared automobile'. Instead, they just transliterate the sound and term as *basi*. Because of the economic influence of Hong Kong, some mainland Chinese have also started to adopt the Hong Kong style of transliteration. Instead of *gōnggòngqìchē*, some have begun to say *basi* to refer to 'bus'. Instead of *chūzūqìchē*, they say *disi*, a Cantonese transliteration of the sound for 'taxi'.

As a result of opening up and the economic reforms since the 1980s, it is increasingly fashionable to say things that sound foreign. Some youngsters may not use *zàijiàn* (see you again) to mean 'bye-bye'. Instead, they may say *baibai* which imitates the English sound.

SYLLABLES, WORDS, AND TONES

Syllables and words

The Chinese language has the reputation of being monosyllabic, which means that every word consists of one syllable. In *wen yan*, i.e. classical written texts, this was certainly the case. Even in Mandarin the rate of occurrence of monosyllabic words, according to one estimate, is 61%, that of disyllabic words is 37%, and multisyllabic words only 2%. In written Mandarin the average number of syllables per word is 1.48.[12]

The impression of Chinese being monosyllabic is reinforced by the writing system in which every syllable has a character and every character has at least one meaning. In English the letters of a word are spelt together as one unit no matter how many syllables the word has. For instance, 'antiestablishmentarianism' is one word and it appears as one unit in print, though *anti*, *establish*, *ism*, and, arguably, *mentarian*, can be interpreted as separate meaningful units. To translate this word into Mandarin we have to say something like:

făn duì yōng hù jì yŏu quán lì tĭ zhì zhŭ yì

There are altogether twelve syllables. We may put all the syllables together as one unit:

fănduìyōnghùjìyŏuquánlìtĭzhìzhŭyì.

Table 3.1   Syllables and words

Sound	Character	Meaning of each character	Meaning of each word
hù shi	护士	look after, person	nurse
yī sheng	医生	medicine, person	doctor
yī fu	衣服	clothe, costume	clothing
xué xi	学习	learn, revise	study
chū zū qì chē	出租汽车	out, rent, steam, vehicle	taxi
zī chǎn jiē jí	资产阶级	capital, property, rank, grade	capitalism

However, in written Chinese there are twelve characters:

反对拥护既有权力体制主义

each of which has at least one meaning. The twelve characters in this case mean 'against', 'towards', 'embrace', 'support', 'exist', 'have', 'power', 'strength', 'body', 'system', 'master', and 'sense' respectively.

The above example may be an extreme case illustrating the point of why Chinese is considered monosyllabic. However, in spoken Mandarin many words are not monosyllabic. There are many disyllabic words such as *hùshi, yīsheng, yīfu,* and *xuéxi* (see the translation below). There are also four-syllable words such as *chūzūqìchē,* and *zīchǎnjiējí.* Of course in print each syllable has its own character. However, each syllable alone does not necessarily have the intended meaning, and the complete two or four syllables have to be spoken together to form a word, as shown in table 3.1.

Neither *hù,* nor *shi* alone can mean 'nurse'; nor can *yī,* or *sheng* mean 'doctor'. In *chū zū qì chē* and *zī chǎn jiē jí* the syllables have to be put together to mean, respectively, 'taxi' and 'capitalism'. In both cases, only when the syllables are together as one unit can they be called a word. Therefore, they are words of more than one syllable. Still, the matter is not that straight-forward. *Yī* and *fú* can independently mean 'clothing' and 'costume'; *xué* can mean 'study'; and *xí* can mean 'revision'.

However, in modern Mandarin *yī* alone is not used as a word, though sometimes *xué* stands alone as a word to mean 'study'.

Syllables and neutral tones

One of the consequences of having multisyllable words in Mandarin is tonal change. What usually happens is that in a two-syllable word, the tone on the second syllable may be dropped. For the four two-syllable words we have shown above, for instance, the tone on the last syllable of each word is not pronounced. Instead, the tone becomes neutral, whether it is first, second, third, or fourth tone. In fact, to produce the last tone distinctively and prominently when saying these words sounds concocted and unnatural. For this reason, there are sometimes considered to be five tones in Mandarin, i.e. the four tones plus a neutral tone. The neutral tone is normally produced with little effort and comes naturally in the flow of speech.

The tendency of having two syllables in a word is also reflected in another phenomenon of word formation. That is the use of *zi* which is added to form two-syllable words.

kuàizi	chopsticks
sháozi	spoon
zhuōzi	table, desk
yǐzi	chair
fángzi	house
érzi	son
dāozi	knife
bízi	nose
lúzi	stove

Zi does not add anything semantically to these words. The function of *zi* is to make them into two-syllable words. Perhaps because it does not have semantic significance, the usual third tone of *zi* is dropped in these words, and it becomes neutral.

The neutral tone also applies to a number of words that have no semantic significance but are grammatically meaningful. These words are usually referred to as grammatical particles. The most commonly used and most important two are *ma* and *le*. *Ma* is a question particle. When it appears at the end of a statement, the sentence becomes a question. For instance, by putting *ma* at the end of the statement 'I am now studying Chinese', it becomes 'Am I now studying Chinese?'.

> *wǒ xiàn zài zài xuéxí hànyǔ* — I am now studying Chinese.
> *wǒ xiàn zài zài xuéxí hànyǔ ma* — Am I now studying Chinese?

Le is a particle used to indicate a sense of completion. The nearest equivalent English grammatical terms are past tense, or present perfect. We will discuss this in detail in the chapter on grammar later. For now, the following example will suffice:

> *wǒ xuéxí hànyǔ* — I study Chinese.
> *wǒ xuéxí le hànyǔ* — I studied Chinese, or I have studied Chinese.

Both *ma* and *le* should be unstressed and no tone is required for them when spoken.

STRESS

In English, the question of which syllable of a word to stress is an important aspect of the sound pattern. For instance, we place stress on the first syllable in 'relative' and the second syllable in 'relation'. If we do not place the right stress on the right syllable the sound is wrong, or we sound foreign. Moreover, in some cases placing stress on the wrong syllable may cause misunderstandings. For instance, to say 'produce' with stress on the second syllable means 'make', or 'manufacture' whereas stress on the first syllable means 'product', or 'things produced'. In other words, stress on the first syllable makes 'produce' a noun and stress on the second syllable turns it into a verb.

Stress plays an important role in Chinese as well, but is not so prevalent as it is in English. For instance, the three-syllable word *xiǎo xuésheng* means 'child student' when the last syllable is unstressed, and in which case the tone of the last syllable becomes neutral. *Xiǎo xuéshēng* means 'primary school student' in which the tone of the last syllable has to be pronounced. For the word *dìdào*, stress on the second syllable gives 'tunnel' or 'underground' whereas stress on the first syllable means 'really good'. *Liànxí* (exercise) is a noun when the first syllable is stressed and becomes a verb when the second is stressed.

Shì (the Chinese equivalent of the verb 'to be') is an agent of stress in a number of sentence patterns. *Wǒ shì xuésheng* means 'I *am* a student'. We can stress *shì* and the sentence will mean 'I am a student'. This pattern of stress is the same in English. However, there is another pattern which has no English equivalent. To simply mean 'I am happy' we cannot say *wǒ shì gāoxìng*. Instead, we have to drop the *shì*. If *shì* is inserted it has to be stressed to mean 'I *am* happy'. To use *shì* in this pattern without stress is ungrammatical.

Rhythm

Previously we have indicated that in a two-syllable word in Mandarin, the second syllable can be unstressed. As a result, the tone of that syllable is dropped and thus becomes neutral. However, when we pronounce three-syllable words in Mandarin, there is a different pattern. Not only must the tone of the last syllable of a three or four-syllable word be produced, but also it should be stressed. For instance the stress should be placed on *shì* in *bàngōngshì* (office), on *shī* in *gōngchéngshī* (engineer), and *xué* in *běijīng dàxué* (Beijing University).

If we categorise stresses into weak (W), medium (M), and strong (S), the pattern for a three-syllable word is M+W+S and the pattern for a four-syllable word is M+W+M+S, as shown in Table 3.2.

There are cases when the pattern is S+M+W. Words like *xiǎo huǒ zi* (young bloke) and *yào fàn de* (beggar) belong to this pattern. This is not surprising since *zi* and *de* are usually unstressed as the former functions as a suffix and the latter is a particle.

Another feature of rhythm is the preference for words with an even number of syllables. Let us take a look at one example. In

Table 3.2

Stress Pattern	Meaning of Each Syllable	Meaning of the word
M W S *bàn gōng shì*	manage, public, room	office
M W S *gōng chéng shī*	work, program, master	engineer
M W M S *běi jīng dà xué*	north, capital, big, learn	Beijing University

Mandarin, there is a grammatical rule by which the opposite meaning of a word can be made by prefixing it with the negative *bù*. Thus, *hǎo* means 'good' and *bùhǎo* means 'bad'. The word *yǒulì* means 'beneficial'. By the same token the word meaning 'not beneficial' ought to be *bùyǒulì*. However, in this case the word meaning 'not beneficial' is *búlì*, resulting from the dropping of one syllable to form an even number of syllables (and a change of a tone).

This tendency of requiring even syllables to be harmonious is also shown in place names. When the name of a county (a county is an administrative unit below province in the Chinese system) has only one syllable, the word *xiàn* (county) is added to form a two-syllable word; but if the name has two syllables *xiàn* is left out.[13]

STUDY QUESTIONS

1. What is *pinyin*? Is it the written language for Mandarin?
2. Why are there initials and finals in *pinyin*?
3. What is a syllable?
4. The number of syllables in Mandarin is very limited. Does that mean the number of words in the language is also limited? Why not?
5. What are tones? What is the main difference between a tonal language and an intonation language?
6. What is the difference between a syllable and a word?
7. What is the relationship between a syllable and a character?
8. Does stress make a difference to meaning in Chinese?

REFERENCE READING

Chao, Y. R., *Mandarin Primer*, Harvard University Press, Cambridge, Mass., 1948.

DeFrancis, John, *The Chinese Language, Fact and Fantasy*, University of Hawaii Press, Honolulu, 1984.

Hirth, Friedrich and W. W. Rockhill, *Chau Ju-hua: His Work on the Chinese and Arab Trade in the Twelfth and Thirteenth Centuries, Entitled Chu-fan-chi*, 1911, Printing Office of the Imperial Academy of Sciences, St Petersburg, reprinted by Cheng-wen Publishing Co., Taipei, 1970.

Kratochril, Paul, *The Chinese Language Today: Features of an Emerging Standard*, Hutchinson University Library, London, 1968.

Laufer, Berthold, 'Sino-Iranica: Chinese Contributions to the History of Civilisation in Ancient Iran' *Anthropological Series*, vol. 15, no. 3, 1919, Field Museum of Natural History, publication 201, Chicago.

Li Sijing, *hanyu r yinshi yanjiu* (A Study on the History of r in Chinese), revised edition, Shangwu yinshuguan, Beijing, 1994.

Norman, Jerry, *Chinese*, Cambridge University Press, first published in 1988 and reprinted in 1997.

Wang Li, Wang Guzhang et al., *xiandai hanyu jiangzuo* (Lectures on Modern Chinese), Zhishi chubanshe, Beijing, 1983.

Xing, Gongwan, et al. (eds), *hanyu yanjiu* (Research on Chinese), vol. 3, Nankai daxue chubanshe, Tianjin, 1993.

Yee, Dennis K., *Chinese Romanization Self-Study Guide, Comparison of Yale and Pinyin Romanizations, Comparisons of Pinyin and Wade-Giles Romanizations*, Honolulu, The University of Hawaii Press, 1975.

ENDNOTES

1   The spelling in brackets here and for several of the following sounds is conventionally adopted.

2   There is evidence that in Old Chinese (first millennium BC) a variety of consonant clusters could occur at the beginning of a syllable and perhaps, in a more limited way, at the end of a syllable.

3   Qian Nairong (ed.), *hanyu yuyanxue* (Chinese Linguistics), Beijing yuyan xueyuan chubanshe, Beijing, 1995, p. 15.

4   This diagram is drawn on the basis of Chao's ideas first developed in Y. R. Chao, A system of Tone Letters, *Le Maitre phonetique*, 45, 1930, pp. 24–7.

5   A. E. Backhouse, *The Japanese Language: An Introduction*, Melbourne, Oxford University Press, 1993.

6   Hirth Friedrich and W. W. Rockhill, *Chau Ju-hua: His Work on the Chinese and Arab Trade in the Twelfth and Thirteenth Centuries, Entitled Chu-fan-chi*, 1911, Printing Office of the Imperial Academy of Sciences, St Petersburg, reprinted by Cheng-wen Publishing Co., Taipei, 1970.

7   Berthold Laufer, Sino-Iranica: Chinese contributions to the history of civilisation in ancient Iran, *Anthropological Series*, vol. 15, no. 3, 1919, Field Museum of Natural History, publication 201, Chicago.

8   Norman Jerry, *Chinese*, Cambridge University Press, first published in 1988 and reprinted in 1997, p. 19.
9   An example cited by Jerry Norman is the Chinese term for television, *dian-shi*, of which the first syllable means <u>electric</u> and the second <u>vision</u>.
10 ibid. p. 20.
11 Chen Yuan, *shehui yuyanxue* (Sociolinguistics), Xuelin chubanshe, Shang-hai, 1983, p. 219.
12 Qian Nairong (ed.), *hanyu yuyanxue* (Chinese Linguistics), Beijing yuyan xueyuan chubanshe, Beijing, 1995, p. 6.
13 Xing Gongwan et al. (eds), *hanyu yanjiu* (Research on Chinese), vol. 3, Nankai daxue chubanshe, Tianjin, 1993, p. 106.

CHAPTER 4
Writing

With the help of *pīnyīn*, a non-native speaker can learn the sound patterns of Mandarin, and therefore learn how to speak it. However, *pīnyīn* was adopted by the Chinese only recently as a kind of orthography to spell the sounds of Mandarin. To be able to read and write Mandarin, one has to learn to read and write **characters**. The same applies to speakers of all other versions of Chinese.

In this chapter we will focus our discussion on the writing system, i.e. Chinese characters. We will discuss the structure and formation of characters, character types, writing styles, character writing in countries other than China, and other related issues.

Hànzì (CHARACTERS)

Hànzì (character) writing is believed to have developed independently within China. Like the Egyptian writing system, Chinese characters evolved from drawing pictures of what were to be represented. No one is sure of the exact date of origin of Chinese characters. The earliest drawing symbols that can be recognised as characters on oracle bones and shells date back to around 1700 BC although symbols drawn on pottery discovered in archaeological finds are even older.[1] However, it may be argued that these early symbols cannot be considered characters. According to Norman, the Chinese script appears as a fully developed writing system in the late Shang Dynasty (fourteenth to eleventh centuries BC).[2]

Nor can the exact number of characters be stated with certainty: *shuō wén jiě zì*,[3] the earliest Chinese dictionary published in the year AD 100, included 9 353 characters; *jí yùn*, which appeared in 1067, contained entries for 53 525 characters; *zhōnghuá dà cídiǎn* (the Chinese Dictionary) published in 1916 collected 48 000 characters; *cí hǎi*, a dictionary published in mainland China in 1979 included 14 872 characters; and *hànyǔ dà zìdiǎn*, the largest dictionary ever printed, appeared in 1986 and has entries for 54 678 characters.[4]

As part of the language reform, some obscure or seldom-used characters were simply discarded in mainland China. In 1952, the Chinese Ministry of Education promulgated a list of 2 000 characters as the minimum number required for literacy.

According to one estimate, the most frequently used 1 500 characters cover 95% of the characters in all writings and the most frequently used 3 800 cover 99.9% of the characters in all writings.[5] Therefore, a knowledge of around 3 000 characters is enough to get by in everyday use. According to one source, the average printing shop stocks around 6 000 characters.[6]

Strokes

Characters as they are in their present form are very different from their earlier form. The process in which Chinese script has evolved from pictures to characters has taken a long time. As the script matured, it became simpler and progressively began to lose some of its pictographic qualities. Rounded and circular or wavelike strokes were gradually transformed into straighter lines and sharper angles. Devices other than pictures were eventually formulated in order to represent concepts and abstract terms which could not otherwise be represented graphically.

It is not my intention, however, to spend a lot of time discussing the evolution of characters in this book. Instead, I will concentrate on a discussion of the present form of characters. Characters are composed of **strokes**, such as a dot, a horizontal line, or a hook stroke. A hook stroke can be a left hook or a right hook, or it can be a straight hook or a bent hook. There are altogether twenty-four basic strokes for writing all the characters. Some characters consist of just one or two strokes whereas some are formed by several strokes. The character for the word 'win', for instance, is written with twenty strokes—贏.

Stroke order

To learn to write individual strokes is quite straightforward and such skills can be acquired easily by imitation. However, to write strokes to form a character, with the strokes added in the right order, is less straightforward. There are some basic rules governing the order of strokes. The basic rules include:

1   write from top to bottom
2   from left to right
3   write the middle stroke first before other strokes on either side
4   when there is a square box or an encirclement, write the left, top, and right sides first and in that order, and then fill in the inside if there is any
5   if the encirclement has to be closed up, write the stroke to close the encirclement last
6   if a horizontal line stroke crosses a vertical line stroke, write the horizontal line stroke first

These rules are not arbitrarily stipulated. It is logical and convenient to write from left to right (assuming everyone is right handed) and from top to bottom. In a classroom situation the Chinese teacher is very strict on school children about stroke order. Many students of Chinese from English-speaking backgrounds, however, do not bother with the stroke order. They just draw up the character using strokes in whatever order they fancy.

In principle there is nothing wrong with the no stroke order approach. However, there are two points to be considered. One is that we can write characters faster with the more logical and convenient stroke order. The second point concerns decoding individual handwriting. When one writes quickly, a character may become cursive; what usually happens is that the stroke that comes first may be connected with the stroke that comes next by an ink trace. Therefore, only when everyone writes the strokes in the same order can cursive writing achieve some uniformity. This uniformity enables handwriting to be decoded. If everyone writes using different stroke order, the cursive style created by the ink traces on different spots will render at least some characters unintelligible to other readers. When one writes cursively this usually is an indication that one writes quickly. In Chinese calligraphy cursive writing is a major art form in which the right order of strokes is an essential element.

RADICALS

Strokes are the building blocks of characters. A single stroke, with few exceptions, does not represent meaning in the system. Some characters are composed of several strokes which do not have any independent meaning. In other words, they are simple non-composite graphs. However, most characters are composite graphs, that is, they are composed of identifiable parts, each of which has a representative meaning internal to the system. This is where the concept of radicals comes in.

A radical is the smallest meaningful unit in a character. Some radicals can be characters themselves while other radicals have meanings but cannot appear by themselves as characters. In this writing system, a radical may consist of one or more strokes and a character may consist of one or more radicals. Moreover, any symbol written in this system is a character if and only if it is associated with a syllable which has a meaning. A radical may have a meaning internal to the writing system, but it cannot be a character unless it is associated with a syllable that has a meaning.

Difference between a character and a radical

The difference between a character and a radical is that the former is a free form whereas the latter is a bound form. A free form is a character in its own right. A bound form, on the other hand, is not a character in its own right, but can be a part of a character. A bound form is similar to prefixes and suffixes in English such as *ex* (as in *ex*-wife) and *ly* (as in beautiful*ly*) in that it has a meaning but cannot be a word in its own right. A character is a free form because it can be independently associated with a syllable that has at least one meaning whereas a radical, as a bound form, has to appear with another radical or a character to form a character. A radical cannot appear by itself in the writing system. Table 4.1 provides an illustration:

Table 4.1 Syllable, character, radical, and the meaning associated with the radical

Syllable and meaning	Character	Radical and associated meaning
qīng green	青	
qíng sunny	晴	日 sun
qīng clean	清	氵 water
qīng dragonfly	蜻[7]	虫 insect
qīng mackerel	鲭	鱼 fish
qíng emotion	情	忄 heart
qīng hydrogen	氢	气 air
qǐng please	请	讠 tongue; language

All the characters have one component in common, i.e. the character associated with the sound of a syllable which means 'green'. Therefore, all the characters are pronounced the same (if we ignore the different tones). With the exception of the character meaning 'green', six characters have a component to the left of the character meaning 'green' and one has a component on the top. These components are called radicals, which indicate the meaning of the whole character they are part of. Thus, the sun makes the weather sunny, water washes things clean, a dragonfly is an insect, a mackerel a fish, emotion comes from the heart, this chemical—hydrogen—has something to do with air, and finally, one has to use language to be polite.

The components that indicate these meanings are called radicals chiefly for two reasons. One is that each of them can be combined with other characters or radicals to indicate a basic meaning. For instance, there are around two hundred characters in the language that have the insect radical as a component, ranging from the character for mosquito to that for snake. Many radicals cannot appear as characters on their own. Of the radicals listed above, those representing 'water', 'heart', and 'language' cannot appear as characters on their own. They are bound forms because they have to be bound with some other component to appear in the writing system. On the other hand, the remainder of the above radicals can appear as characters on their own.

The exact number of radicals in the language is a matter of debate. In *shuō wén jiě zì*, 540 radicals were listed. In the great *kāngxī* dictionary published in 1716, there were 214 symbols categorised as radicals. Since then some dictionaries have included more, and others include less symbols. In *cí hǎi*, 250 symbols are classified as radicals.

Is the Chinese script phonetic?

Two further points need to be highlighted here. First, it is clear that the radicals in the above illustration may be called **significs** since they indicate meaning and the character associated with *green* functions as a **phonetic** since it gives the sound for all these characters.

Second, the great majority of Chinese characters are like those illustrated above in that they are not purely arbitrary symbols bearing no relationship to one another, but, rather, are made up of a relatively small number of components. According to one estimate, more that 80% of characters consist of two parts, like the examples shown in table 4.1: one part that is signific and the other part phonetic.[8]

It has to be pointed out at this juncture that the format with the signific on the left and the phonetic on the right is only one of several character-structure formats. Indeed, in a character the phonetic can appear on the left and hence the signific on the right. Or it can have the signific on the top and the phonetic on the bottom. The relation can even be one inside and the other surrounding it on the outside.[8]

A legitimate question to be raised here is: Can the Chinese script be considered phonetic? In other words, since there are symbols in 80% of the characters that indicate how the words are pronounced, the Chinese script cannot be said to be totally unrelated to the sound system. I do not intend to answer this question here since it requires considerable discussion on related theoretical issues.

Radicals and character index in a dictionary

To summarise, there are two basic requirements for a symbol to be a radical. First it has to have some root meaning. Second, it can be combined with other symbols to form characters.

According to these requirements, a symbol, be it composed of one stroke or more, cannot be a radical if it does not have a meaning that plays a semantic role in the character in which it appears. However, in many Chinese dictionaries, a dot stroke and a vertical line stroke are also classified as radicals even though they do not represent meanings in the characters in which they appear.

The fact that this happens has something to with how characters are indexed in a Chinese dictionary. It is of little help to look up a character in an alphabetically ordered dictionary without knowing the sound of the character. The usual solution to this problem is to index characters according to radicals. Thus, all characters which have the symbols for insect will be grouped together, and all characters which have the water radical as their component will be put into another group, and so on. In each group, characters are then ordered according to the number of strokes the character is made up of, ordered from the least to the most number of strokes.

In order to find the pronunciation and definition of a character in a dictionary, one must first identify the radical which is part of that character. From the radical index one is then able to find the group to which the character belongs. Thus, in order to find a character with the insect radical, one must refer to the radical index to find out on which page characters having the insect radical are located. Finally, in order to locate the needed character amongst many, one must count the number of strokes in the character (the counting of which, by the way, does not include the number of strokes of the radical itself) and go to the relevant section. Sectioning of characters by stroke number enables quick location. If the number of characters containing a certain radical is only small, one may not even find it necessary to count the strokes since the target character will be found easily by simply taking a glance at the group in which it appears.

The problem with this system is that in order to look up a character in a dictionary you will need at least some knowledge of what radicals are and which part of the given character is the radical to be indexed. With some practice, this should not be a problem for most of the characters in the language. However, there are some characters that do not have an easily identifiable radical. In these cases, they either have to be indexed independently or an arbitrary decision has to be made about which part of the character is to be taken as the radical. Alternatively, as mentioned above, dots or vertical lines are sometimes called radicals, even though they have no semantic role, in order to facilitate dictionary entries.

TYPES OF CHARACTERS

Classification of characters was systematically carried out by the great Chinese philologist Xu Shen (58–147?) who compiled the first Chinese dictionary *shuō wén jiě zì*. Xu Shen had classified characters into six types. For the purpose of our discussion, it is not necessary to go into the details of these six types. Instead, we will discuss some of his basic ideas.

Pictograms
Because the earliest forms of characters were drawings of objects—traces of these drawings can still be found in some characters today—those types of characters may be called pictograms. For example, the earliest symbol for the sun is a drawing of something like the sun, which eventually evolved into the present form 日. The symbol for the moon now is 月, which had its origin in a drawing shaped like a half moon. The symbol for a tree is 木, indicating the shape of a tree.

Figure 4.1 contains three examples of how the original pictures gradually evolved into the characters of today.[10]

Ideographs
As a language communication system, pictograms are very limited in their use since we cannot adequately draw pictures of all things, let alone ideas and concepts.

The types of characters representing ideas or concepts are very often called ideographs or ideograms. For instance, when the symbols for the sun 日 and the moon 月 are combined, they form a new character 明, which represents the concept 'bright', as the light of the sun makes the day bright and moonlight lights

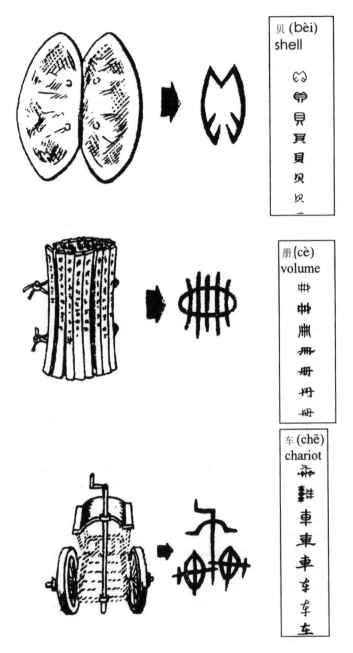

Figure 4.1 Ideographs

up the night sky. When two of the symbols for a tree 木 are put together, the resulting character (林) means 'forest'.

Here are two more examples. The character for 'small' is 小, that for 'big' is 大, and the character for 'sharp point' is 尖, meaning from big to small to form a sharp point. The character for 'not' is 不, that for 'straight' is 正, hence the character for 'crooked' is 歪.

The characters for numbers illustrate the logic of ideograms as well as their limitations. For instance, the character for one is 一, two 二, and three 三. Obviously, this logic cannot be applied to all numbers. Characters for four 四 and five 五, and so on are therefore more arbitrary.

Self-explanatory characters

Another type of character that goes a little beyond simple, direct representation of ideas or concepts is the self-explanatory character. Examples that are often used in textbooks are the characters for above 上, and below 下. In a sense the shape of the two does indicate the concept of above and below, but only by comparison, and they are by no means obvious.

Internal borrowing

Another type of character evolved from internal borrowing. Take the example of 花, the character for 'flower'. In this character, the top part is meant to represent plant, and the bottom part is pronounced *huà*, which is the pronunciation of the word for flower *huā* (the tone is different). So in this character one part represents the meaning and the other part represents the sound. However, this character is also the written form for the word 'spend' which is also pronounced as *huā*. The meaning of the two words are not related at all, and the fact that 花 is the written form for both 'flower' and 'spend' is a result of internal borrowing.[11]

Sounds and ideas: Representation by characters

The majority of characters are composed of a signific and a phonetic part as illustrated and discussed above in the example of the character for flower. Therefore, it is not categorically true to say that characters are not phonetic, i.e., that they are totally detached from how the words are pronounced.

It can be argued, however, that the phonetic component is not nearly as helpful as the alphabetic script, such as *pīnyīn*, in learning how a word is pronounced. Radicals do represent objects, ideas, or concepts. Take, for example, the radicals which represent water, language, plant, air, person, and so on—we have to stretch our imagination to think that these radicals are naturally associated with the idea, or concept, or thing that they represent. Even though a radical of three dots and hence three drops of water is quite well represented, in most cases, an idea or concept is often arbitrarily attached to a radical.

As the evolution progresses, these symbols become more and more arbitrary. Therefore, to associate the right idea or concept with the right character also involves memorisation. We cannot expect a learner to guess what idea, concept, or thing a character represents by simply looking at its shape.

From the pedagogical point of view, however, it is very useful to work with some images or associations of a character to help in memorisation. Very often the teacher can employ this as a teaching method. The students themselves can also work out their own images and associations so as to remember characters more easily. That is why it is useful to memorise the meanings of radicals as a learning technique.

WRITING STYLES AND CALLIGRAPHY

As modern characters have evolved from drawings, not only have the original shapes disappeared, but also writing styles have changed greatly. The print style normally seen in the print media is called *kǎi shū* (regular script) in which every character is written to fit in a square. The counting and ordering of strokes is also based on this style.

In reality, however, with the exception of beginners, very few people write in this style. What happens is that once you start to write fast you tend to connect one stroke with the next. Hence the *cǎo shū* style, which is cursive handwriting, arises. The degree of cursiveness depends on how fast one writes and how skilful one becomes. There are other styles of writing such as seal style and classic style. However, these styles are not practiced by the majority of people and they require special expertise.

Căo shū is the basic form of calligraphy although one can also utilise the *kăi shū* style. Everyone can do *căo shū* for the very reason that everyone has his or her own style of writing. Despite the fact that there is some basic uniformity which is imposed by stroke order, some calligraphy handwriting is difficult to decode and even guesswork through context needs training and practice.

The Chinese value calligraphy highly. They look upon calligraphy as a form of art, like drawing and painting. They also think practising calligraphy can help one relax and achieve harmony with nature. Many Chinese believe calligraphy reveals personality and inner self. They believe that whether one is aggressive, assertive, patient, inspiring, or vulgar, these elements of personality will be conveyed through calligraphy. The calligraphy of Mao is often said to be unconstrained and bold, whereas that of Lu Xun (the great critic of Chinese tradition) is seen to be precise and sharp.

The Chinese also believe that good calligraphy is a sign of cultural maturity and high educational attainment. Immature and childish handwriting is often considered to show low levels of education and cultural standards. This is not surprising since in traditional China scholars spent a great deal of their lives practising and writing calligraphy. Even in contemporary China a semi-literate soldier-general who has hardly read a book in his life likes to spend time practising calligraphy so as to show that he is culturally sophisticated. A Chinese politician also may like to display his or her calligraphy to boost popularity.

VERTICAL AND HORIZONTAL WRITING AND PUNCTUATION

In Chinese there are two directions for writing: vertically, beginning at the top right corner of the page and proceeding downwards in columns to the left; or horizontally, as in English, proceeding from the top left corner across to the right. Which cover of a book in Chinese is the front therefore depends on the format in which the book is written. In other words, a book written in the vertical format will be read from the back to the front by European standards, whereas a book written in the horizontal format will be read from front to back.

Traditionally all written materials were written vertically. Since the new culture movement started at the beginning of this century, horizontal writing has been adopted as part of anti-tradition revolutionary change. In mainland China most books and written materials are written horizontally, though vertical writing appears occasionally in newspaper columns as well as in reprints of Chinese classics. In Hong Kong and Taiwan, where official rhetoric has been less anti-tradition, more books and written materials are written vertically. It is also worth pointing out that since the end of the Mao era, various aspects of Chinese tradition have been re-emerging, and, as a consequence, more and more books and written materials are being written in the vertical format.

However, one aspect of change that seems irreversible is the use of punctuation marks. In traditional Chinese writing there were no punctuation marks. Nowadays, as in English, there is a full range of punctuation marks, such as commas, quotation marks, exclamation marks, and colons. There are, however, some differences. The mark adopted for a full stop is written as a circle rather than the dot in English. There is also a book title mark (<< on the left of the title and >> on the right) and a slight pause mark 、 which English does not have. This mark is used for a pause that is supposed to be shorter than that denoted by a comma, for instance, pauses between items in a list.

COMPLEX AND SIMPLIFIED CHARACTERS

As discussed previously, many Chinese considered it necessary to reform their language as a process of nation-building. One of the main agenda for such a project was to do something about the characters. Characters were the target of revolution because they do not correspond to the sounds of the words they represent and hence are not alphabetic. Therefore, it imposes a great burden on the learner to memorise several thousand different characters and it takes a long time to write a character, especially the ones comprising many strokes.

Before the Communist revolution in 1949 many Chinese of different political persuasions thought it necessary to get rid of characters altogether and adopt an alphabetic system instead. However, by the late 1950s, even the most radical of all revolutionaries, the Communists, abandoned the project of replacing characters with an alphabetic system. Instead, the task of reform has been concentrated on simplifying characters in the hope that the simpler the characters the easier it will be for the populace to memorise them.

Simplification of characters in mainland China

In 1935 the then Nationalist government promulgated a list of 324 simplified characters for official use but, due to conservative opposition, support for this reform was withdrawn in the following year. The Communist Chinese government took the task of simplification very seriously. Over a number of years and with a high level of planning a government Committee for Chinese Writing Reform achieved some degree of character simplification. First, some obscure and rarely used characters were simply taken out of circulation. Second, uniformity was imposed by abolishing variations of characters with the same sound and meaning. These two measures reduced the total number of characters in the language. Third, some characters and radicals were simplified so as to have fewer strokes.

For several years the Committee for Chinese Writing Reform added to the number of simplified characters to serve as the national standard. By 1964 a definitive list was published. The list called *jiǎnhuà hànzì zǒngbiǎo* (A Comprehensive List of Simplified Characters) contained 2 236 simplified characters, roughly one-third of the total characters required to write modern Chinese. In 1986, the list was republished with some modifications. It contains 2 235 simplified characters.[12]

Table 4.2 has examples showing the differences between simplified and traditional characters. The first line consists of eight simplified characters used in mainland China and on the second

Table 4.2 Highlighting the differences between some simplified and complex characters

湾	穷	让	体	艺	发	点	飞
灣	窮	讓	體	藝	發	點	飛
bay	poor	let	body	art	develop	dot	fly

line are the corresponding complex characters used in Taiwan and Hong Kong. Underneath are the individual meanings of each character.

How are characters simplified?

Several techniques were used to simplify characters. One was to replace the original component of a character with a component of fewer strokes but which had the same sound as the given character. For example, the simplified character for 'art' is 艺. The component 乙 is pronounced as *yǐ* which is also the pronunciation of 藝 (although the tone is different), the complex character for art. Thus, 乙 is used to replace the entire middle and bottom components of the complex character and only the top component of the complex character remains.

Another technique used was simply to take one section of a complex character and use it as the simplified one. The complex form for 'to fly' is 飛 and the simplified is simply 飞, a part of the original one.

Some simplified characters had been invented and used by the Chinese people long before the official simplification initiative of the present government. According to one estimate, in publications which appeared in the Yuan, Song, Ming, and Qing dynasties there were more than six thousand simplified characters in use and more than three hundred of them are the same as the simplified ones in use today.[13] These simplified characters used to be considered vulgar and non-standard by the intellectual establishment. The Communist Chinese government sanctioned these characters and made them official.

Some simplified characters existed side by side with complex ones in classical Chinese, such as the two characters for *cóng* 从 and 從[13] (from), *zhòng* 众 and 眾 (the masses), *wàn* 万 and 萬

(ten thousand), and *bǐ* 笔 and 筆 (Chinese writing brush).[15] All that was needed in this case was to abolish the complex characters and to retain the simplified ones.

Some characters get simplified simply because cursive forms are adopted. When one writes fast, a character may become cursive and some of its strokes may be lost as a result. Gradually, the cursive form is adopted. The evolution of 言 to 讠 is an example in case.

Simplification of characters has been an on-going process and in a sense the process began as soon as drawings became writings. According to Qi, the very process of simplification was pushed by unofficial writing.[16] As the process went on the characters became abstract and therefore appeared less pictographic and more arbitrary. The users of characters have continued the process of simplification because of the convenience and speedier writing of the simpler characters.

Issues and problems with simplification

There is a difference in attitude between the governments of mainland China and Taiwan towards simplified characters. The mainland government not only sanctioned the current simplified characters but also actively created new ones. In contrast, the Nationalist government in Taiwan resists the change even today despite the fact that the Singapore government has adopted the simplified system.

The effects of simplification are far from obvious. Without sophisticated research it is very difficult to prove that the simplification of characters has improved literacy rates. In Hong Kong and Taiwan where complex characters have been preserved, and in Japan for that matter, the literacy rate is considerably higher than it is in mainland China. Such a comparison is somewhat unfair however, since Hong Kong, Taiwan, and Japan have higher levels of economic development than mainland China, a fact which must partly account for their higher literacy levels.

The simplification of characters has created some problems. To start with, the mastery of both the complex and simplified forms has become necessary: complex to read written materials published prior to the Communist revolution, and those published in present-day Hong Kong and Taiwan; simplified for people in Taiwan and Hong Kong if they want to read materials published in mainland China—they need skills to decode simplified characters. The situation poses the same problem for foreigners who want to learn Mandarin: having to learn both forms of characters if they want to read written materials published in both Taiwan and China.

Another argument against simplification is that simplified characters may be easier to write, but they are not necessarily easier to remember. Usually, the more strokes a character has the more distinctive it becomes as more strokes create more features. Distinctiveness jogs the memory and reduces confusion. Moreover, some simplified characters have lost their residual pictographic or ideographic features which may have helped in remembering them. For instance, the complex character for 'listen' has as the ear radical 耳 as a part . The simplified character, however, is written as 听. The right-hand side component of the simplified character 斤 is pronounced *jīn* and represents the word for a unit of weight—half a kilogram. The end result is that for a word meaning 'listen' the ear radical is replaced by the radical for mouth, 口!

CHARACTERS IN OTHER COUNTRIES

Apart from Taiwan, Hong Kong, and Singapore where the majority of the people are ethnic Chinese, characters were also used in Japan, Vietnam, and the Korean Peninsula in the past and are still used in Japan and South Korea today.

Korea

According to one account, the Koreans started using characters as early as the fifth century.[17] The Koreans did not just borrow Chinese characters, they also invented their own characters. By the mid fifteenth century, the Koreans developed the Korean alphabet, *hangŭl*. As a consequence the Korean language consisted of a mixture of Chinese loan words (known as *hanja* in Korean) and the native Korean alphabet. In 1948, however, the North Korean government abolished characters altogether.

Nowadays, while North Koreans do not use characters at all, South Koreans still use a certain number.

Japan

The precise time when the Japanese started using characters is also uncertain. What seems certain, however, is that it was from Korean immigrants that the Japanese learned about Chinese characters.[18] Apart from creating their own characters, like the Koreans did, the Japanese used Chinese characters in four major ways. One way was to adopt Chinese words in script (character), meaning, and also roughly in pronunciation. Second, some Chinese words were borrowed in script (character) as well as meaning but with different pronunciations. Third, the Japanese borrowed Chinese characters only but attached different meanings and pronunciations to them. Chinese characters borrowed in these ways belong to the category called *kanji*. Finally, there is what is called the *kana* script, which was developed using Chinese characters or radicals as syllable writing. The two types of *kana* script are called *hiragana* (based on the cursive Chinese script) and *katakana* (based on the regular Chinese script) in Japanese.

The Japanese have also made an effort to simplify *kanji*. Since the Meiji Reform the Japanese government has tried to restrict the use of *kanji*, and has attempted to limit the number of Chinese characters used in Japanese writing. In 1981, for example, the Japanese government sanctioned a reduced list of 1 945 characters to be used in textbooks and publications.[19]

Vietnam

Although relations between Vietnam and China date back to the second century BC, Vietnam has never completely adopted Chinese characters. They developed a writing system called *chũ nôm* that made use of some unchanged Chinese characters, but in which most characters were Vietnamese-created. However, even after Vietnam became an independent state from China in AD 939, Chinese cultural and linguistic influences were still extensive. This was because China, time and again, exercised suzerainty over Vietnam until the late nineteenth century when

Vietnam became a French colony. Even after the French colonised Vietnam, Chinese characters, together with French and Vietnamese, were used by some people. Since 1945 a Romanised version of Vietnamese (developed by European missionaries in the seventeenth century) finally became official and characters were completely phased out.

STUDY QUESTIONS

1. How many characters do you have to know to be literate in Chinese?
2. Why is stroke order important in writing characters?
3. What is a radical? What is the main difference between a radical and a character?
4. In what way can a character be argued to be phonetic?
5. How does one look up a character in a dictionary?
6. Is a character necessarily a word? Why?
7. Are characters arbitrary signs? Why?
8. Does simplification of characters help a student to learn to read and write?
9. In which countries other than China were characters once used and in which countries does character usage still occur?

REFERENCE READING

Ann, T. K., *Cracking the Chinese Puzzles*, vol. 1, Stockflows Co., Ltd, Hong Kong, 1982.

Aria, Barbara, *The Nature of the Chinese Characters*, East Rowville, NSW, Simon and Schuster,1991.

Bolts, William G., 'Early Chinese Writing', *World Archaeology*, no. 17, 1986, pp. 420–36.

Chen, Ping, 'Modern Written Chinese in Development', *Language and Society*, 22 (4), Dec. 1993, pp. 505–37.

——, 1999, *Modern Chinese*, Cambridge University Press, Cambridge.

Chen, Yulong, Yang, Tongfang et al., *han wenhua lungang-jian shu zhongchao zhongri zhongyue wenhua jiaoliu* (An Outline of Chinese Culture and Sino-Korean, Sino-Japanese and Sino-Vietnamese Cultural Exchange), Beijing daxue chubanshe, Beijing, 1993.

Driscoli, Lucy and Kenji, Toda, *Chinese Calligraphy*, Paragon Book Reprint Corp., New York, 1964.

Fazzioli, Edoardo, *Understanding Chinese Characters, A Beginner's Guide to the Chinese Language*, English Translation, William Collins Sons & Co. Ltd, London, English Translation 1987.

Georges, Jean, *Writing the Story of Alphabets and Scripts*, English translation, Thames and Hudson Ltd, London, and Harry N. Abrams, Inc., New York, 1992.

Guan Erjin and Tian Lin, 'ruhe shixian hanzi biaozhunhua', (How to standardise the use of characters), *zhongguo yuwen*, 2, 1981, pp. 35–42.

He Jiu Ying, Hu Shuangbao and Zhang Meng et al. (eds), *zhong guo han zi wen hua da guan* (Aspects of Chinese Character Culture), Beijing daxue chubanshe, 1995.

Li Leyi, *hanzi yanbian wu bai li* (Tracing the Roots of Chinese Characters: 500 Cases), Beijing, Beijing Language and Culture University Press, 1993.

Li Xiaoding, *hanzi shihua* (On the History of Chinese Characters), Taipei, Lianjing,1977.

Lindqvist, Cecilia, *China, Empire of the Written Symbol*, London: Harvill, 1989.

Qi Xigui, *wenzixue gaiyao* (An Outline Study of Characters), Shangwu yinshuguan, Beijing, 1988.

Shao Jingmin and Shi Youwei (eds), *wenhua yuyan zhongguo chao* (the Tide of Cultural Linguistics in China), Yuwen chubanshe, Beijing, 1995.

Su Peicheng, *hanzi jianhua yu fanti zi dui zhao zidian* (A Dictionary of Traditional and Simplified Characters in Contrast), Beijing, Zhongxin Chubanshe, 1992.

Wang Tiekun et al., *hanzi guifan tongsu jianhua* (Lectures on Standardisation of Common Characters), Renmin ribao chubanshe, Beijing, 1994.

ENDNOTES

1 T. K. Ann, *Cracking the Chinese Puzzles*, vol. 1, Stockflows Co., Ltd, Hong Kong, 1982, p. VI, and He Jiu Ying, Hu Shuangbao, and Zhang Meng et al. (eds), *zhong guo han zi wen hua da guan* (Aspects of Chinese Character Culture), Beijing daxue chubanshe, 1995, p. 8.

2 Jerry Norman, *Chinese*, Cambridge University Press, 1988, p. 58.

3 This is not a dictionary in the sense generally understood in the West. Instead, it largely classifies and explains the origin and composition of characters. *Wen* here means simple non-composite graphs and *zi* means composite graphs. *Shuo* means talk about and *jie* means explain.

4 He, Hu, Zhang et al. (eds), *zhong guo han zi wen hua da guan*, p. 74.

5 Wang Li, Wang Guzhang et al., *xiandai hanyu jiangzuo* (Lectures on Modern Chinese), Zhishi chubanshe, Beijing, 1983, p. 49.

6 Guan Erjin and Tian Lin, ruhe shixian hanzi biaozhunhua, (How to standardise the use of characters), *zhongguo yuwen*, 2, 1981, pp. 147–53.

7 The syllable represented by this character is a bound morpheme in that it has to be combined with another syllable to mean 'dragonfly'. However, the point about the structure of the character is valid.

8 Li Xiaoding, *hanzi shihua* (On the History of Chinese Characters), Taipei, Lianjing, 1977.

9 Qi Xigui, *wenzixue gaiyao* (An Outline Study of Characters), Shangwu yinshuguan, Beijing, 1988, p. 7.

10 Li Leyi, *hanzi yanbian wu bai li* (Tracing the Roots of Chinese Characters: 500 Cases), Beijing, Beijing Language and Culture University Press, 1993, p. 376.

11 Qi Xigui, *wenzixue gaiyao* , p. 166.
12 Su Peicheng, *hanzi jianhua yu fanti zi dui zhao zidian* (A Dictionary of Traditional and Simplified Characters in Contrast), Beijing, Zhongxin chubanshe, 1992, p. 2.
13 Li Xiaoding, *hanzi shihua* (On the History of Chinese Characters), Taipei, Lianjing, 1977.
14 The first one in each pair is obviously simplified.
15 Qi Xigui, *wenzixue gaiyao*, p. 302.
16 Qi Xigui, *wenzixue gaiyao*.
17 He, Hu, Zhang et al. (eds), *zhong guo han zi wen hua da guan*, p. 374.
18 He, Hu, Zhang et al. (eds), p. 384.
19 He, Hu, Zhang et al. (eds), pp. 388–9. According to Jerry Norman, After the Second World War, the number of Chinese characters to be used was limited by law to a list of 1 850. Norman, 1988, p. 78.

CHAPTER 5
Vocabulary

WORDS

We have discussed the sound and writing systems of Mandarin in the previous two chapters. The sound and writing systems of any language are simply ways of representing linguistic meaning. A sound, or a written symbol by itself, does not have any inherent linguistic meaning. A link has to be established between a sound or a written symbol and a meaning for the former to be linguistic. Because such links are arbitrary, a non-native language has to be strenuously learned. Only when such a link is established can a sound or a written symbol represent a meaning and thus be called a word.

Vocabulary is a stock of words in a language. A word may represent an object such as the name of a person or a thing; but a word may also represent an idea or a concept. These words are our way of referring to ourselves and the world around us. We call these words lexical words.

Lexical words versus grammatical or functional words
There is another set of words in any language which are used for grammatical purposes only. The word *to* in English is such a word. In the sentence 'I am going to China', the function of *to* is grammatical; and, as a matter of fact, the meaning of the sentence can be conveyed without *to*. Without *to*, however, the sentence would be ungrammatical. We call this set of words grammatical words or functional words because they are internal to a system of grammar.

The precise number of lexical words in any language is difficult to determine because vocabulary is open-ended and new terms are continually being added to meet new needs. According to one estimate, the English language has a staggering one million items.[1] The largest modern dictionary of Japanese, the *Nihon Kokugo Daijiten*, contains some 400 000 entries.[2] A figure comparable to this is the half a million entries that are contained in the Chinese dictionary *zhōnghuá dà cídiǎn.* 中华大词典

No one needs to use all the words in a language and some lexical items are never encountered in everyday use. Still, to be able to use, or at least to recognise, the more than 100 000 most frequently used vocabulary items listed in the Chinese dictionary *cí hǎi* involves a tremendous amount of memory work.

Native speakers of English may find it easier to learn vocabulary items from most other European languages than those of Mandarin because most European languages are genetically and culturally related to English and share a vocabulary which is cognate. A dictionary can give one or more simple definitions, (or translation if it is a bilingual dictionary) of any vocabulary item. However, many vocabulary items involve cultural assumptions which cannot easily be defined in a dictionary. Chinese words and English words, therefore, cannot always be equated on a one-to-one basis. That is why the vocabulary items of a foreign language have to be learned in context. To construct sentences by looking up words in a dictionary alone may give rise to some very strange combinations.

Words and characters

It is worth repeating at this stage that in Chinese a written word is not the same as a character. A character always has at least one meaning, but a written word may consist of more than one character. In Mandarin, a written word is often formed by two characters which have the same meaning. In 衣服 (clothing), 学习, (study) and 画画 (to paint), each has two sounds which are represented by two characters that mean, more or less, the same thing. 无产阶级 (without property grade rank) has four characters, but it has a one-word meaning— 'proletariat'.

WORD CLASSES

To divide words into classes is a method of analysing a language. This division is useful for students because it helps in learning grammar. Words are grouped as different classes (usually called parts of speech) according to their properties and the ways they function in sentences.

Although how words in a language are grouped together depends largely on definitions, there are universal features that all languages share and features which only some languages share. For instance, however we define them, both English and Chinese can group lexical words into nouns, verbs, adverbs, and so on. The following discussion of word classes focuses on comparing Mandarin with English for the benefit of English native speakers learning Chinese.

Nouns

Words are grouped on the basis of two criteria: semantic properties (meaning), and syntactic properties (structural function; that is, how they appear in a sentence). Semantically, nouns denote objects, things, persons, ideas, or concepts. Syntactically, a noun can be the subject of a sentence or the object. For instance, in 'John likes whales', *John* is the subject and *whales* is the object of the sentence. In these respects the function of nouns in Mandarin and English is the same.

Nouns in both English and Mandarin may be specified or modified by numerals, as shown in the following:

> *sān gè rén* (three people)
> *yī liàng chē* (one car)

They may be modified by a demonstrative as in:

> *zhè xiē shū* (these books)
> *nà tiáo gǒu* (that dog)

Both in English and Mandarin a noun can be modified by an adjective, such as:

> *gāo shān* (high mountain)
> *píng dì* (level ground)

There are, of course, structural properties which are not shared between English and Mandarin. Unlike their English counterparts, Mandarin nouns do not reflect the difference in number (singular versus plural). In Chinese the difference between singular and plural is made either through the context, or by a numeral. Only in a few cases, where nouns denote human beings, is the particle *men* added to indicate plurality. Thus, *wǒ* is 'I' or 'me' and *wǒmen* is 'we' or 'us', *háizi* is 'child' and *háizimen* is 'children'.

Verbs
Subject and predicate
Semantically, most verbs denote actions and activities. Syntactically, a verb, together with other elements, forms the predicate of a sentence. A sentence is often described as having two parts: the subject and the predicate. In 'John likes whales', *John* is the subject and *likes whales* is the predicate. Likewise, in 'The handsome and hard working John likes all kinds of whales', *the handsome and hard working John* is the subject and *likes all kinds of whales* is the predicate.

There are sentences in which the predicate is not formed by an action verb. For instance, in 'John is handsome', *John* is the subject, but the predicate, *is handsome*, has nothing to do with any action. In this case the predicate is not about what the subject does, but about what the subject is like. In English the lexical item from which '*is*' is derived is sometimes called the copula, or verb 'to be'. It can take many forms: *is, am, was, are*, or indeed, *were, should be, will be, has been, would have been*, and so on, depending on the number, person, and tense.

The nearest equivalent of the verb 'to be' in Mandarin is *shì*, which never changes, no matter what number, person, or tense is involved. Whether lexical items such as *shì* are verbs can be debated, but what they have in common with action verbs is that they are essential parts of the predicate in a sentence.

Adverbs modifying verbs
Verbs may be modified by adverbs. Thus, for 'He works hard', the Chinese equivalent is *tā* (he) *nǔlì* (hard) *gōngzuò* (work), and

for 'He suddenly stood up' the Chinese is tā (he) *tūrán* (suddenly) *zhàn qǐlái le* (stood up).

However, there is an important difference between the role of an adverb in Chinese and that in English. In Chinese, the position of an adverb in a sentence is very rigid: it has to appear before the verb and usually after the subject. In English, however, an adverb may appear either before or after the verb: 'Suddenly he stood up', or 'He stood up suddenly'.

Absence of inflection in Chinese

Another important difference between Mandarin and English is that verbs in the former do not inflect. In English, verbs inflect to show differences in number, person, and tense:

> He/She work*s*
> We work
> I *am* work*ing*
> They *were* work*ing*
> You work*ed*

and so on. As the italicised bits show, the verb 'work' changes form depending on the number, person, and tense. In Chinese the sound as well as the character for 'work' remains the same whether or not it involves past or future tense, or singular or plural subject.

Transitive versus intransitive verbs

A verb may be transitive or intransitive. A transitive verb is able to take a direct object as part of a predicate in a sentence, whereas an intransitive verb cannot. Verbs like 'go' and 'work' are intransitive in English because they do not have a direct object. For instance we can say 'We are going', but we cannot say 'We are going China', or 'He works it'. We have to say 'We are going *to* China' and 'He works *at* it'.

Verbs like 'make' in English are transitive as they have to take a direct object. We cannot say 'He makes', but we can say 'He makes a good statesman'. Some verbs are both transitive and intransitive, such as 'stop': 'She stops' (intransitive) and 'She stops the car' (transitive). In Chinese, *qù* (go) is both transitive and intransitive, so are *zuò* (make) and *tíng* (stop); on the other hand, *gōngzuò* (work) is an intransitive verb.

The dissyllabic process (having two syllables as one word) has given rise to a feature in regard to transitivity versus intransitivity in Chinese. We need to spend some time explaining this.

Traditionally, at least in written texts, many verbs in Chinese were monosyllabic; that is, one syllable for one word, such as *huà* (to paint), and *chàng* (sing). In modern colloquial Mandarin many words including verbs consist of two syllables. Thus 'to paint' is *huà huà* (paint a painting), and 'to sing' is *chàng gē* (sing a song). Hence, 'She sings' is very often not *tā chàng*, but *tā chàng gē*, and 'She paints' is not *tā huà*, but *tā huà huà*.

The result of this is that verbs like *chàng gē* and *huà huà* cannot take another object. In other words, a verb is combined with an object to become a verb in its own right, but the second syllable still functions as an object. As a result, when we want to attach another object after verbs of this kind, the object that is a part of the verb has to be dropped. For instance, the following Chinese sentences are ungrammatical:

tā huà huà wǒ (She paints me.)
tā chàng gē liúxíng gēqǔ (He sings pop music.)

The grammatical sentences should be:

tā huà wǒ
tā chàng liúxíng gēqǔ.

in both of which the second syllable of the verb is dropped.

Adjectives

Semantically, adjectives are words which describe qualities. Syntactically, they are used either to modify nouns or, as in English, to be combined with the verb to be to form the predicate in a sentence. In 'Red apples are sweet', both <u>red</u> and <u>sweet</u> are adjectives, both describing the quality of the subject. In English, many adjectives are identifiable by the fact that they share derivations such as *-ive*, *-ful*, *-ty*, *-al*, and so on. Beauti*ful*, administrat*ive*, pret*ty*, and economic*al* are all adjectives. In other words, by looking at words which have these derivations we know that they are adjectives.

However, not all adjectives have these derivations and some words which have these derivations are nouns. 'Security', for instance, is a noun. Like verbs, adjectives in English may have inflections, as in, 'prettier' and 'prettiest', but adjectives of more than three syllables do not inflect; for instance, it is ungrammatical to say 'beautifuller' or 'beautifullest'.

An adjective particle in Chinese

In Mandarin, adjectives, like verbs, do not have any inflection. Nor is there any special derivation to identify an adjective. There is, however, a functional word (or grammatical word) which is used to link the adjective and noun when an adjective modifies a noun. That grammatical word is *de*.

To mean 'handsome man/men' we say *piàoliang de nánrén*. *Piàoliang* means 'handsome' and *nánrén* (male person) means 'man' or 'men'.

Absence of the verb 'to be' in Chinese

Notice that when an adjective is used as the predicate in a sentence, no verb to be (*shì*), is required. In English we have to say 'Someone *is* handsome' or 'They *are* handsome', or 'You *were* handsome'. In Mandarin it is ungrammatical to say:

> *tā shì piàoliang* (He is handsome.)
> *wǒmen shì piàoliang* (We are handsome.)

Instead, we have to say:

> *tā piàoliang* (literally 'he handsome')
> *wǒmen piàoliang* (literally 'we handsome')

to mean 'He is handsome' and 'We are handsome' respectively.

Syntactically speaking, that is, in terms of how they appear in a sentence, there is therefore no difference between an adjective and a verb as predicate in Mandarin, as in *wǒmen gōngzuò* ('We work'—a verb predicate) and *wǒmen hěn gāo* ('We are very tall'—an adjective predicate). In other words, in a sentence which has what is usually called an adjective as part of the predicate, the adjective does not require the verb 'to be' in Mandarin. In English, various forms of the verb 'to be' are required depending on the person and number of the subject and the tense of the sentence.

Adverbs

Adverbs are used in Mandarin, as they are in English, to modify verbs, adjectives, or adverbs. In *tā fēicháng piàoliang* (She is extraordinarily beautiful), *fēicháng* is an adverb modifying an adjective. In *tā piàoliang de dǎ wǎngqiú* (He plays tennis beautifully) *piàoliang de* is an adverb modifying a verb. In English an easy way to identify many adverbs is by the derivation -*ly*: beautiful*ly*, economical*ly*, semantical*ly*.

There is no such morphological way of identifying an adverb in Chinese. Instead, as the sentence *tā piàoliang de dǎ wǎngqiú* shows, the particle *de* is an indication of *piàoliang* being an adverb. Notice that *piàoliang* in *piàoliang de nánrén* (handsome men) is an adjective whereas *piàoliang* in *tā piàoliang de dǎ wǎngqiú* is an adverb. The difference is entirely structural: When *piàoliang* modifies a noun such as *nánrén* it is an adjective, but when it modifies a verb such as *dǎ* it is an adverb.

An adverb particle in Chinese

It appears that words such as *piàoliang* can either be an adjective or an adverb depending how they appear in a sentence. When such words, followed by *de,* modify verbs they are adverbs, and when they modify nouns they are adjectives (again followed by *de*). When they are adverbs they always precede verbs and when they are adjectives they always precede nouns.

Hence the difference between the adjective *de* and the adverb *de* is shown by its syntactic properties: if it appears before a noun, it is an adjective particle and if it appears before a verb it is an adverb particle. In written Mandarin, two different characters are assigned to the two *de*s: 地 for the adverb *de*, and 的 for the adjective *de*.

Stative verbs

Notice that in our discussion about the category of adjectives we have shown that there is no syntactic difference between the category of verbs and that of adjectives in Mandarin. Just as a verb does not inflect (change its form) in accordance with differences in the subject in terms of person, number, and tense, an adjective does not require any inflection of the verb 'to be'. In fact, as shown a moment ago, it does not even require the verb 'to be' in Mandarin. The difference, therefore, between a verb and an adjective is entirely semantic: roughly speaking, one category of words (verbs) denotes action, and the other (adjectives) denotes qualities.

On the other hand, in our discussion of adverbs in this section we have shown that whether words such as *piàoliang* are adjectives or adverbs is entirely dependent on syntactic functions: if they modify a noun they are adjectives, and if they modify a verb they are adverbs. It is for these two facts—the fact they are structurally not different from verbs, and the fact that they can either be adjectives or adverbs—that words such as *piàoliang* are sometimes called stative verbs.

The term stative verb, therefore, can explain these two facts: the first that the words belonging to this category are the same as verbs syntactically (that is, no requirement of the verb 'to be' and there is no inflection); and second that they are different from verbs semantically (that is, they denote qualities rather than actions).

Finally, just to reiterate, these so-called stative verbs can either be adjectives or adverbs depending on how they appear in a sentence. If they appear before a noun they are adjectives and if they appear before a verb they are adverbs. Therefore, the classification of these words depends on their context within a sentence.

Particles

Particles are functional words which are internal to the grammar. In other words, they are used to carry out grammatical functions in a given language. In English, some prepositions such as 'to', 'for', 'on', and 'at' function as particles. In Chinese there are half a dozen important particles, and *de* discussed above is one of them. We will have more discussion on particles in the next chapter.

WORD FORMATION

The boundary line of what a word is cannot always be clearly defined. Is 'work mate' one word or two words? Sometimes, the two elements are spelt together to indicate unity, such as 'headline'. Sometimes a hyphen is used to indicate that they are single words, such as 'first-hand', but at other times they are not, such as 'first class', or 'first lady'.

Monosyllable versus multisyllable words

The situation in Chinese is even more complex. Because every syllable in Chinese has a corresponding character and every character has to be written separately, every character looks like a symbol for a word. In fact, not every syllable is a word in Mandarin and many words need more than one syllable to make sense. However, even if we write in *pīnyīn* instead of characters the word boundary becomes no clearer. This is clearly shown by the different ways of writing Chinese names using alphabet letters. The standard way of writing the name for Mao is Mao Zedong, but some still write it as Mao Ze-dong.

We may argue that the four syllables *wú* (without) *chǎn* (property) *jiē* (grade) *jí* (rank) meaning 'proletariat' should be spelt together as *wúchǎnjiējí* since it is one word. Should we push this argument further, we may even want to write 'the People's Republic of China' as *zhōnghuárénmíngònghéguó*, although each of the seven syllables has at least one distinctive meaning: *zhōng* (middle), *huá* (Chinese), *rén* (person), *mín* (people), *gòng* (share), *hé* (together), and *guó* (country). The most sensible solution in this case is perhaps to spell the name in three separate entities: *zhōnghuá* (China), *rénmín* (people), *gònghéguó* (republic).

Morphemes, syllables, and characters

The best approach to syllables in Mandarin is in terms of morphemes. A morpheme is the smallest linguistic unit with meaning. Thus in 'beautifully' there are three morphemes: *beauti*, *ful*, and *ly*, each of which has a meaning. Both *beauti* and *ful* have lexical meanings whereas *ly* only has a grammatical meaning, i.e. derivation of an adverb.

A morpheme that can appear independently as a word is called a free morpheme and a morpheme that cannot appear independently as a word is called a bound morpheme. *Beauty* is a free morpheme, and so is *full* (ignoring the variations of spelling when they are parts of the word 'beautiful'). *Ly*, however, is a bound morpheme because it has to appear with another morpheme to make a word.

By this definition, therefore, almost every syllable in Mandarin—with the exception of some loan words such as *pútao* meaning 'grapes'—is a morpheme (note that this is not the case in English), and every morpheme has a corresponding character in the written language.

Accordingly, there are many monosyllabic words in Mandarin, although it should be pointed out that a lot of them have to be used as such in the right contexts either linguistically or pragmatically. For instance, the word for house can either be two syllables—*fángzi,* or one syllable—*fáng,* depending on the context. To say 'one house', the word for house has to be two syllables, i.e. *yí gè fángzi,* and to say *yí gè fáng* is unacceptable; but in 'the person who buys houses', the word for 'house' can be one syllable, *mǎi fáng de rén.*

There are words which always need more than one syllable to make sense. Words like *pútao* (grapes), *méiguì* (rose), *bōlí* (glass), and *kāfēi* (coffee) are examples. For each of these words, one syllable cannot be separated from the other because once separated each syllable becomes meaningless. In other words, each of these syllables is not a free morpheme. Most of these words are nouns and are borrowed from other languages. The same applies to the loan words discussed in chapter 4.

Another group of words that need more than one syllable to make sense are called conjunctions. A common one is the word meaning 'when', as shown in the following example:

Table 5.1 Conjunctions

Chinese sentence	Literal translation	English translation
dāng wǒ chīfàn deshíhòu	dang I eat meal deshihou	When I was eating

Dāng is sometimes omitted and when it is *deshíhòu* means 'when'. There are a number of words of this kind, such as *yī* ... *jiù* (as soon as), and *lián* ... *dōu* (even).[3]

COMPOUND WORDS

The majority of words in Mandarin are formed by morphemes which are free. These words are usually two-syllable compounds.

Compound words of two free morphemes

The majority of compound words consist of two free morphemes. In fact, a lot of these compound words are formed by two morphemes which have more or less the same lexical meanings. Apart from words like *xuéxí* (learn study) meaning 'study', *huàhuà* (paint a painting) meaning 'to paint' which we have discussed previously, there are words like:

gāngcái (just-just) meaning 'just now'
shēngyīn (sound-sound) meaning 'sound'
qíguài (strange-strange), 'strange'

Each of the two syllables not only has a lexical meaning, but also can function as an independent word in the right context.

Some compound words are formed by free morphemes of different meanings. In words like:

yīshēng (medicine person) meaning 'doctor'
dōngxi (east west) meaning 'things'
hútu (paste spread) meaning 'muddled' or 'confused'

each syllable is a morpheme which has at least one meaning and each can function as a word by itself.

Multisyllable compound words: Loan words

Many compound words of more than two syllables are formed as a consequence of new ideas and concepts introduced into the language, especially from the West. Consider the following:

1   *mǎkèsī zhǔyì*

2 *gòngchăn dăng*
3 *zhōngchăn jiējí*

In (1) the first three syllables are the transliteration of Marx, and *zhŭ* (main) together with *yì* (meaning) means *ism*. (2) is the word for 'communist party', which literally means 'share property clique'. (3) means 'middle class' (middle-property-grade-rank).

Many of these concepts were introduced into the language when Western books were translated into Chinese. Very often, the translator had to work hard to find suitable words for these concepts. The first great modern translator of Western books Yan Fu confessed that he sometimes had to spend days working out the translation of a single term.

If the translation of a term becomes commonly accepted it becomes a word in the language. When the concept of democracy was first introduced, some tried the technique of translating the English pronunciation, as *demokelaxi*. But the term was not popular. As a sign of desperation, as well as amusement perhaps, some writers in the 1930s termed democracy *dé xiānsheng* by taking the sound of the first syllable of the word and adding the Chinese term for 'Mr'. Fortunately, the Japanese had tackled the problem of introducing Western ideas into their language before the Chinese. The Chinese were therefore able to adopt these ready-made Japanese character words into their own language with considerable ease. Thus, the term for democracy was finally settled by adopting the Japanese word which rendered it in two Chinese characters *mínzhŭ* (people-master). At the beginning of this century there was a continual process of China reborrowing characters from Japan to form new words.

Numeral compounds
The Chinese are fond of forming compound words with numerals. For each of the numbers from one to ten, hundreds of words are formed beginning with a numeral. In *A Concise Chinese–English Dictionary of Chinese Proper Names and Terms* published in 1992, more than thirty thousand lexical entries are included. Of these entries, more than 1 500 begin

with a numeral. A dictionary that contains only words starting with a numeral lists 2 760 entries.[4] The following are some examples starting with the numbers one to ten.

> *yī nián dào tóu* (one-year arrive-end) meaning 'throughout the year'

> *èr jìn zhì* (two-enter system) meaning 'binary system'

> *sān K dǎng* (three-K clique) meaning 'Ku Klux Klan'

> *sì miàn bā fāng* (four-face eight-directions) meaning 'all around'

> *wǔ guān* (five organs) meaning 'the five features of eyes, ears, nose, mouth, and tongue'

> *liù cháo* (six-dynasty) meaning 'the Six Dynasties' in Chinese history

> *qī qī bā bā* (seven-seven eight-eight), which means 'disorderly'

> *bā fāng* (eight directions) meaning 'all directions'

> *jiǔ jiǔ biǎo* (nine-nine table) meaning 'the multiplication table'

> *shí zì jià* (ten-character frame) to mean 'a cross'

A word may consist of nothing but numbers:

> *yì wǔ yì shí* (one-five-one-ten) meaning 'systematically' or 'full details'

Some Sinologists have noted the Chinese love of numbers.[5] The classic Confucian tenets are referred to as *sān gāng wǔ cháng* (the three cardinal guides and five constant virtues) as specified in the Confucian ethical codes, and the complete collection of a particular set of classic books is termed *sì kù quán shū* (four-store complete book).

In contemporary China, the practice of naming things using numbers has been pushed even further by the Communist government. Terms such as the following are very common:

1 *yí dòu èr pī sān gǎi* (one struggle two criticise three reform)

2 *sì xiàng jī běn yuán zé* (four kind basic original rule)

3 *sì rén bāng* (four-person gang)

(1) is a term used in the Mao era to refer to the Communist Party technique of first the ideological struggle session, second self-criticism and finally thought reform. (2) refers to 'the four cardinal principles of socialism, proletarian dictatorship, Communist leadership, and Marxism-Leninism and Mao Zedong Thought' laid down by Deng Xiaoping to halt the process of the collapse of Communist rule. (3) means 'the Gang of Four' referring to the four principal radicals during the Cultural Revolution. These terms are all standard jargon in everyday use.

LOAN WORDS

For the names of foreign places and people, the usual practice is to transliterate the sounds. Thus, the term for 'Washington' is *huáshèngdùn* and the term for 'Australia' is *àodàlìyà*.

Even when solving the problem of translation by transliteration, the Chinese will try to find characters which not only correspond to the sounds but also denote meanings as near as possible to the original. The term invented by Lin Yutang for the English word 'humour' is *yōumò* (seclusion quiet), the term for 'miniskirt' invented by Zhao Yuenren (or Y. R. Chao) is *mínǐ qún* (fascinate you skirt). The term for Mickey Mouse is *mǐ lǎoshǔ* (rice-mouse). Terms like these capture the sounds as well the meanings of the original words to some extent, and Chinese people like these types of loan words.

With the exception of very few words such as: *shāfā* (sofa), *báilándì* (brandy), *dídītì* (DDT), *nígǔdīng* (nicotine), *xuějiā* (cigar), *pūkè* (poker), *wǎ* (watt), *nílóng* (nylon), *bāléiwǔ* (ballet), and *àikèsīguāng* (X-ray), the transliteration of sounds for words other than names of people and places is not frequent. Butter, for instance, was first translated as *baituo*, whereas Esperanto (the name of an artificially invented language) was translated as *aisibunandu*. Both of these show attempts to capture the sounds of the original words. However, these translations were later dropped and, *nǎi yóu* (milk-oil), for 'butter' and *shìjiè yǔ* (world-language) for 'Esperanto' came to be adopted.

Proper names, i.e. names of places, people, and institutions are different. Thus, the term for McDonalds is *màidāngláo* and that for Bolshevik is *bùěrshíwéikè*. For these terms none of the syllables denotes an intended lexical meaning. A term that transliterates the sounds quite accurately and, at the same, time reflects the intended meaning is the Chinese word for Coca-Cola, *kěkǒu kělè* (good taste and happy!).[6]

Chinese, like other languages, borrows items of vocabulary from other languages all the time. *Hārbīn*, the capital of Heilongjiang Province, is a word from the Nuzhen people, an ancient tribe in the north, who were supposedly the predecessors of the modern Manchu nationality. *Hārbīn* means 'glory' in Nuzhen, but now it has lost its previous meaning and simply denotes the city in Mandarin. *Wūlǔmùqí*, the capital of Xinjiang Province, is a Mongolian term meaning 'excellent pasture land'. *Xīshuāngbǎnnà*, likewise, does not have any meaning in Mandarin except the name of a town in Yunnan Province. The term is borrowed from the Dai language meaning 'the twelfth basin'.[7]

Although Chinese continues to borrow words from other languages, it is still very resistant to outside influence. Chinese is a very exclusive language in that it cannot borrow terms from alphabetic languages (apart from proper names) without a process of transformation. Therefore, it may not always be easy to determine which words in the language are loan words and which are not.

REDUPLICATION

Reduplication of syllables to form words happens in many languages. In English, for instance, there are words such as 'papa', 'hush-hush', 'pooh-pooh', or slightly modified reduplications such as 'mishmash'. Reduplications in English, however, are rare. In contrast, there are many words formed by reduplicating syllables in Mandarin. Reduplication may apply to a noun, a verb, or an adjective. In fact, reduplication in Chinese is a grammatical phenomenon that deserves special discussion.

Reduplicated names

Apart from the usual ones like *māma* (mother), *bàba* (father)—the kind of reduplications that may appear in other languages—there exists a handful more in Mandarin such as *yéye* (grandpa), *năinai* (grandma), *gēge* (elder brother), *mèimei* (younger sister), and so on. Many Chinese like to have reduplicated personal names because they convey a sense of affection, like nicknames in English. There must be thousands of Chinese whose personal names are *Máomao,* or *Tíngting,* or *Fāngfang.*

We may also observe that all the giant pandas donated by China to other countries have reduplicated names such as *Qīngqing* or *Jīngjing.*

Reduplicated verbs

Reduplication regularly applies to verbs in Mandarin. For a monosyllabic verb, the syllable can be repeated to mean the same thing, thus making it a two-syllable word. A word with two syllables that do not sound the same can also be repeated to make a four syllable word. For instance, for the verb *xuéxí* (to study), the reduplication is *xuéxí xuéxí.*

Although a reduplicated verb means the same as the non-reduplicated one, reduplication of verbs has semantic consequences. By repeating the same verb, the speaker actually intends to reduce the force conveyed by the verb, and thus soften the tone. Therefore, to reduce the tone in giving a command, one can repeat the verb. Instead of saying *shuō* (Speak!) one may say *shuō shuo,* which can be translated as 'You had better speak', or 'I suggest you speak'. Equally, in contrast to *wǒshuō* (I will speak), *wǒ shuō shuo* means 'Let me speak'.

When a monosyllabic verb is reduplicated, *yī* (the word for 'one') may be inserted in between. Thus, we can say *shuō yi shuō,* which is exactly the same as *shuōshuo.* The use of *yī* is a matter of personal choice. For two-syllable verbs, however, *yī* should never be inserted when reduplication takes place.

Finally, there are some verbs which cannot be reduplicated: verbs describing mental state such as *xǐhuān* (like), verbs of existence such as *yǒu* (exist), and verbs denoting process or change such as *kāishǐ* (begin), and *biànhuà* (change).

Reduplicated adjectives

Adjectives (or stative verbs in the right context) can also be reduplicated to achieve the effects of vividness, or picturesqueness. *Hóngshū* (red book) is just a book that is a red colour, but *hóng hóng de shū* brings focus to the colour.

Notice that the process of reduplication of adjectives is different from that for action verbs. In a two-syllable adjective, the two syllables need to be separated to be repeated. For instance, *gāoxìng* (high-mood), meaning 'happy', is reduplicated as *gāogāo xìngxìng,* not *gāoxìng gāoxìng.* When *gāoxìng* is repeated as *gāoxìng gāoxìng* it becomes a verb. *Ràng wǒmen gāoxìng gāoxìng* (let us happy happy) means 'Let us have some fun'.

Reduplicated measure words (or classifiers)

It is appropriate here perhaps to introduce, however briefly, the concept of a measure word before we discuss its reduplication. The types of words often referred to as measure words or classifiers have some similarity with what are sometimes called collective nouns in English. For instance, we need to say 'a piece of news', but not 'a news', nor 'two news'. In general, a classifier or measure word is not usually required in an English expression which containsa numeral. In other words, there is no need for a measure word in between the noun and the numeral, for example in 'three books'. However, that is exactly what we have to do in Chinese: between a numeral and a noun there must be a measure word to link them up.

More discussion will be devoted to measure words in the next chapter. What concerns us here is that when reduplicated, a measure word takes on the meaning of a universal quantifier. In other words, by reduplicating any measure word, it comes to mean the universal 'every'. Let us take a common measure word *gè* as an example:

Yí gè píngguǒ (one *ge* apple) means 'one apple'
liǎng gè píngguǒ (two *ge* apple) means 'two apples'
sān gè píngguǒ (three *ge* apple) means 'three apples'

and so on. If *gè* is reduplicated and we say *gè gè píngguǒ* it means 'every apple'. Thus, *nián nián* (year-year) means 'every year' or 'year after year', *tiān tiān* (day-day) means 'everyday', and *tiáo tiáo* (piece-piece) means 'every piece'.

AFFIXES

Affixes include prefixes, suffixes, and infixes. In languages like English it is reasonably straightforward to identify affixes. For instance, in 'unlikely' there is a prefix *un* and a suffix *ly*. These affixes usually do not function as words themselves, Moreover, they operate at vocabulary level—they are not grammatical words in a sentence.

In Mandarin, however, the situation is more complex. To start with, many of what may be considered to be affixes do function as words themselves. Second, some that appear to be affixes operate beyond vocabulary level and have grammatical functions at sentence level. Therefore, some of these need to be discussed in terms of what are called grammatical particles.

Prefixes

One of the most commonly used prefixes is *dì* which, when it precedes a numeral, makes any numeral an ordinal number. Thus *dì yī* is 'first', *dì èr* is 'second', *dì sān* is 'third', and so on. In a sense, the morpheme *bù* (no, not) can also be called a prefix because it can be prefixed to most adjectives, causing them to mean the opposite. Thus, *dàodé* is 'virtuous', or 'moral', and *bú dàodé* means 'immoral'. Other prefixes include *lǎo/xiǎo* which are typically prefixed to surnames to form nicknames, or for informal terms of address.

Here are some more prefixes. *Chū* is one of them. When it is prefixed to the first ten numerals, it means any of the first ten days of any lunar month. Thus, *chū yī* means the first day of whichever month is referred to; *chū èr* means the second day of the month referred to, and so on.

Another one is *kě*. When *kě* is prefixed to a verb it makes the verb into an adjective which has meaning equivalent to the English suffix *able*. Thus, *kě* can be prefixed to *ài* (love) and *kě ài* means 'lovable'; and *kě zuò* (the syllable *zuò* means 'do') means 'do-able'.

Another common pair of prefixes is *hǎo* (good) and *nán* (difficult) which, when prefixed to certain verbs or stative verbs, form adjectives that are antonyms. Thus, *hǎo chī* (*chī* means 'eat') means 'delicious' and *nán chī* means the opposite. *Hǎo kàn* (*kan* means 'look') is 'pretty' or 'handsome', whereas *nán kàn* means 'ugly'.

Since every syllable (except some loan words) that exists in Chinese has at least one meaning and since the majority of them can join another to form a word, it is difficult to say whether they are affixes in the conventional sense.

Take the examples of *hú, yáng,* and *wài guó*. In pre-modern times *hú* (which had a derogative connotation) was used to refer to foreigners or things foreign. Hence many things imported to China were given a name with *hú* as a prefix. A foreigner was *hú rén* (foreign person), the word for 'carrot' *hú luóbo* (foreign turnip), and that for 'walnut' *hú táo* (foreign peach). The derogative connotation is extended to expressions such as *hú shuō bā dào* (foreign say eight talk) meaning 'talk rubbish' and *hú zuò fēi wéi* (foreign work negative deed) meaning 'misbehaviour'.

Since the nineteenth century *hú* has been replaced by *yáng* ('ocean' and, therefore, 'overseas'). Hence a 'foreigner' is *yáng rén,* 'petrol' is *yáng yóu* (foreign oil), and 'match' is *yáng huǒ* (foreign fire). In contemporary Chinese, *yáng* has been replaced again by *wài guó* (outside country). Hence a 'foreigner' is *wài guó rén*. Can we say that these are affixes or just parts of compound words?

Suffixes

What is a suffix in Mandarin is not a straightforward issue either. The question involves whether an element appearing at the end of a word is a suffix or a particle. Certain people argue that some of these elements are suffixes while others argue that they are particles.[8] What is adopted in this book generally is that an element is a suffix if it functions at vocabulary level, and it is a particle if it functions at sentence level. Admittedly, however, there are cases that may not be so easily defined. Chapter 6 deals with what are considered to be particles.

The most common suffixes are *zi* and *r*. The original meaning of *zi* is 'human being'. In classical Chinese, *zi* was used to show respect to a learned person. Thus the founder of Confucianism was called *Kǒngzǐ,* the alleged founder of Daoism, or Taoism, was called *Lǎozǐ,* the legalist scholar was called *Xúnzǐ,* and the military strategist who wrote the famous military treaty *Sūnzǐ bīngfǎ* (The Art of War by Sunzi)—*Sūnzǐ;* they are all still known by these names today. The first syllable of each of these names was in fact the surname.

However, the semantic connotation of *zi* is different in modern Mandarin. *Zi* is no longer used to denote respect. If anything it is the opposite. Children and names of small objects such as tools or articles may have *zi* attached. Thus, we have *háizi* (children), *kuàizi* (chopsticks), *dāozi* (knife), and so on. Notice that each of these words has the same meaning without *zi* although in Mandarin they would require another syllable to form a word.

r as a suffix is used more among the northern Chinese, and it may be suffixed to a verb, such as *wánr* (to play), in which case it does not make a semantic difference. One can also add *r* to a noun such as *huār* (flower). When *r* is added, the sound immediately preceding *r* is dropped. For instance, in *wánr,* the *n* is not pronounced. Instead, it is pronounced as *wár.*

However, the phenomenon of *r* is far more complex than is suggested in the last paragraph.[9] To start with, in some cases the addition of *r* can change the category of a word as well as the meaning. For instance, consider the following:

huó (to live) *huór* (work)
dài (bring or take) *dàir* (ribbon)
fāng (square) *fāngr* (method)
zǎowǎn (eventually) *zǎowǎnr* (morning and evening)
gè (a measure word) *gèr* (size)

yībān (usually) *yībānr* (the same as)
xìn (letter) *xìnr* (news)

Clearly, in many cases, the meanings of a word with *r* and without *r* are related. For instance the word meaning 'eventually' is related to 'either morning or evening'. The above examples do show, however, that *r* is a suffix, even though in most cases *r* is semantically insignificant and just adds a syllable to a word.

What are we to make of *r*? On the one hand one can add *r* to many words to sound like a northerner; but the word does not change meaning. On the other hand *r* can be semantically significant. In other words, in this second case whether an *r* is added or not forms a different word. Therefore, it appears that when *r* is semantically significant it is a suffix. Moreover, I would suggest that the semantically significant *r* occurs only in northern dialect which is not Mandarin.

There are other suffixes such as *men*, the plural suffix for pronouns and names referring to human beings, and *tou* (head, end). Thus, *wǒ* means 'I' or 'me' and *wǒmen* is 'we' or 'us'. *Háizi* can either mean 'child' or 'children' depending on the context, but *háizimen* only means 'children'. When *tou* is added to *wài* (out) as *wàitou,* it means 'outside', and when added to *lǐ* (in) as *lǐtou,* it means 'inside'.

Other suffixes include *xué* which means 'the study of something', or *-ology* in English, for instance:

rénlèi (human kind) *rénlèi xué* (anthropology)
shèhuì (society) *shèhuì xué* (sociology)

Another one is *jiā* which is more or less equivalent to *-ist* in English. For example, *kēxué* is 'science' and *kēxuéjiā* is 'scientist'.

Infixes

Infixes are very rare in English. One example is 'bloomin' in 'abso-bloomin-lutely' in colloquial discourse.[10] Some Chinese grammarians[11] argue that Mandarin has infixes in what are called potential complement structures. For example in *chī bu xià* (literally meaning 'eat not down') and *chī de xià* ('eat can down') both *bu* and *de* are fixed in the middle. The former means 'cannot finish eating' and the latter 'can finish eating'. There is a large number of expressions formed by inserting either *bu* or *de* in the middle. For a more detailed discussion of this phenomenon see chapter 6.

Chéng yǔ (SET PHRASES)

Chěng yǔ (literally meaning accomplish language) is a class of words which do not have ready English equivalents. The nearest counterparts are idioms or idiomatic expressions. They are called *chéng yǔ*—accomplished, or ready-made language—because they have fixed forms and constant meanings, and they are, therefore, often referred to as set phrases. Some of these expressions have been in use for thousands of years without any change.

Chéng yǔ are sometimes referred to as four-character phrases because the majority of these idiomatic expressions consist of four syllables and therefore four characters. The exact number of *chéng yǔ* in the language is not clear. In *liù yòng chéng yǔ cí diǎn* (a Six-Way Definition Dictionary of Cheng Yu), more than 4 600 entries are listed.

Some *chéng yǔ* have straightforward meanings in that one can understand it by knowing the meanings of the individual sylla-bles. For instance, *wàn zǐ qiān hóng* (ten-thousand-purple thou-sand-red) means a riot of colour, or a blaze of colour. However, the majority of *chéng yǔ* have specific meanings handed down through Chinese history, which cannot be understood without knowing the history behind them.

Almost every *chéng yǔ* contains a story, a legend, or a moral tale and the phrase that sums up the story is meant to be a moral lesson or some wisdom learned from experience. For instance, *shǒu zhū dài tù* (stay with tree wait rabbit) tells the story of a farmer in ancient China who happened to pass a tree when a rabbit ran into the tree and killed itself. The farmer, very happy that he could have a good meal from the rabbit without having to do anything, decided to sit by the tree and wait for another rabbit to kill itself in the same way. The moral is that past experience cannot always be a guide for future actions and one cannot always expect reward without work. The story was told as a moral lesson in essays by Han Feizi (280–233 BC). Here are some more. *Qīng chū yú lán* (green out from blue) literally means that the colour blue is the base of the colour green, although green may be better than blue. The moral lesson being that a student may have to learn from the teacher, but the former may overtake the latter. This was told in *Shǐ Jì*, the first historical treatise in China written by Sima Qian (appeared in about 100 BC).

Another *chéng yǔ* is told by Mencius, which is *bá miáo zhù zhǎng* (pull shoot help grow). It tells the story of a farmer who, impatient with his young crop for not growing fast enough, pulls the shoots up to make them taller. The crop, of course, withered and died. The moral is that if one does something just for a short-term effect, the eventual outcome can be a complete disaster. A phrase like this can be used conveniently in a modern context. Some may argue, for instance, that extreme economic rationalism is *bá miáo zhù zhǎng*, because it may have long term social and environmental consequences which are detrimental to society.

Clearly, two general points can be made about *chéng yǔ*. One is that they have historical origins and their meanings in most cases cannot be worked out by simply knowing the meanings of the individual morphemes. To gain full comprehension of a *chéng yǔ*, one has to know the story or legend from which it derives. The second point is that once you know the meaning of a *chéng yǔ*, it becomes a code which is very economical to use because it is so precise. For many of them, both the literal meaning and metaphorical meaning contained in a set phrase have only four syllables and therefore four characters. But it would take a long paragraph if expressed in plain language.

By learning *chéng yǔ* at school, children begin to learn about the long and rich history of China. This can, perhaps, partly explain the fact that the Chinese are not only very proud of their historical heritage, but also tend to take a historical view of the things that happen around them.

In everyday conversation people usually use only the most common *chéng yǔ*. In the written language, however, many more *chéng yǔ* are employed. In fact, some Chinese believe that the extensive use of *chéng yǔ* is a sign of superior learning. One consequence of this tendency is that when *chéng yǔ* are used to excess, the written language can become stale and rigid.

When used creatively, however, the style can be very effective. One of the reasons why Mao Zedong held such a spell over his colleagues is, I believe, because his style of writing skilfully combined Chinese historical heritage with contemporary Chinese circumstances. The political rivals of Mao within the Communist Party of China, the Soviet-trained Chinese leaders, were never able to achieve this.

HOMOPHONES

Because Chinese is a tonal language many words consist of the same sounds, and they become different words only by virtue of their different tones. The sound of *fei*, for instance, with the first tone can mean 'fly', the same sound with the second tone can mean 'fat', while the third tone can mean 'bandit', and the fourth tone 'waste'. Because of the tonal differences we cannot say they are homophones.

There are, however, a large number of real homophones where different words share not only the same sounds but also the same tones. For instance, there are more than half a dozen morphemes for the sound [*lì*]. These morphemes can function independently as words; but they can also become parts of other words and such combinations in which [*lì*] is a part run into hundreds. However, homophones in Chinese do not cause serious problems in communication because the grammatical as well as the situational context will make it clear which word is meant. This is also why a non-native speaker can make him or herself understood even with some mistakes in tones. In the written language, of course, the question of homophones does not arise.

INFORMAL, FORMAL, AND CLASSICAL VOCABULARY

As discussed previously, the difference between written and spoken Mandarin was so great before the new culture movement at the beginning of this century that they were virtually two different languages. The gap has been narrowed a great deal by *bái huà* (plain language) writings as a result of the new culture movement and Communist ideology in demoting high culture while promoting popular culture. Some differences, however, still remain.

Informal versus formal language

There are very few linguistic honorific niceties in Mandarin. In fact, unless one is absolutely familiar with the subtlety of the uses of different particles, one may have the impression that the language is very rude. There is really only one word to address people politely and formally, which is *nín* (you sir, you madam). *Nín* is used a lot in Beijing and some parts of northern China, but it is hardly used by southerners.

The word, *zánmen,* meaning 'we' or 'us', is informal and always used in speech whereas *wǒmen* can be used in both formal and informal styles. The other difference between *zánmen* and *wǒmen* is that the former includes the person who listens whereas the latter does not necessarily do so. This is logical since *zánmen* is only used in speaking and the listener is present when the utterance is made.

As well as the extensive use of *chéng yǔ,* vocabulary in the formal language also tends to use monosyllabic words. In the written language monosyllabic words make the writing more condensed, succinct, and more precise. In spoken language, many disyllabic words, consisting of two morphemes with the same meaning, ease the burden of comprehension in a flow of speech on the part of the listener. On the other hand, in written language redundant information is not required for adequate communication since the reader can always decode it at his or her own pace.

Classical Chinese

Because classical Chinese exists only in the written form, its vocabulary is mostly monosyllabic, and its style succinct, with short sentences in which every word carries the full load of information. For instance, to translate one of the Confucian sayings *sān rén xíng bì yǒu wǒ shī yān* (three person walk must have me teacher), we may have to say something like *yàoshì wǒ gēn liǎng ge rén yìqǐ zǒulù, yídìng yǒu yí ge rén néng zuò wǒlǎoshī* which means 'If I walk with any two people there must be one of them who can be my teacher'. Here the great teacher Confucius, by simply using eight morphemes, was able to convey his wisdom of humility.

Function words in classical Chinese

In classical Chinese, words were not only used in their most succinct form, but there were also many grammatical words which no longer function in modern Mandarin and have been replaced either by modern function particles or by other grammatical means. Four words of this kind in classical Chinese deserve discussion here. They are *zhī*, *hū*, *yě*, and *zhě*.

Zhī (之)

In classical Chinese *zhī* has the important function of making the possessive case, something like 'of' in English. Thus, *xīng* (spark) *xīng zhī* (of) *huǒ* (fire) means 'a spark of fire'. The colloquial equivalent of *zhī* in modern Mandarin is *de* though *zhī* is still sometimes used in written language. A hotel may display a sign with four characters *lǚ kè zhī jiā* (travel guest-s home) to advertise their service. Replacing *zhī* with *de* for the signboard would be perfectly grammatical, but not appropriate because it is too colloquial.

Hū (乎)

Hū was used in classical Chinese to function as a question mark (there are no punctuation marks in classical Chinese). Consider the following:

> *láng* (wolf) *láng hū* (Is it a wolf?)
> *gǒu* (dog) *gǒu hū* (Is it a dog?)
> *láng hū gǒu hū* (Is it a wolf or a dog?)

Yě (也)

Yě is used in classical Chinese to indicate the declarative mood, that is, indicating that the speaker is making a judgement or statement.

A neutral statement *rén nǎi dòngwù* (person be animal) meaning 'human beings are animals' is an uncommitted statement which can be made into a judgement or an opinion by the speaker by adding *yě*, like the English sentence 'Human beings are animals!' with an exclamation mark, as opposed to a full stop. On the other hand, *rén nǎi dòngwù hū* is a question: 'Are human beings animals?'.

Zhě (者)

The grammatical particle *zhě* in classical Chinese has a number of functions. One of them is like the agent derivational suffix 'er', or 'or' in English such as writ*er* and act*or*. In English the derivation may simply be referential and it need not denote an action. For instance, whatever precedes is form-*er* and whatever follows is latt-*er*. *Zhě* has a similar function, for example:

zuò (make) *zuò zhě* (author)
shì (wait) *shì zhě* (waiter)
qián (front) *qián zhě* (former)
hòu (back) *hòu zhě* (latter)

In modern spoken Chinese some of the functions of *zhě* are replaced by *de*. Thus, 'the former' is *qiánmiàn de* and 'the latter' is *hòumiàn de*. Here *miàn* is added because the words for both 'front' and 'back' are disyllabic words in the spoken language.

Zhī hū zhě yě has now become a set phrase to refer to classical Chinese. The best way to describe someone who uses too much archaic and stale language is to say that his or her language is too *zhī hū zhě yě*.[12]

More function words in classical Chinese

There is another set of classical vocabulary which is used to show one's humbleness. One of them is the word *nú,* meaning 'slave'. In gentry households in traditional China, a wife was supposed to address her husband by saying *nú* (your slave) instead of 'I'. Other words of humility include:

bǐ rén (humble person) meaning 'I, the humble one'
xiǎo rén (little person) meaning 'I, the insignificant person'
zài xià (at below) meaning 'I, the one below you'
zhuō zuò (unworthy work) meaning 'My unworthy work'

In Mandarin, however, the use of *nú* disappears, though words like *xiǎo rén* and *zhuō zuò* are sometimes still used, especially in written language.

MEANING, REFERENCE, AND TRANSLATION

The meaning of any word lies in its use, not in a dictionary. Dictionaries only record some of the meanings in use. Even the best dictionary cannot record all the meanings. Very often the meaning of a word cannot be defined in isolation, as the following quote from *Alice in Wonderland* illustrates[13].

'There's glory for you!'
  'I don't know what you mean by "glory"', Alice said.
  Humpty Dumpty smiled contemptuously. 'Of course you don't till I tell you. I meant there's a nice knock-down argument for you!'
  'But "glory" doesnt mean "a knock-down argument"', Alice objected.
  'When *I* use a word', Humpty Dumpty said, in a rather scornful tone, 'it means just what I choose it to mean—neither more nor less'.
  'The question is', said Alice, 'whether you can make words mean so many different things'.

A word conveys its meaning in linguistic context and cultural context. Because meanings manifest themselves in linguistic context, we need to learn the vocabulary through sentences and texts. Because words also embody elements in a culture we need to understand the culture of the native speakers to master the language thoroughly.

Meaning

Every native speaker is a walking dictionary because every word that a native speaker uses may contain meanings not listed in a dictionary. It is easy for a native speaker to use the word 'kitten', for instance, but to define what a kitten is can be a troublesome task: an animal which is young; a young feline animal that has four legs, is furry, and so on. Moreover, some meanings associated with a term are culture-specific. For instance, the Chinese may not understand why some English speaking people try to avoid the number thirteen. Equally, an Australian will not comprehend why some Chinese speakers do not like the number four.

Many Chinese are very particular about the number four because the pronunciation for 'four' is *sì* which is the same as the sound of the word for 'death'. Some people in Hong Kong spend a fortune purchasing a car registration plate which has three or more eights. They believe eight is a lucky number because the sound of eight, *bā*, rhymes with the sound *fa*, which means 'prosperity'. Some Chinese will never buy a house located in a cul-de-sac because they believe a cul-de-sac is *sǐ hútong*, a dead end for career, prosperity, and for the family.

Learning a foreign language involves acquiring cultural assumptions and becoming familiar with another culture and human existence. In order to learn a foreign language really well one has to be prepared to be engaged with the culture embodied in that language. Nowadays this usually involves living in the country or region where the language is spoken, or having a relationship with someone who is a native speaker of that language. In the days before globalisation and when transport was not so convenient, one might have learnt a foreign language, at least the written form of that language, by means of a dictionary.

The celebrated Arthur Waley, who, according to some, made some of the best translations of classical Chinese poetry into English had never set foot in China. He even declined an official invitation to visit China because he feared that he might be disappointed, and that his fascination and love for the classical Chinese literary world might be destroyed by ugly, modern reality. In any case, Waley had a relationship with the culture, which the language embodied, albeit an imaginary one.

Reference

All words, including pronouns, proper names, and the names of ideas, refer to something; and so long as we know what is referred to we can communicate without having to know all properties of the referent. For instance, scientists know that water is composed of hydrogen and oxygen; but we know water as an element essential for drinking and bathing. For such words, a one-to-one translation is usually sufficient for learning a foreign language. If you are told that *shuĭ* in Mandarin means 'water', you will know what *shuĭ* signifies.

However, even these kinds of terms may have special meanings related to the lifestyle and culture of a particular community. We will not be able to understand what these different terms mean unless we understand their lifestyle and culture. Therefore, more than a word-for-word translation is required to understand terms referring to ideas and concepts which are culture-specific. For instance, the direct translation of the concept of democracy in Mandarin is *mín zhŭ* (people-master); but how the Chinese understand the term may be vastly different from how it is understood in the West. Indeed, for some Chinese the concept is still alien. The same is true of privacy, for which Mandarin still lacks a straightforward term.

Translation

When a concept or idea is first introduced from a foreign culture it may sound alien, but that does not mean the language cannot cope with it. When and if an idea becomes part of the culture, the word for it will then be just as natural as the word in the original language. However, since cross-cultural fertilisation is a long and continuous process, at any point in the history of linguistic exchange there are always cultural barriers to translation. For instance, it is very difficult to translate the term *dào jiào* into English. For many speakers of English, the translated term, 'Taoism', for this Chinese concept does not mean anything until elaborate explanations are given, or experience encountered.

Xiào, sometimes translated as 'filial piety', is another case in point. 'Filial piety' communicates very little to the average speaker of English about what *xiào* means in Chinese. The above are two examples which embody a whole set of assumptions about traditional Chinese culture.

The same is true of modern terms in Mandarin. The term *hù kŏu,* translated as 'household register', does not inform speakers of English about the administrative and ideological assumptions involved in the term. Equally, terms like *jiěfàng qián* (before liberation) and *jiěfàng hòu* (after liberation), which mean 'before 1949' and 'after 1949' respectively, involve a whole range of historical and ideological assumptions embodied in official Communist discourse.

NAMES

In any language naming has its own system due to accustomed cultural practice. In English, the first name is usually the name of the individual, the middle name, if there is one, may be taken from a close relative, and the final name is the surname. In Mandarin, however, the first name is the surname. There are also different ways of naming places and institutions in Chinese.

Personal names

The majority of Chinese names have three syllables, the first one being the surname although there are some two-syllable surnames, which results in some names having four syllables. In rural China, many villages are clan villages and therefore everyone has the same surname. Some of the villagers may also share the same middle name which is the generation name. Usually, a clan village has a record book of all the people born in the village and generation names are decided collectively well in advance so that every male of the same generation is automatically given the same middle name. Only the last name is the individual name.

The way in which a personal name is given reflects the tremendous changes as well as continuities in contemporary China. Clan naming still persists in rural China despite several decades of anti-tradition rhetoric in Communist China. However, clan culture does not exist in cities which are comprised of immigrants from all over China. In fact, many city dwellers have two-syllable names: surname first and personal name last but without a middle name. A tendency for having names with reduplicated syllables, especially for females, is more evident in cities. Another feature of naming in both rural and urban contemporary China is that a woman does not change her surname when she marries. Indeed, in many urban families, children may be given their mothers' surnames.

Another aspect of naming, which still persists in rural areas, is the importance attached to what names mean.[14] Parents may give their children, especially boys, very unworthy nicknames such as 'doggy', 'piggy', or 'rotten head', hoping the child may live longer by having an unworthy name. This practice is derived from a belief that one dies because a ghost takes life away. The idea is that ghosts will not be attracted to people with unworthy names and thus the child will survive and live long. This is practised even today in Hong Kong, or among Chinese communities overseas.

Place names

In naming places the Chinese like to let the name show some properties of the object named. Thus the name *Huáng Hé* (Yellow River) suggests it contains water that is yellow. The Yangtze is called *Cháng Jiāng* (long river) because it is very long. *Cháng Chéng* is translated as 'Great Wall' in English; but in Chinese it means 'long wall' because it is very long indeed!

In English we may refer to a state in Australia as Victoria, or Tasmania, but we do not have to say Victoria State, or the State of Victoria. This is precisely what we have to do in Mandarin, however. We have to say *wéiduōlìyà zhōu* to translate 'the state of Victoria'. Chinese also add *shěng* to refer to a province, for instance, *Yúnnán shěng* (Yunnan Province); *shì* to refer to a city, for instance, *Shànghǎi shì* (Shanghai city). We add *qū* if it is a district, and if it is the name of a county we may add *xiàn* (county). All of these are meant to indicate the quality or attribute of a particular name.

WRITING ADDRESSES AND DATES

The Chinese write addresses in exactly the opposite order to English. The Chinese start with the larger entity, the collective, and move down to the individual whereas in English, the name of the individual comes first. If a letter is to be delivered overseas, the post office looks for the nation first, and whoever is the individual recipient is of no significance. Only when the letter arrives in the country will the postman look at the city, and then the street, and so on.

The same applies to writing dates. Unlike English, dates in Chinese start from the large and proceed to the small, and from the general to the specific. Thus, the year is written first, then the month, then the day.

DICTIONARIES

A good dictionary is one that has exemplary sentences as illustration. Word-to-word translation on a one-to-one basis can be very misleading. For an English-speaking learner of Mandarin, it is always helpful to get a dictionary which lists vocabulary in alphabetical order using *pīnyīn*. However, the written language of Mandarin is not *pīnyīn* and an alphabetical index is useful only when one knows how to pronounce the character. Otherwise a radical index and stroke counting is required. Therefore, one has to learn the technique of finding a character by radicals and strokes which has been discussed in chapter 4. Most modern dictionaries of Chinese list words in alphabetical order in the text, but also include a radical index at the front of the dictionary.

STUDY QUESTIONS

1. What is the main difference between a lexical (or content) word and a grammatical (or functional) word?
2. What is inflection? Does Chinese have inflection?
3. Very often in Chinese we do not know whether a word is an adjective or an adverb until in context. What contexts make a word an adjective and what make an adverb?
4. What does it mean to say that there is no verb 'to be' (or copula) in Chinese?
5. What makes a stative verb different from an action verb?
6. Is Chinese a monosyllabic language?
7. What is the relationship between a morpheme and a character?

8. How does Chinese handle loan words?
9. What kind of words can be reduplicated in Chinese?
10. Does Chinese have prefixes and suffixes or are there only particles?
11. What is a *chéng yǔ*?
12. There are many homophones in Chinese. How is ambiguity avoided?
13. How do Chinese personal names differ from those in English?

REFERENCE READING

Alleton, Viviane, *Les Chinois et la Passion des Noms* (The Chinese Passion for Names), Paris, Aubier, 1993.

Chao, Y. R., *A Grammar of Spoken Chinese*, University of California Press, Berkeley and Los Angeles, 1968.

Hartmann, R. R. K. and F. C. Stork, *Dictionary of Language and Linguistics*, London, Applied Sciences Publishers Ltd, reprint, 1973.

Hu, Jerome P. and Lee, Stephen C., *A Basic Chinese Vocabulary*, Longman Cheshire, Melbourne, 1989.

Kennedy, George A., 'Word-Class in Classical Chinese', in *Selected Works of George A. Kennedy*, Far Eastern Publications, New Haven, 1964, pp. 423–33.

Li, Chi, *General Trends of Chinese Linguistic Changes under Communist Rule*, Studies in Chinese Communist Terminology no. 1, East Asia Studies, Institute of International Studies, University of California, Berkeley, California, July 1956.

Li, Sijing, *hanyu r yinshi yanjiu* (A Study on the History of r in Chinese), revised edition, Shangwu yinshuguan, Beijing, 1994.

Pulleyblank, Edwin G., *Outline of Classical Chinese Grammar*, Vancouver, UBC Press, 1995, reprint 1996.

Ramsey, Robert S., *The Languages of China*, New Jersey, Princeton University Press, 1987.

Xie, Wenqing, 'erhua xianxiang de gongneng fenxi', (An analysis of the Function of the Phenomenon of r) in *hanyuyan wenhua yanjiu* (Study on the Cultural Aspects of the Chinese Language), Nankai daxue hanyuyan wenhua xueyuan, vol. 4, Tianjin Renmin Chubanshe, Tianjin, 1994.

ENDNOTES

1 R. R. K. Hartmann and F. C. Stork, *Dictionary of Language and Linguistics*, reprint, Applied Science Publishers Ltd, London, 1973, Chinese version translated by Huang Changzhu et al., Shanghai cishu chubanshe, Shanghai, 1981, p. 379

2 A. E. Backhouse, *The Japanese Language: An Introduction*, Melbourne, Oxford University Press, 1993, p. 65.

3 Jia, Putian, shilun xiandai hanyu gudingshi de leixing he jiben tedian, (On the Categories and Basic Features of Set Expressions in Modern Chinese), in *hanyuyan wenhua yanjiu* (Study on Cultural Aspects of the Chinese Language), Nankai Hanyuyan wenhua xueyuan, Tianjin renmin chubanshe, Tianjin, 1994, pp. 49–64.

4 See Yi Xiaolin, *han yu shu mu ci cidian* (A Dictionary of Words Starting with a Numeral), Beijing, Zhong hua shu ju, 1993. There is, in China, a tradition of compiling dictionaries which only contain numeral words. For instance *xiao xue gan zhu* (Elementary Collection) compiled by Wang Yinglin appeared as early as the Song Dynasty. Others include *chun shu shi tuo* (A Selection of Words) by Zhang Jiushao in the Ming Dynasty and *du shu ji shu lue* (A Selection of Numeral Words) by Gong Mengren in the Qing Dynasty.

5 Lowell Dittmer and Chen Ruoxi, *Ethics and Rhetoric of the Chinese Cultural Revolution*, Studies in Chinese Terminology, no. 9, Berkeley, California, University of California, Center for Chinese Studies, Institute of East Asian Studies, 1981.

6 According to Ramsey, when Coca-Cola was first marketed in China in the 1930s, the company sponsored a highly publicised contest to find the best term in Chinese for the soft drink. *Kekou kele* was finally settled on; the owner of the entry won a $50 prize. See S. Robert Ramsey, *The Languages of China*, New Jersey, Princeton University Press, 1987, p. 60.

7 Wang Li, Wang Guzhang et al., *xiandai hanyu jiangzuo* (Lectures on Modern Chinese), Zhishi chubanshe, Beijing, 1983, p. 98.

8 Wang Li, Wang Guzhang et al., 1983, pp. 111–12. Yuen Ren Chao, *A Grammar of Spoken Chinese*, University of California Press, Berkeley and Los Angeles, 1968, pp. 219–56.

9 Xie Wenqing, 'erhua xianxiang de gongneng fenxi', (An analysis of the Function of the Phenomenon of *r*), in *hanyuyan wenhua yanjiu* (Study on the Cultural Aspects of the Chinese Language) Nankai daxue hanyuyan wenhua xueyuan, vol. 4, Tianjin Renmin Chubanshe, Tianjin, 1994, pp. 1–12. The following discussion is largely based on this paper, and most of the examples are drawn from it. For a monograph dealing with the evolution of *r* see Li Sijing, *hanyu r yinshi yanjiu* (A Study on the History of *r* in Chinese), revised edition, Shangwu yinshuguan, Beijing, 1994.

10 R. R. K. Hartmann and F. C. Stork, *Dictionary of Language and Linguistics*, reprint, Applied Science Publishers Ltd, London, 1973, Chinese version translated by Huang Changzhu et al., Shanghai cishu chubanshe, Shanghai, 1981, p. 169.

11 Qian Nairong (ed.), *hanyu yuyanxue* (Chinese Linguistics), Beijing yuyan xueyuan chubanshe, Beijing, 1995. p.107.

12 Some say *zhi hu ye zhe*.

13 Lewis Carroll, illustrated by John Tenniel, *The Annotated Alice, Alice's Adventures in Wonderland and Through the Looking Glass*, New York, Bramhall House, 1960, pp.268–9

14 The fact that Chinese place great importance on names has drawn attention from Western scholars. See, for instance, Viviane Alleton, *Les Chinois et la Passion des Noms* (The Chinese Passion for Names), Paris, Aubier, 1993.

CHAPTER 6

Grammar

GRAMMAR: STRUCTURAL RULES

The vocabulary of a language is a stock of words that denote things, objects, qualities, actions, or events. When we communicate, however, we do not just say or write words at random; we structure them to make sentences, which are rule-governed. These rules are rules of grammar.

Some rules of sentence structure are shared by a number of languages, but there are also language-specific rules which are characteristic of one particular language. When the first Europeans encountered Chinese language they were very puzzled by the fact that it does not distinguish word classes by form and that there are not many morphological processes such as inflection. They considered Chinese to be without structure and exceedingly defective.[1]

Grammar: What is different about Chinese?
When European linguists in the early nineteenth century divided languages into three major types, Chinese was classified as an isolating language, as opposed to agglutinating languages like Turkish, and inflecting languages like Indo-European languages. Chinese was classified as one of the isolating languages because it lacks many morphological processes that are common in inflecting languages, for example pluralisation, subject–verb agreement, tense, and gender. Linguists at that time thought that Chinese was a simple and primitive language because it lacked these familiar features.

This perception of Chinese by Western scholars even influenced the view of some Chinese towards their own language. Chinese grammarians therefore started using Western linguistic terms to analyse Chinese.[2] Some Chinese grammarians, for instance, as noted by Ramsey, advocated the use of three different characters to distinguish words meaning 'he', 'she', and 'it'. The pronunciations of the three characters are exactly the same, i.e. *tā*, because in Chinese there is no gender distinction and therefore there is only one third-person pronoun in the language. Some even went further to invent two different characters for the male and female 'you', which again were pronounced in exactly the same way. Three different characters were also invented to distinguish the three different uses of the particle *de*, one for the genitive (or possessive) and adjective *de*, one for the adverb *de*, and one for the complement *de*. The Chinese also began to adopt a set of punctuation marks for the written language.

While these adoptions reflect efforts by the Chinese to learn from the West, they do not in any way alter the fact that Mandarin has its own rules of grammar. Apart from the fact that Chinese is rich in compound words as discussed in chapter 5, the language has grammatical or functional words which play an important role in sentence construction by linking words together and by establishing formal relationships between words in sentences. Like any other language, when words in Mandarin are combined in sentences they must be arranged in a particular order.

THREE MAJOR FEATURES OF GRAMMAR

Of the three main features in grammar, that is word order, morphological process, and grammatical functions expressed by functional words, languages differ only in detail and in the relative weight assigned to them. In Mandarin the lack of a comprehensive morphological process, i.e. inflection, is compensated by function words. In other words, some meanings and information conveyed by inflections in languages such as English are expressed by functional words in Mandarin.

For example, the past tense in English can be conveyed by inflecting the verb with -*ed*, say in 'I finish*ed*', and perfect aspect by inflecting 'have' and the verb, as in 'I *have* finish*ed*'. In Mandarin these meanings are conveyed by the functional word *le*. The Chinese equivalent of 'I finished' or 'I have finished' is:

1 *wǒ wánchéng le* (I finish le)

The fact that *wǒ wánchéng le* may be translated as either 'I finished' or 'I have finished' indicates that Chinese lacks formal morphological processes. In isolation the sentence can be ambiguous. However, from another point of view, it is more economical because the sentence will not be ambiguous in a particular context.

One characteristic of Mandarin, therefore, is that in comparison with English, it relies less on formal inflection, but more on context. To continue with the same example, the difference between the present perfect and simple past can be made by adverbial words in Mandarin. Consider the following:

2 *wǒ gāng wánchéng le* (I just finish le) 'I have just finished'.
   (present perfect)
3 *wǒ zuótiān wánchéng le* (I yesterday finish le) 'I finished
   yesterday.' (simple past)
4 *wǒ míngtiān wánchéng le* ... (I tomorrow finish le) 'After
   I finish tomorrow ...' (future)

Clearly the lack of inflection for the present perfect, simple past, and future in (2), (3), and (4) respectively is made up for by the adverbs. Even when there is no such adverbial word in a sentence, the difference between present perfect and simple past can be made by pragmatic contexts.

WORD ORDER

Of the three major grammatical features we shall start with that of word order. Generally speaking, word order in Mandarin is the same as that in English. That is, the subject precedes the verb, which is followed by the object, and we can schematise the order as S+V+O. For the English sentence 'John loves Mary' the equivalent Chinese is *Yuēhàn ài Mǎlì* (John love Mary). Clearly the word order is the same.

Sentences like 'John loves Mary', however, are prototypic, and not all sentences correspond exactly to this pattern. For example, sentences can be formed without an object, or even without a verb. In 'John is handsome', there is no action verb and the predicate is formed by a copula, that is, the verb 'to be' and an adjective.

Verb versus adjective

In sentences like 'John is very tall' the predicate is formed by the verb 'to be', an adverb, and an adjective. An important difference between Chinese and English is that there is no need for an equivalent of the verb 'to be' in Chinese to establish the link between the subject and adjective. The Chinese equivalent of 'John is very tall' is:

Yuēhàn hěn gāo (John very tall)

The word order of this type of sentence in Mandarin, therefore, is that of subject followed by the adverb which is, in turn, followed by the adjective.

There is a Chinese equivalent of the English verb 'to be', which is *shì;* but *shì* cannot be used as a link word in this type of sentence. Many students of Chinese from English backgrounds tend to insert *shì* every time they make a Chinese sentence of this type because this is what they do in English. When *shì* is used in this kind of sentence it should be stressed as an emphatic element. Thus, *Yuēhàn shì hěn gāo* means 'John IS very tall', not just 'John is very tall'. If the emphatic meaning is not intended the sentence is ungrammatical.

Stative verb revisited

Recall that in the last chapter we introduced the term stative verb. We suggested that it is for this syntactic or structural reason (as opposed to semantic reason) that words like 'tall' in this type of sentence are not adjectives but stative verbs in Chinese.

The reason for saying these words are not adjectives but stative verbs is that structurally they behave in the same way as verbs do in Chinese: they do not inflect and they do not require a linking word such as *shì*. However, semantically, these types of words are different because they denote qualities rather than actions. Hence the term 'stative verb'.

Transitive versus intransitive

A transitive verb takes an object in a sentence. When a verb does not take an object, it is called intransitive. Just as in English, there are verbs in Mandarin which cannot take an object in a sentence. 'Work' in English is an intransitive verb that cannot be directly followed by an object. For instance, we cannot say 'I will work it', but we can say 'I will work at it'. The verb 'work' cannot take the object 'it' directly. Nor can its Chinese equivalent *gōngzuò*.

What is different between Chinese and English is that some adjectives (or stative verbs) in Chinese can be transitive because they can take a direct object. In:

> *wǒ hěn gāoxìng zhè jiàn shì* (I very happy this matter) 'I am very happy about this matter'.

zhè jiàn shì (this matter) is the direct object of the adjective *gāoxìng* (happy). This is not so in English since 'happy' cannot be followed by 'this matter' directly, and it requires a preposition 'about' to link them together. By the way, this is further evidence that adjectives in Chinese behave structurally in the same way as verbs do.

PHRASES

So far we have only discussed word order in simple sentences in which the subject, the verb, and the object all consist of one word each. A subject or an object may consist of many words. When they do they form what we call phrases, such as noun phrases, adverb phrases, and preposition phrases. In these phrasal constructions there is also the question of word order.

Noun phrases

A noun can function as a subject or an object in a sentence. Very often the subject or object consists of more than one word. A noun may be modified by an attributive adjective, by a demonstrative pronoun, by a genitive, or by a relative clause, as the following examples show:

1 Attributive adjective modifier:
   hóng shū (red book) meaning 'red book'
2 Demonstrative pronoun modifier:
   nà běn shū (that volume book) meaning 'that book'
3 Genitive modifier:
   Yuēhàn de shū (John **genitive-particle** book) meaning
   'John's book'
4 Relative clause modifier:
   wǒ zuì xǐhuan de shū (I most like **clause-particle** book)
   meaning the book that I like most

All four are noun phrases and each has a noun as its head and each of them can either function as a subject or an object in a sentence. For purpose of discussion, in each noun phrase, the noun that is modified by any other elements is called the head noun. In sentences (1) to (4) *shū* (book) is the head noun.

In fact, we may construct a long noun phrase by combining all of the modifying elements headed by *shū:*

5 *wǒ zuì xǐhuan de nà běn Yuēhàn de hóng shū* (I most like
   clause-particle that **volume** John **genitive-particle** red **attribu-
   tive-adjective** book) meaning 'that red book that belongs to
   John that I like most'

Note that 'that red book that belongs to John that I like most' is not a sentence because there is no predicate. Instead it is a noun phrase which can either function as a subject or an object in a sentence, as shown in the following:

6 *That red book that belongs to John that I like most* was
   published last year.
7 Last year, Oxford University Press published *that red book
   that belongs to John that I like most.*

The italicised part is the subject in (6) and object in (7). More importantly, note that both in English and Chinese the demonstrative and attributive adjective modifiers appear before the head noun in the noun phrase. The difference between English and Chinese in terms of word order is that in Chinese a relative clause always appears before the head noun in a noun phrase whereas in English it appears after. In other words, in Chinese anything that modifies a noun has to appear before that noun.

Adjective phrases

In Mandarin when an adjective is modified by an adverb, the adverb usually appears before the adjective. For example, in *hěn rè* (very hot) and *fēicháng rè* (extraordinarily hot), the adverb in both phrases, as in English, appears before the adjective.

Adverb phrases

An adverb phrase may be just an adverb, or a time adverbial, or a place adverbial. An adverb phrase may be used to modify a verb, or the subject in a sentence, or even used to modify the whole sentence. For example:

1 The plane landed smoothly.
2 Probably he was late.
3 Only I like it.
4 He worked at home yesterday.

The adverb 'smoothly' in (1) modifies the verb; the adverb 'probably' in (2) modifies the whole sentence; the adverb 'only' in (3) modifies the subject; and in (4) <u>yesterday</u> is a time adverbial and <u>at home</u> is a place adverbial.

As shown by these examples, adverb phrases, depending on their functions, may appear anywhere in an English sentence: before the subject, before the verb, after the verb, and so on. However, this is not the case in Chinese. Instead, any adverb or adverb phrase has to appear before the verb in a Chinese sentence.

1 *fēijī píng wǒn de zháolù le* (plane smooth **particle** land **particle**) 'The plane landed smoothly.'
2 *kěnéng tā wǎn le* (probably he late **particle**) 'Probably he was late.'
3 *zhǐ yǒu wǒ xǐhuan tā* (only I like it) 'Only I like it.'
4 *tā zuótiān zài jiā gōngzuò* (he yesterday at home work) 'He worked at home yesterday.'
5 *zuótiān tā zài jiā gōngzuò* (yesterday he at home work) 'He worked at home yesterday.'

If we place *zuótiān* (yesterday) or *zài jiā* (at home) at the end of the sentence, that is, after the verb, the sentence is ungrammatical.

Preposition phrases

A preposition phrase usually consists of a preposition appearing before a noun. By definition, to say that a language has prepositions is to say that this is the word order in such phrases. The identification of prepositions in Chinese is complicated by the fact that most of them are derived historically from verbs. Indeed, many of them can still function as main verbs today. In (3) and (4) above, for instance, *zài* is a preposition; however in (5):

> 5 *tā zài jiā* (he be+at home) meaning 'He is at home.'

zài functions as the main verb.

The above discussion shows that in Mandarin the word order in a statement sentence is S+V if the verb is intransitive; S+V+O if there is an object in the sentence; and Adv+S+V+O, or S+Adv+V+O if there are adverb phrases in the sentence. Therefore, a general rule governing word order in Mandarin is that a modifying phrase must be placed before what it modifies in a statement sentence.

QUESTION SENTENCES

Generally speaking, as a tonal language, Chinese does not use intonation in asking questions. Indeed, raising the intonation of a sentence to ask a question in Chinese, as some native speakers of English tend to do, often leads to the incorrect rendering of tones. Nor does Chinese require a change of word order to construct question sentences; for instance, the statement in English 'This is a book' becomes a question when the word order is changed into 'Is this a book?'. There is no such transformation in Chinese.

There are generally three ways of asking questions in Chinese. One is by using what are called question particles; another is to use interrogative words. The third type of question is what can be called A+NOT+A sentences and is discussed shortly.

Question particles

There are three very commonly used question particles in Mandarin: *ma*, *ne*, and *ba*. Any statement sentence becomes a question sentence when *ma* is placed at the end of it. For instance:

1 *zhè shì yì běn shū* (this is one **volume** book)
2 *zhè shì yì běn shū ma* (this is one **volume** book ma)

(1) is a statement meaning 'This is a book', and (2) is a question meaning 'Is this a book?'

The function of *ne* is the same as *ma* and it is usually placed at the end of a noun or phrase to ask short questions, like 'how about' in English, as shown in (3):

3 *nǐ ne* (you ne) 'How about you?'

The third question particle is *ba*, which is again placed at the end of a sentence to ask about assumptions or presuppositions. The use of *ba*, again, can be shown through examples:

4 *nǐ chī le ma*? (you eat le ma)
5 *nǐ chī le ba*? (you eat le ba)

(4) is a straightforward question meaning 'Have you eaten?' whereas (5) means something like 'You have eaten, I suppose?'.

Interrogative words

Just as in English, in Chinese question sentences can be constructed by using interrogative words. In English these interrogative words are sometimes called *wh*-words because they all begin with *wh*.

In English *wh*-words always appear at the beginning of a question sentence no matter what part of the sentence is questioned. When the object of a sentence is questioned the *wh*-word in the object position is, as it were, moved to the beginning of the sentence. In Chinese, however, no such movement is required. For instance, instead of '*What* do you have?' or '*Who* do you like?' in which the object of each sentence is questioned, the word order of the equivalent Chinese sentences should be:

nǐ yǒu shénme? (you have what)
nǐ xǐhuan shéi? (you like who)

in other words, both the interrogative words *shénme* and *shéi* remain in the object position.

A+NOT+A questions

A question sentence in Chinese can also be constructed by repeating a verb or an adjective in a sentence, but with a negative in between: thus the formula A+NOT+A. 'A' here stands for any verb or adjective and 'not' stands for the negative. A+NOT+A is just a formula to represent the structure of this type of question sentence. The following examples show how A+NOT+A question sentences are formed:

Table 6.1 Formation of a A+NOT+A question sentence

Chinese sentence	Literal translation	English translation
jīntiān lěng bù lěng	today cold not cold	Is it cold today?
nǐ yào bú yào chī	you want not want eat	Do you want to eat?
nǐ chī méi chī	you eat not eat	Did you eat/Have you eaten?

Lěng, yào, and *chī* are repeated in the three examples in the above table each with a negative in between.

Note that there are two negatives in Mandarin: *bù* and *méi. Bù* is a negative in sentences that denote present or future tenses, whereas *méi* is a negative used in sentences that convey what may be termed past tense or perfect aspect. However, when a negative is used with an adjective, *bù* is always used irrespective of whether the sentence denotes past or present tense; for instance, *bù* is used in a sentence about the past:

> *zuótiān lěng bù lěng (yesterday cold not cold) meaning 'Was it cold yesterday?'*

To use *méi* here would render the sentence ungrammatical.

Tag and choice questions

The A+NOT+A formula also applies to tag questions. 'Is it good?' in Mandarin is *hǎo bù hǎo* (good not good), and 'Is it OK?' is *xíng bù xíng* (OK not OK).

Finally, choice question sentences can be constructed by using a choice question word. The Chinese equivalent of 'Shall I go or will you come?' is *wó qù háishì nǐ lái* (I go or you come).

WORD ORDER OF PASSIVE SENTENCES

So far we have discussed only the word order of active sentences. In passive sentences, however, the word order is different. In English the syntactic difference between an active and a passive sentence is, with few exceptions, straightforward. In an active sentence, the agent or the doer of the action appears in the subject position, whereas in a passive sentence the object of the action appears in the subject position. In a prototypic passive sentence, the copula, or the verb 'to be' is used together with the past participle (usually in the form of -*en*), and the agent or doer appears after *by* if the agent needs to be specified.

1 We ate the cake.
2 The cake *was* eat*en by* us.

(1) is an active sentence and (2) is a passive sentence. The italicised words are prototypic elements of a passive sentence. In both sentences, the object of the action is the cake which is in the object position in (1), but in the subject position in (2).

Bèi and passive in Chinese

The word order of a passive sentence in Mandarin is like that in English. The difference is that there is no verb inflection such as -*en*, nor is the verb 'to be' used; only *bèi*, a particle similar to *by*, is used to form a passive in Chinese. The Chinese equivalents of (1) and (2) are (3) and (4) respectively

3 *wǒmen chī le dàngāo* (we eat le cake)
4 *dàngāo <u>bèi</u> wómen chī le* (cake bei us eat le)

Word order in a passive sentence in Chinese is clearly object-subject-verb (O+S+V). Note that this is different to English. The word order of a passive sentence in English is O+V+S.

Ràng, gěi, and *jiào*

The passive particle *bèi* has three variants, *ràng, gěi,* and *jiào.* In (4) *dàngāo bèi wómen chī le*, the passive particle *bèi* can be replaced by any one of the three variants and the sentence will mean the same thing.

Word order of bǎ-structure

Another particle which needs to be discussed in connection with word order is *bǎ*. The way it is used is called the *bǎ*-structure because there is not an accurate alternative term for it. The meaning of *bǎ* is very difficult to explain in English, but will be clear in the examples below. For the time being we will focus on the syntax, i.e. what it does in word order.

What *bǎ* does is move the object of a sentence to the front of the verb, immediately after the subject, as the following shows:

Table 6.2   Word order of *bǎ*-structure

Chinese sentence	Literal translation	English translation
wǒ hē le chá	I drink le tea	I drank some tea.
wǒ bǎ chá hē le	I ba tea drink le	I drank the tea.

The word order of the *bǎ*-structure sentence is therefore S+O+V. Now what does *bǎ* do semantically? In other words what does *bǎ* do to make the meaning of the two sentences in the above table different? The difference in meaning is shown by the English translation. The difference in meaning is shown by the English translation. The lack of a definite article in Mandarin (there is no word such as 'the' in Chinese) is, at least in this case, compensated by the use of *bǎ*. In other words, in such sentences, the difference in meanings—as shown in the English translation—is borne out by either the absence or presence of *bǎ*.

In the *bǎ*-structure, the predicate must contain a verb and the verb in the sentence is usually an action verb. Verbs of mental state or cognition, for instance, cannot be involved in *bǎ*-structures. It is ungrammatical to say, for example:

wǒ bǎ xióngmāo xǐhuan (I *bǎ* panda like)

to mean 'I like the panda'. The S+V+O structure *wǒ xǐhuan xióngmāo* must be used. For verbs of this kind, the *bǎ*-structure cannot be used.

Word order of duì-structure

For a predicate which involves a stative verb there is a particle similar to *bǎ*, which also changes an S+V+O structure into an

S+O+V one. This particle is *duì*, and again, for lack of a precise definition, we may call the usage of *duì* the *duì*-structure.

To mean, for instance, 'I am very happy about this matter', we may say in Chinese:

wǒ hěn gāoxìng zhè jiàn shì (I very happy this **piece** matter)

The same meaning can be expressed by a sentence involving *duì*:

wǒ duì zhè jiàn shì hěn gāoxìng

Clearly the word order has changed into S+O+V.

INFLECTION

Inflection is about shapes and meanings of different grammatical forms of the same word. In English inflection is mainly found in verbs, adjectives, and nouns, as shown below:

verbs: (walk, walks, walking, walked; think, thought; sing, sang, sung)

nouns: (tree, trees; child, children)

adjectives: (hot, hotter, hottest)

The most complicated form of inflection in English is the copula, or the verb 'to be', which is illustrated as follows:

be, is, was, am, are, were, shall be, will be, should be, would have been, may be, might have been, and so on.

Lack of inflection in Chinese

In English a verb may inflect to denote the past, present, or future tense. A verb may also inflect to indicate the first person, second person, and third person, singular or plural. All these kinds of inflections are absent in Chinese. The first person, second person, or third person, singular or plural are expressed by the personal pronouns alone in Chinese. According to the logic of Chinese grammar, we may say that meanings conveyed by verbal inflections in English are really redundant.

Chinese clearly does not have a grammatical category of tense. However, speakers of Chinese naturally need to talk about events which have happened in the past, or which will happen in the future. One way in which speakers of Chinese can easily achieve explicit temporal reference is by using temporal adverbs, or future auxiliaries:

míngtiān (tomorrow)
zuótiān (yesterday)
xià xīngqī (next week)
huì/jiāng (will)

Sense of time and notion of aspect are also expressed in Chinese by grammatical words such as particles that we will discuss shortly.

Inflection or grammatical words?

There are a number of grammatical words in Chinese which express grammatical meanings, some of which are expressed by inflections in English. However, there are a number of suffixes in Chinese which may be discussed in terms of inflection. One is the plural suffix *men*.

Men is mostly used with pronouns to form plurals. It is unstressed and therefore has a neutral tone. However, *men* cannot be suffixed to just any nouns to make them plural. It can be used only to indicate the plural noun denoting human beings or occasionally animals. Even for personal pronouns *men* is not used very often and plurals are usually indicated either by the sentence context or situational context. Indeed, very often it can be ambiguous if a sentence is looked at in isolation from context.

Native speakers of Chinese do not bother to make a difference between plural and singular unless it is required situationally. When situation requires specification of plurality *men* is used, but only when the noun refers to human beings or animate objects, such as *xiānshengmen* (gentlemen) as opposed to *xiānsheng* (gentleman), and *háizimen* (children). Occasionally, *men* is used to make an animate noun plural, for example *hóuzimen* (monkeys).[4] We cannot suffix *men* to an inanimate noun to form the plural form. We cannot say, for instance, *zhuōzimen,* to mean the plural 'tables', or *fángzimen* to mean 'houses'.

There are other suffixes discussed in chapter 5. Clearly, morphemes like *men* can be used to inflect only a small number of words in the language. One question, however, is whether these are suffixes that can be considered to be suffixes in the English sense of the word, or shall we just say that they are grammatical words in the context of the Chinese language?

GRAMMATICAL WORDS

A substantial lack of inflection in Chinese means that meanings and functions otherwise carried out by inflection have to be expressed by alternative ways in the language. This is done by grammatical words in Chinese.

Grammatical words are those which have grammatical or functional meanings only within the grammar system of a particular language. They are sometimes called structural words or form words, as opposed to content words or lexical words which derive their meanings from the objects or things to which they refer and whose meanings are not based on any particular grammar system. It is very important to learn grammatical words in Mandarin because they, among other things, make up for the absence of inflection.

Particles

Particles are one type of grammatical word[5] and there are a number of them in Mandarin. We have already discussed *ma, ne,* and *ba* in relation to the word order of question sentences. These words are called question particles because they have the function of turning statement sentences into interrogative sentences.

The passive sentence particle *bèi* and its variants *ràng, gěi,* and *jiào,* and *bǎ* (in what is called the *bǎ*-structure) have also been dealt with. Two particles which have the function of changing an S+V+O sentence into an S+O+V one, *bǎ* and *duì,* have also been discussed. The particles to be explored next are *le, guo, zai, zhe,* and *ne* (not the same as the question particle *ne*).

Particle le

Le is one of the most important particles in the language. Syntactically speaking the properties of *le* are quite straightforward: it appears either immediately after the main verb (there may be more than one verb in a sentence) or at the end of a sentence. When *le* occurs in the former context we call it the verbal *le*, and when it occurs in the latter context we may call it the sentence-final *le*.

When the verb in a sentence has an object, there may be two *le*s in the same sentence: one immediately after the main verb, and one at the end of the sentence. However, in a sentence where the verb does not take an object, whether *le* is verbal or sentence-final is indistinguishable since *le* will be at the end of the sentence. In such sentences, the two *le*s fuse for phonological reasons into one token *le*.

Semantically speaking, however, *le* is far from straight-forward. It is one of the most difficult grammatical words in the language to grasp conceptually because its functions are so subtly varied. Very often when it appears after the main verb the sentence conveys an event of the past. It would therefore be easy to get the impression that *le* is restricted to past events and thus be viewed as a past tense particle. At other times, however, a sentence with *le* may be interpreted as denoting present or past perfect aspect. For example:

wǒ mǎi le sān běn shū (I buy le three volume book)

can be interpreted either as 'I bought three books' or as 'I have bought three books' depending on the contextual circumstances.

What appears even more confusing with *le* is that it may occur in a sentence which has nothing to do with either past or past tense, nor present perfect aspect. For example:

Yuēhàn chī le fàn jiù kàn diànshì (John eat le food then watch television)

is a simple present sentence expressing a habitual event: 'John watches television after he finishes his meal'. Here *le* has nothing to do with the past tense. On the other hand, if a sentence expresses a habitual event of the past, no *le* may be required. The Chinese equivalent of 'Last year John often watched television' is:

Yuēhàn qùnián chángcháng kàn diànshì (John last year often watch television)

and if *le* appears the sentence would be ungrammatical.

Verbal le

An attractive view of the function of the verbal *le* is to say that it does not express past but rather perfectiveness, an aspectual notion. Aspect is a grammatical category concerned with the internal structure of events rather than their temporal location relative to the time of utterance. Viewed in this light, we are in a better position to understand why *le* can occur in sentences which may express past, present, and future events.

Since *le* is aspectual it is not concerned with either past, present, or future relative to the time of utterance. Rather it expresses the notion of completion irrespective of whether the event took place in the past or will take place in the future. Thus, there cannot be a *le* in:

Yuēhàn qùnián chángcháng kàn diànshì (John last year often watch television)

because habitual action, past or present, has no sense of completion. On the other hand, there is a *le* in:

Yuēhàn chī le fàn jiù kàn diànshì (John eat le food then watch television)

even though the sentence expresses a present habitual event. *Le* is used here because the second event of watching television does not take place until the first event of having a meal is completed. In terms of internal structure, there is a sense of completion of the event of finishing a meal.

To continue with the same notion of the aspect of completion, *le* is typically used with verbs, which by virtue of their meanings have a sense of completion, such as *sǐ* (die) and *wàng* (forget). For the same reason, *le* cannot occur in a sentence expressing ongoing action. *Le*, for example, cannot occur in:

tā zài liú húzi (he zai[6] grow beard)

which is the Chinese equivalent of 'He is growing a beard'.

Sentence-final le

So far we have only discussed the verbal *le*; that is, *le* which appears immediately after an action verb. *Le*, however, can also occur at the end of a sentence and it does this even when part of the predicate of the sentence is not an action verb but an adjective. This is what we call the sentence-final *le*.

Sentence-final *le* has a number of functions—which are, arguably, not grammatical but pragmatic. According to Li and Thompson, the variety of functions the sentence-final *le* has are communicative. It is claimed that the communicative function of *le* is to signal a currently relevant state.[7] 'Currently relevant' here means the time relevant to the speech situation—past, present, or future. The sentences in table 6.3 can be answers to the questions 'Why is John not at home now?', 'Why was John not at home yesterday?', and 'Why will John not be at home next week?' respectively:

Table 6.3 Sentence-final *le* structure

Chinese sentence	Literal translation	English translation
1 *Yuēhàn chūqù mǎi dōngxi le*	John out go buy things le	John has gone out shopping.
2 *zuótiān Yuēhàn chūqù mǎi dōngxi le*	yesterday John out go buy things le	John went out shopping yesterday.
3 *xià xīngqī Yuēhàn jiù zài zhōngguó le*	below week John then at China le	Next week John will be in China.

The notion of 'currently' in (1), (2), and (3) is identified with present, past, and future respectively. 'Relevant' here means that John's absence is relevant to the speech situation and the speaker is trying to say something that is relevant to that situation. Without *le* at the end of the sentences they are simple statements of facts. With *le*, they are offered as an explanation for why John is absent. This communicative function of *le* can be further illustrated by the contrast in table 6.4, in which the predicates are in fact formed by a stative verb:

Table 6.4 Communicative function of *le*

Chinese sentence	Literal translation	English translation
tiānqì lěng	weather cold	It is cold.
tiānqì lěng le	weather cold le	It has become cold.

As the English translations show, the second sentence means that the coldness of the weather has some relevance to the current situation. Thus, for example, one could use this sentence to suggest that warm clothing is needed, or one could use it to comment on the sudden change of weather, or that it was warm just then but cold now, and so on. Indeed, the precise interpretation of the second sentence depends on the speech situation.

However loose and varied speech situations involving the use of *le* may be, they can be broadly grouped into five categories, which are discussed briefly below.

Change of state of affairs
When a sentence-final *le* is added to a statement, the speaker intends to show the changed state of affairs which is relevant to the speech situation. The contrasting pairs in table 6.5 are good examples.

Table 6.5 Change of state of affairs

Chinese sentence	Literal translation	English translation
1 *wǒ zhīdào*	I know	I know.
wǒ zhīdào le	I know *le*	Now I know/I see.
2 *wǒ lèi*	I tired	I am tired.
wǒ lèi le	I tired *le*	I am tired now.
3 *méi yǒu*	not have	There is no ...
méi yǒu le	not have *le*	There is no ... any more.
4 *Yuēhàn hěn gāo*	John very tall	John is very tall.
Yuēhàn hěn gāo le	John very tall *le*	John has grown very tall.

Correcting a wrong assumption
Another use of sentence-final *le* is to refer to assumptions in a relevant speech situation. For instance, both (1) and (2) below mean 'You are wrong'. But by saying (1) instead of (2):

   1 *nǐ cuò le* (you wrong *le*)
   2 *nǐ cuò* (you wrong)

the speaker intends to express the sense of 'Let me correct you', or 'Let me make it clear to you that you are wrong'.

In response to an invitation for you to eat something, you may say

wǒ yǐjīng chī le (I already eat *le*)

which can be translated as 'I have already eaten', but at the same time implies something like 'I am not hungry'.

Specific state of affairs

Some states of affairs may be specifically relevant to both the speaker and hearer. For example, you may say 'I have bought a house' by using two *le*s, one verbal and one sentence-final:

wǒ mǎi le fángzi le (I buy *le* house *le*)

However, you will not use the sentence-final *le* when you tell a stranger that you have bought a house. Without the sentence-final *le*, *wǒ mǎi le fángzi* is a simple statement. With the sentence-final *le*, *wǒ mǎi le fángzi le* is spoken with the assumption that the listener knows something about the affair.

Equally, as a general statement, you could say:

1 *Yuēhàn tài zìsī* (John too selfish)

meaning 'John is too selfish' referring to his personality in general. But when you discuss a specific action by John that is considered to be selfish you may say:

2 *Yuēhàn tài zìsī le*

Although the English translation may still be 'John is too selfish', by saying (2) which uses the sentence-final *le* the specific relevance is clearly made to both the speaker and the listener of the speech situation.

Imminent action

Sentence-final *le* is often used together with adverbs such as *kuài* (quickly) or auxiliaries such as *yào* (will) to express an action or event which is to take place soon. Thus, 'We will be arriving in Beijing soon' is:

wǒmen yào dào Běijīng le (we will arrive Beijing *le*)

and the Chinese equivalent of 'The plane is taking off soon' is:

fēijī kuài qǐfēi le (fly machine quick take off *le*)

Other situations
Sentence-final *le* can be used in some other speech situations.
For example it may be used with negative imperatives as in:

1 *bié wàng le* (do not forget le) meaning 'do not forget'
2 *bié shuō huà le* (do not say speech le) meaning 'shut up'
3 *bié zhǎo le* (do not look le) meaning 'do not look (for it)
   anymore'

Without *le*, (2) would mean 'Be quiet' and (3) would just mean
'Do not look for it'.

Le is also often used in sentences which express excessiveness
such as:

4 *wǒ tài gāo le* (I too tall *le*) 'I am too tall.'
5 *wǒ chī de tài duō le* (I eat *de*[8] too more *le*) 'I have eaten too
   much.'

In these sentences, however, the excessiveness is expressed by
the word *tài* (too), and therefore *le* is used to convey some extra
information. For example (5) may not just mean I have eaten too
much. The speaker may also, depending on the pragmatic context, want to say something like 'I cannot have any more' or 'It
was foolish of me to have eaten so much'.

The use and understanding of the sentence-final *le* is, therefore, very subtle and depends on the pragmatic situation. It is for
this reason that sentence-final *le* is generally not used in written
expository or descriptive prose and it is rare in formal spoken
language situations such as news reports, speeches, lectures, and
proclamations. This is only logical since the use of *le* is very
dependent on situational context.

Le is also not used when the speaker is simply asserting a general truth, or describing ongoing situations involving no change,
or reporting simple events that happened in the past, or simple
future events, requests, suggestions, and commands.

Particle guò

Guò is often called the 'experience' particle, and it is used to indicate that an event has been experienced with respect to some reference time.

Guò, however, can be a verb by itself that means 'to experience' or 'to go through'. Only when *guò* is suffixed to a verb is it considered a particle. Its functional meaning is clearly associated with its meaning as a verb.

The examples in table 6.6 show not only the difference as well as the association of the two categories to which *guò* belongs, but also the subtlety of its meaning when *guò* is used as a particle.

Table 6.6 Particle *guò*

Chinese sentence	Literal translation	English translation
1 *wǒ zài yīngguó guò le bā nián*	I at UK experience *le* eight year	I lived in the UK for eight years.
2 *Yuēhàn qù le zhōngguó*	John go *le* China	John went to China.
3 *tā qù guo zhōngguó*	he[a] go *guo* China	He has been to China.
4 *tā yǒu le nǚ péngyou*	he have *le* female friend	He now has a girlfriend.
5 *tā yǒu guo nǚ péngyou*	he have *guo* female friend	He used to have a girlfriend.

a *Ta* in fact is gender neutral and it can either be she or he in Chinese. It is translated as he here simply because a choice has to be made in English.

In (1) *guò* is used as a verb, and in (3) and (5) it is used as a particle, just as *le* is in (2) and (4). The contrast in meanings shown by the English translation clearly demonstrates the grammatical function of *guò* as a particle and its association with the function of being a verb.

Particle zài

Zài is often referred to as a progressive particle, and it is used to indicate an event or action in progress. Unlike other particles which are either suffixed to a verb or placed at the end of a sentence *zài* is prefixed to a verb. Thus, while *wǒ xiě* (I write) means 'I write', *wǒ zài xiě* (I zài write) means 'I am writing'. Note that there is no formal grammatical element in *wǒ zài xiě* to indicate tense and the English translation of it can also be 'I was writing' in the appropriate context.

Zài can also be used as preposition before a noun, meaning 'at' or 'on'. Indeed, *zài* can be interpreted as 'be at' or 'be on', as can be seen in:

> *Yuēhàn zài jiā* (John zai home) meaning 'John is at home.'
> *shū zài zhuōzi shàng* (book zai table above) meaning 'The book is on the table.'

In these sentences *zài* functions both as a preposition and as the verb 'to be'. Another way of saying the same thing is that in Chinese the verb 'to be' is not required in these kinds of sentences.

When the prepositional use and progressive use of *zài* are both possible in a sentence the interpretation of *zài* can be ambiguous, as shown in the example below:

> *wǒ zài túshūguǎn gōngzuò* (I *zai* library work)

This can either be interpreted as 'I work at the library' or 'I am working at the library'. Note that there cannot be two *zài*s in one sentence, and *wǒ zài túshūguǎn zài gōngzuò* is ungrammatical.

Particle *ne*

Ne (with a neutral tone) is another progressive particle, but it is restricted to the colloquial language and its interpretation is more speech-situation dependent. The other difference between *ne* and *zài* is that whereas the latter is prefixed to a verb the former is always placed at the end of a sentence.

Finally, very often *zài* and *ne* are used together in one sentence. For instance, in response to 'What are you doing?', which can be *nǐ zuò shénme ne* (you do what *ne*), the speaker may say:

> *wǒ zài kànshū ne* (I *zai* look book *ne*) meaning 'I am reading'.

Particle *zhe*

Whereas *zài* and *ne* are particles indicating ongoing actions or events, *zhe* (also with a neutral tone) is a particle indicating ongoing state.

Zhe is used particularly with an activity verb signalling states associated with the meaning of the action implied in the verb. Structurally, *zhe*, just as with *le*, is suffixed to a verb. The minimal pairs in table 6.7 show the difference between the use of *zài* and *zhe*:

Table 6.7 Particle *zhe*

Chinese sentence	Literal translation	English translation
wǒ zài ná liǎng běn shū	I *zai* take two volume book	I am taking two books.
wǒ ná zhe liǎng běn shū	I take *zhe* two volume book	I am holding two books.
Yuēhàn zài zhā lǐngdài	John *zai* wear tie	John is putting a tie on.
Yuēhàn zhā zhe lǐngdài	John wear *zhe* tie	John is wearing a tie.

Finally, *zhe* is often used to indicate states or manners expressed by one verb which accompanies the activity expressed by another verb in a sentence. Consider the following pair:

1 *wǒ zhàn zhe shuōhuà* (I stand *zhe* speak)
2 *wǒ hē zhe kāfēi kàn diànshì* (I drink *zhe* coffee watch television)

(1) can be interpreted as 'I talk standing up', and (2) as 'While drinking coffee I watch television'.

The three particles de

In previous chapters we have come across the three *de*s, but without a detailed analysis. They are discussed here together in this section not only because they have important grammatical functions, but also because they are pronounced the same way. Just like certain other particles they are among the few words in Mandarin that have a neutral tone and each of them is represented by a distinctive character.

The three *de*s are the adverb particle, the adjective particle, and the complement particle.

The adverbial de
The adverbial *de* is the easiest of the three to handle. It appears before the verb and is suffixed to a stative verb. In other words, this *de* makes a stative verb into an adverb when *de* is suffixed to the stative verb and when it appears before the verb. *Gāoxìng* (happy), for example becomes 'happily' when *de* is suffixed to it in:

> *Mǎlì gāoxìng de chànggē* (Mary happy de sing)

which means 'Mary sings happily'. This is more or less the same as in English: when *ly* is suffixed to some adjectives they become adverbs.

The adjectival de
It has been mentioned previously that in Mandarin the so-called adjectives do not behave differently syntactically from verbs. That is the main reason why we call them stative verbs. However, these words are semantically like adjectives in English. Semantically, for example, *gāoxìng* (happy) obviously belongs to a class which is different from the class that contains words such as *qù* (go). Therefore, there is a justification for calling words like *gāoxìng* adjectives.

An adjective, however, can only be a modifier of a noun and therefore it has to appear before a noun in Chinese. When it does the adjective particle *de* is suffixed to it. Note that in the last section we have shown that a stative verb becomes an adverb by virtue of the fact that *de* is suffixed to it and that it appears before a verb in a sentence. Equally, a stative verb becomes an adjective by virtue of the fact that *de* is suffixed to it and it appears before a noun in a sentence. We call the *de* adjectival simply because the stative verb that goes with it functions as an adjective. Now consider the following:

> 1 *gāoxìng de gōngzuò* (happy *de* work)
> 2 *gāoxìng de Yuēhàn* (happy *de* John)

In (1) *gāoxìng de* becomes 'happily' because it appears before a verb whereas *gāoxìng de* in (2) becomes 'happy' because it appears before a noun. *Gāoxìng* by itself may just be called a stative verb and it can be part of a predicate in (3) for example:

3 *Yuēhàn hěn gāoxìng* (John very happy)

which means 'John is very happy'. Therefore, whether a stative verb in Mandarin is an adjective or an adverb depends on the syntactic context. Similarly, whether *de* is adverbial or adjectival also depends on syntactic context.

This context-binding quality of *de* is also illustrated by its function in relative clauses. In English a relative clause can be connected by a relative clause pronoun such as 'which', 'when', and 'what'. For example, in the 'The book *which* is published by Oxford University Press', 'James, *who* is the best student in the class', and 'In 1989 *when* the Berlin Wall came down' the italicised words are all relative clause pronouns. In Mandarin there are no such relative clause pronouns and all relative clauses are connected by *de*.

Table 6.8 *de* as a relative clause pronoun

Chinese sentence	Literal translation	English translation
Niújīn dàxué chūbǎnshè chūbǎn de shū	Oxford University Press publish *de* book	the book which was published by Oxford University Press
bān shàng zuì hǎo de xuésheng Zhānmǔsī	class in most good *de* student James	James, who is the best student in the class
Bólín qiáng dǎo xià de yī jiǔ bā jiǔ	Berlin Wall fell down *de* 1989	In 1989 when the Berlin Wall fell down

Clearly in these syntactic contexts, *de* functions as a relative clause pronoun. Semantically speaking, these relative clauses are like adjectives because they modify nouns. Therefore, in the framework of Chinese grammar we may still call this use of *de* adjectival.

The complement de

The complement *de* is more complex and therefore is dealt with in a separate section after some points related to it are discussed first.

MEASURE WORDS (M)

A measure word (or classifier as it is sometimes called) is a grammatical word which measures or classifies a noun. In English, 'pride', 'drop', and 'piece' are measures or classifiers for 'lion', 'water', and 'information' respectively. In English there are some nouns that require a particle of this kind. To be grammatically correct we have to say, for instance, 'a piece of information' rather than 'an information'.

However, for most nouns in English no measure word is required. For example, 'a table', 'a person', 'two dogs', and so on do not require a measure word. In Mandarin, however, whenever a noun is preceded with a numeral or a demonstrative pronoun a measure word is required. For example, to mean 'two books' we have to say *liǎng běn shū* (two M book), and to mean 'that dog' we have to say *nà zhī gǒu* (that M dog).

As the two examples illustrate, a measure word appears in between the noun and the numeral or between the noun and the demonstrative pronoun. If the noun phrase has both a demonstrative and a numeral, the word order is: demonstrative, followed by the numeral, followed by the measure, and then the noun.

There are hundreds of measure words in Mandarin although it is not clear what the exact number is.[9] This is the case because different measure words are required for different groups of nouns. Which nouns require which measure words depends on the perceived nature and attributes of the nouns. There is a specific measure word for round things, a measure word for bulky things, and so on. It requires some effort to learn which measure words go with which nouns.

The most commonly used measure is *gè*, which can be used with nouns of very different categories such as 'person', 'nation', 'table', and 'house'. These nouns have their own specific measure words; but it is also grammatically correct to use *gè* with them. A rule of thumb is that it is totally unacceptable not to use a measure word and a wrong one is better than none. Therefore, some speakers use *gè* most of the time, especially in spoken language.

Another point about measure words is that some nouns, such as the names of the days and year, are considered to be measure words themselves. In other words, it is wrong to say the following:

yí ge tiān (one M day) to mean 'one day'
zhè ge nián (this M year) to mean 'this year'

because *tiān* and *nián* themselves are measure words. Thus, 'one day' is *yī tiān* (one day) and 'two years' is *liǎng nián* (two year).

Another point to be remembered is that when a measure word is reduplicated it becomes a universal quantifier, as discussed in the previous chapter. For example *nián nián* is 'every year' and *tiān tiān* is 'every day'.

Finally, *gè* can be used as a universal quantifier for a range of nouns. Whatever follows *gè gè* becomes 'every' something. For example *gè gè rén* (M M person) is 'every person' and *gè gè guójiā* (M M nation) is 'every nation'.

AUXILIARIES

Many particles in Mandarin can be called auxiliaries in that they assist verbs to express grammatical functions such as tense, aspect, and mood. For example, *le* has the same function that the auxiliary *have* plus *-en* has in English in sentences such as 'I *have* written a book'; *zài* and *ne* have the same function that the auxiliary verb 'to be' plus *-ing* has in English in the sentence 'I *am* reading this book.'

The difference is that in English these auxiliary elements have different forms depending on tense, person, and number whereas in Chinese no such inflection takes place. In other words these elements do not change form in Chinese and they, therefore, are called particles. There are a number of auxiliaries in English which do not change form either, for example prepositions such as 'to', 'for', 'with'; and conjunctions such as 'and' and 'but'. In what follows the Chinese equivalents of these auxiliaries are discussed.

Directional auxiliaries

Directional auxiliaries are those that indicate directions when they are used with verbs. Six directional auxiliaries are discussed in this section; they are *lái, qù, shàng, xià, cóng, and lí.*

Lái *and* qù

Lái (come) and *qù* (go) can function as proper verbs themselves and it is by extension of their verbal meaning that *lái* is used to have the grammatical meaning of 'towards the speaker' and *qù* the meaning of 'away from the speaker'.

To illustrate the use of this pair, let us compare them using the verb *jìn*, meaning 'enter'. To say 'Enter!' when the speaker is inside the room, the Chinese equivalent is *jìn lái* (enter come); but to say it when the speaker is outside the room it is *jìn qù* (enter go). Similarly, 'Bring it to me' is *ná lái* (bring come), and 'Take it away' is *ná qù* (bring go).[10]

Shàng *and* xià

Shàng (up/above) and *xià* (below/down) are used in similar ways to English. *Pá shàng* (climb up) is 'climb up'; *pá xià* (climb down) is 'climb down'; *pá shàng shān* (climb up mountain) is 'climb the mountain', and so on.

The pair *lái /qù* and the pair *shàng/xià* can be used together. For example, *zǒu shàng lóu qù* (walk up stairs go) is 'go upstairs' if the speaker is downstairs; but *zǒu shàng lóu lái* (walk up stairs come) means 'come upstairs' when the speaker is upstairs.

A point to remember is that these directional auxiliaries, unlike their English equivalents, have verbal qualities and they can function as verbs. For example, *shàng qù* means 'go up', and *xià lái* means 'come down'. This is why auxiliaries like these are sometimes called co-verbs in Chinese grammar.

Cóng *and* lí

Cóng can be translated as 'from' in English whereas, loosely translated, *lí* means 'away from'. *Cóng* is often used with *dào* (to), as in *cóng Běijīng dào Shànghǎi* (from Beijing to Shanghai) and *cóng qùnián dào xiànzài* (from last year till now).

Cóng and *lí* are not interchangeable although in translation the difference usually is not shown. For instance, in:

wǒ jiā lí gōngyuán bù yuǎn (my home *li* park not far)

the concept of away from is not shown in words in the English translation of the sentence which is 'My home is not far from the park.'

Conjunctions and prepositions
Two conjunctions and two prepositions are discussed here. The two conjunctions are *hé* and *gēn* and the two prepositions are *gěi* and *tì*.

Hé *and* gēn
Hé and *gēn* can both be translated as 'and' or 'with' in English. For example:

wǒ hé/gēn nǐ yìqǐ qù (I *he/gen* you together go) meaning 'I will go with you.'
Yuēhàn hé/gēn Mǎlì shì hǎo péngyou (John *he/gen* Mary are good friend) meaning 'John and Mary are good friends'.

The difference between them is that *hé* is more formal than *gēn* in its usage.

Gěi *and* tì
Gěi and *tì* are another pair, which can be translated as 'to' or 'for' in English, for example:

wǒ tì /gěi nǐ zuò (I *ti/gei* you do) meaning 'I will do it for you'.

However, *gěi* is more often used to mean 'to' while *tì* as 'for' or 'on behalf of'.

wǒ yào gěi nǐ shuōhuà (I want *gei* you speak)

can mean both 'I will speak to you' and 'I will speak for you'. On the other hand, *wǒ yào tì nǐ shuōhuà* is more likely to be translated as 'I will speak on your behalf.'

Comparison auxiliary

Bǐ, the comparison auxiliary, is derived from the verb *bǐ* (compare), as shown in the following examples:

> *wǒ bù néng gēn nǐ bǐ* (I not can with you compare) meaning 'I cannot be compared with you'.
> *Máo bǎ dìguózhǔyì bǐ zuò zhǐ lǎohǔ* (Mao *ba* imperialism compare as paper tiger) meaning 'Mao likened imperialism to a paper tiger'.

In these sentences *bǐ* is used as a verb.

As an auxiliary, *bǐ* is involved in various sentence constructions as table 6.9 shows.

Table 6.9 Comparison auxiliary *bǐ*

Chinese sentence	Literal translation	English translation
1 *Yuēhàn bǐ Mǎlì gāo*	John *bi* Mary tall	John is taller than Mary.
2 *xiǎo bǐ dà měilì*	small *bi* large beautiful	Small is more beautiful than large.
3 *gōngzuò bǐ xián zhe jiànkāng*	work *bi* idle *zhe* healthy	To work is healthier than to be idle.
4 *Mǎlì bǐ Hǎilún pǎo de kuài*	Mary *bi* Helen run *de*[a] fast	Mary runs faster than Helen.

[a]This *de* is what is called a complement particle which will be discussed shortly

(1) compares two nouns, (2) two adjectives, (3) two verbs, and (4) two adverbs. In Chinese *bǐ* expresses all the grammatical meanings expressed by derivatives in English: tall*er*, healthi*er*, fast*er*, and *more beautiful*.

COMPLEMENTS

The term complement itself is not difficult to grasp: it is anything which completes the whole. In terms of grammar, a complement is something that cannot be left out in an expression. This can be illustrated by an English example. 'She became' is not complete; it needs a complement to make a whole sentence. 'President', for instance, is a complement to make a whole sentence 'She became president'. On the other hand, an adjunct, though also part of a sentence, can be left out. 'Last year' is an adjunct and it can be added to make a sentence 'She became President last year'; but when left out, the sentence is still complete.

In a standard textbook of English grammar, complements are dealt with in terms of other grammatical categories. In Mandarin, however, complement structures have distinctive features, partly because they involve the use of *de*. As we shall see shortly, some features of complement structures in Mandarin do not have English equivalents and are difficult to translate.

Potential complements

Potential complements are verbal complements. They are called potential complements because all these phrasal verbs denote potentiality or capability, as illustrated in table 6.10:

Table 6.10   Potential complement

Chinese	Literal translation	English translation
tīng de jiàn	listen *de* perceive	can hear
zhǎo de dào	find *de* reach	can find
shuì de zháo	sleep *de* attain	can sleep
zuò de wán	do *de* finish	can finish doing
xué de hǎo	learn *de* good	can learn well
kàn de dǒng	read *de* understand	can understand (by reading)
jì de zhù	memorise *de* fix	can remember
chī de bǎo	eat *de* full	can have enough (eating)
tán de lái	talk *de* come	can be on good terms
kǎo de shàng	take examination *de* up	can pass the examination
zuò de xià	sit *de* down	can sit down
shàng de qù	up *de* go	can go up
zǒu de shàng qù	walk *de* up go	can walk up
chī de xià	eat *de* down	can eat (something) up
kàn de chū	look *de* out	can detect

The English translation 'can' indicates potentiality here, not permission. Note that, unlike English phrasal verbs which consist mostly of a verb and a preposition, verbal complements in Chinese may consist of two verbs, a verb and a stative verb, or a verb and a preposition. All of them are connected by *de* in the middle.

Finally, the meaning of potentiality in the above verbal phrases can be expressed by *néng* (can). In fact, the meanings of all of them except *tán de lái* can be expressed by replacing *de* with *néng*, in which case *néng* has to appear as the first item of these verbal phrases, not in the middle of the phrase as *de* does, as in *néng kàn chū*.

The negative counterparts of these verbal complements are formed by replacing *de* with *bù* in the middle, to mean that something cannot be done or is not possible. Thus, *tīng bú jiàn* means 'not be able to hear' and *tán bù lái* means 'cannot be on good terms'.

Clause complements

When a clause follows *de* to complete a sentence we call this kind of construction a clause complement. In these sentences, the clause complements usually express the extent, degree, or quality expressed by the verb which precedes *de*, as shown by table 6.11:

Table 6.11   Clause complements

Chinese translation	Literal translation	English translation
tā gāoxìng de dà xiào	he happy *de* big laugh	He was so happy that he laughed loudly.
tā kū de yūn guò qù le	he cry *de* faint pass go *le*	He cried so much that he fainted.
tā sǐ de zhòng yú Tàishān	he die *de* heavy over Tai Mountain	He died in such a way that the significance of his death is heavier than Mount Tai.

As can be seen from the translation, the function of *de* is contextual and the translation of it depends on the context of every sentence.

Comparison complements

By definition, a comparison complement involves *de* in comparison sentences. In such sentences what appears after *de* complements what appears before *de*.

Just as clause complements express degree or extent of the consequence of some action or state of affairs, comparison complements express the degree of comparison such as more or less and how much more or less. Of course, comparison involves more than one subject, and the comparison particle *bǐ* (see previous discussion on this particle) is required to link up the comparison. Thus the Chinese equivalent of 'John runs faster than Mary' is:

Yuēhàn pǎo de bǐ Mǎlì kuài (John run *de bi* Mary fast)

The word order can be slightly altered to mean the same thing:

Yuēhàn bǐ Mǎlì pǎo de kuài (John *bi* Mary run *de* fast)

Note that in both types of sentences, *de* appears immediately after the verb.

Intensifying or degree complements

In a comparison sentence, we have seen that when a complement is connected by *de*, which appears between the verb (or stative verb) and the complement, it expresses the extent or degree of some action or state of affairs. The same pattern applies to some words of intensity or degree which function as complements and are followed by *de* in a sentence:

Table 6.12 Intensifying or degree complements

Chinese sentence	Literal translation	English translation
wǒ lèi de hěn lìhai	I tire *de* very serious	I am extremely tired.
tā shuō de fēicháng hǎo	he speak *de* extraordinary good	He speaks extraordinarily well.
wǒ ké de yào sǐ	I thirsty *de* want die	I am terribly thirsty.
Běijīng de dōngtiān lěng de bùdéliǎo	Beijing *de* winter cold *de* exceedingly	It is exceedingly cold in winter in Beijing.

Note that these intensity or degree complements can be formed by either a stative verb, a verb, or an adverb.

Directional complements

Directional complements consist of a verb and a word of direction such as 'towards', 'away', 'up', and 'down'. They resemble English phrasal verbs except that directions in Chinese can be expressed by a verb. These complements are different from potential complements in that they do not contain *de*. Here is a list of examples:

Table 6.13 Directional complements

Chinese	Literal translation	English translation
guān shàng	close up	turn off/close
zuò xià	sit down	sit down
jìn lái	enter come	come in
chū qù	out go	go out
dài lái	take come	bring here
dài qù	take go	bring away
shàng lái	up come	come up
xià qù	down go	go down

Resultative complements

Resultative complements are similar to directional complements in that they do not involve *de*. Strictly speaking, resultative complements are formed either by two verbs, or a verb and a stative verb. Usually the first verb is the action and the second verb or stative verb is the result of the first. Again let us illustrate the structure by examples:

Table 6.14 Resultative complements

Chinese	Literal translation	English translation
kàn jiàn	look perceive	see
tīng jiàn	listen perceive	hear
xiě wán	write finish	finish writing
gǎo hǎo	handle good	get done
tīng dǒng	listen understand	understand (by listening)
dǎ kāi	beat open	to open
shuō dìng	say fix	promise
ná zhù	take hold	hold firm to

Table 6.14 Resultative complements (continued)

Chinese	Literal translation	English translation
shuō duì	say correct	say it right
hē bǎo	drink full	drink one's fill
xiě qīngchu	write clear	write clearly

In the English literal translation, each of these resultative complements has two words: a verb followed by a verb, an adjective, or an adverb. The first verb is the action and the second word is what is accomplished by the action. 'Look', for instance, is the action of trying to see; and only when perception is accomplished does it mean 'see'.

A SUMMARY OF THE THREE *DE*S

We are now in a position to review the differences between the three *de*s. When *de* appears in between a stative verb (or adjective in terms of English grammar) and a noun it makes the stative verb into an adjective (thus the term adjectival *de*); when it appears in between a stative verb and a verb it makes the stative verb into an adverb (thus the term adverbial *de*); and finally when it appears after a verb (or a stative verb) followed by either a sentence, a verb, or an adverb it is heading a complement (thus the term complement *de*).

This triple function of *de* is best illustrated by the following examples:

Table 6.15 Three functions of *de*

Chinese sentence	Literal translation	English translation
tā shuō liúlì de zhōngwén	she speak fluent *de* Chinese	She/he speaks fluent Chinese.
tā liúlì de shuō zhōngwén	she fluent *de* speak Chinese	She/he speaks Chinese fluently.
tā zhōngwén shuō de liúlì	she Chinese speak *de* fluent	(not directly translatable)

De is adjectival in the first sentence, adverbial in the second, and a complement in the third. The third sentence is left untranslated because there is no exact equivalent in English. It can either be translated as the first or the second, although neither of them can be considered a satisfactory translation. A more appropriate translation may be 'He speaks Chinese in such a way that it is fluent'. The word order in the third sentence, unlike that in the first and second, is S+O+V because there is a general rule in Chinese syntax that the verb cannot be followed by two phrases. Thus, *zhōngwén*, the noun phrase in the third sentence has to be moved to the front of the verb.

QUANTIFIERS

Quantifiers are words that express quantities, such as 'every', 'all', 'any', 'some', and numerals.

Numerals as quantifiers

Let us start with the numerals. There are ten words for the numbers from one to ten in Mandarin, and the rest are formed by combinations. Eleven is *shí yī* (ten one), twelve is *shí èr* (ten two), and so on. Twenty is *èr shí* (two ten), thirty is *sān shí* (three ten), etc. Thirty-one is *sān shí yī* (three ten one) and thirty-two is *sān shí èr* (three ten two), and so on.

A distinctive feature in using numeral quantifiers is that every time a numeral quantifies a noun it has to be followed by a measure word, as discussed previously. The universal quantifier *měi* (every) also requires a measure word when it quantifies a noun except when a noun is a measure word itself. Nouns such as *tiān* (day) and *nián* (year), for instance, as seen earlier, are measure words themselves. For words which are not measure words themselves, a measure word is required, for example in *měi zhāng zhuōzi* (every M table) for 'every table' and *měi jià fēijī* (every M plane) for 'every plane'.

Dōu as a quantifier

Dōu is a very useful and yet difficult grammatical word in the category of quantifiers in Chinese. There is no word-to-word translation for it because *dōu* can mean 'all', 'both', 'neither', or 'any' depending upon the context, as the following examples show:

Table 6.16 *Dōu* as a quantifier

Chinese sentence	Literal translation	English translation
tāmen wǒ dōu xǐhuan	them I *dou* like	I like them all.
tāmen dōu bù xǐhuan zhōngguó cài	they *dou* not like Chinese food	None of them like Chinese food.
Yuēhàn hé Mǎlì dōu xǐhuan zhōngguó cài	John and Mary *dou* like Chinese food	Both John and Mary like Chinese food.
Yuēhàn hé Mǎlì dōu bù xǐhuan zhōngguó cài	John and Mary *dou* not like Chinese food	Neither John nor Mary likes Chinese food.
wǒ shéi dōu xǐhuan	I who *dou* like	I like everyone.
wǒ shéi dōu bù xǐhuan	I who *dou* not like	I do not like anyone.

Clearly *dōu* cannot be translated without proper context. First, it depends on whether the sentence is affirmative or negative. Second, it depends on the number of the noun that *dōu* quantifies. In an affirmative sentence if the number of the noun *dōu* quantifies is more than two, *dōu* is interpreted as 'all', as in:

sān ge rén dōu xǐhuan kàn diànshì (Three people all like to watch television.)

and if the noun denotes just two *dōu* is interpreted as 'both', as in:

liǎng ge rén dōu xǐhuan kàn diànshì (Both people like to watch television.)

In a negative sentence, if the noun *dōu* quantifies is a number of more than two it is interpreted as 'none', as in

sān ge rén dōu bù xǐhuan kàn diànshì (None of the three people like to watch television.)

and if the noun denotes just two *dōu* is interpreted as 'neither', as in:

liǎng ge rén dōu bù xǐhuan kàn diànshì (Neither of the two people likes to watch television.)

The first sentence in table 6.16, for instance, is ambiguous because we do not know whether 'them' entails two people or more.

In a sentence that has an interrogative word as a quantifier, *dōu* is interpreted as 'every' or 'any' in an affirmative sentence and as 'not' in a negative one. The functions of *dōu* in this respect need more detailed discussion. However, before we proceed to these functions, we need to discuss interrogative words as quantifiers.

Interrogative words as quantifiers

One important and interesting property of interrogative words (or *wh*-words) is that they function as quantifiers in certain contexts. These contexts can arise from within affirmative or negative sentences. In an affirmative sentence their quantification interpretations are set out in table 6.17 which includes most, but not all, of the interrogative words.

Table 6.17 Interrogative words

Chinese	Literal translation	English translation
shéi	who	anybody
shénme	what	anything
něi	which	any
shénme shíhòu	when	anytime
nǎlǐ	where	any place
zěnme	how	any way
wèishénme	why	any reason
duōshǎo	how many/much	no matter how much/ many
gànmá	what for	no matter what for

The last two sentences in Table 6.16 illustrate well how interrogative words are used as quantifiers in contexts. Here are two more illustrations:

1 *Wǒ nǎlǐ dōu qù* (I where *dou* go)
2 *Wǒ duōshǎo qián dōu yào* (I how much money *dou* want)

The first sentence can be interpreted as 'I will go anywhere' in which case the interrogative word 'where' becomes 'anywhere'.

(2) can be interpreted as 'I want it no matter how much it costs' in which case the interrogative word 'how much' becomes 'no matter how much'.

The role of *dōu* in interrogative quantifiers

An important point to note is that when these interrogative words function as quantifiers they are used with *dōu*. In fact, we can say that it is *dōu* which makes them quantifiers. In terms of word order, an interrogative word appears before *dōu*, which appears before the verb.

Since these interrogative words become the quantifier, 'any', we can term them as universal quantifiers because 'any' means inclusive. *Dōu*, therefore, can be termed as a universal quantifier particle in these contexts. As a universal quantifier particle, *dōu* has a variant which is *yě*. In any of the above sentences *dōu* can be replaced by *yě* and they are interchangeable.

Note that interrogative words can be quantifiers without *dōu*; but must be in a negative context. Consider the following pair:

> *wǒ bù mǎi shénme* (I not buy what)
> *wǒ bú qù nǎlǐ* (I not go where)

The first sentence can be interpreted as 'I don't buy anything', and the second as 'I don't go anywhere'. However, when *dōu* appears in a negative context, the interpretation becomes all exclusive.

> *wǒ nǎlǐ dōu bú qù* (I where *dou* not go)
> *wǒ shénme dōu bù mǎi* (I what *dou* not buy)

The first can mean 'I will go nowhere' and the second 'I will buy nothing'. Therefore, we see again that *dōu* marks universality in a sentence.

Finally, *dōu* also has an effect on word order: in a sentence where *dōu* appears, the quantifier in the object position moves to the front of the verb, as shown by the comparison between the two sentences without *dōu* and the two sentences with *dōu* used in the above examples.

SENTENCES

In this chapter we have so far discussed three aspects of grammar: word order, morphological processes (inflections), and grammatical words, which are essential grammatical elements in language. As we have seen, Mandarin lacks inflection which is common in Indo-European languages. However, grammatical functions expressed by inflection in languages like English are accomplished by means of word compounds and grammatical words such as particles in Chinese. In this section, we are concerned with three basic types of sentences: simple sentences, compound sentences, and complex sentences.

Simple sentences

A simple sentence consists of a subject and a predicate. A command sentence such as *zuò!* (Sit!) may appear to have no subject; but in fact the subject is the understood *nǐ* (you).

A subject can be a noun, a pronoun, or even a verb. However, in English when a verb functions as a subject it has to appear in the form of a gerund or with 'to'. For instance, we either say '*Eating* in a restaurant is expensive' or '*To* eat in a restaurant is expensive.' It is ungrammatical to say 'Eat in a restaurant is expensive'.

In Chinese, however, it is grammatical to use the infinitive verb without the gerund *ing* or 'to' as a component of the subject. The simple reason is that there is no morphological process of *ing*, or infinitive 'to' in Chinese. The Chinese equivalent of 'To eat in a restaurant is expensive' or 'Eating in a restaurant is expensive' is:

> *zài fànguǎn lǐ chīfàn hěn guì* (at restaurant in eat very expensive)

The predicate of a sentence in Mandarin may be just a verb, a verb plus an object, or an adjective. Therefore we may say there are two types of simple sentences in Mandarin: verbal sentences and adjectival sentences. A verbal sentence consists of a subject and a verb, or a verb plus an object. An adjectival sentence consists of a subject and an adjective, with or without some other elements. The following are examples of verbal sentences.

Table 6.18   Verbal sentences

Chinese sentence	Literal translation	English translation
1 *wǒ gōngzuò*	I work	I work.
2 *Yuēhàn xiě hànzì*	John write Chinese character	John writes Chinese characters.
3 *gōngzuò bāngzhù xiāohuà*	work help digestion	Work helps digestion.

The subject in (1) is the pronoun *wǒ*, in (2) a name *Yuēhàn*, and in (3) the noun *gōngzuò*. The predicate is a verb in (1), a verb plus an object in (2), and a verb and an object in (3).

Expansions

However the above three are prototypic, simple sentences. In real communicative situations, sentences can be very long because each part of the sentence may be expanded. Take (2) as an example. The subject *Yuēhàn* may be modified by an adjective, or a clause, or both; the verb may be modified by an adverb; and the object *hànzì* may also be modified, as the following example shows

> *nèi gè gāogāo de chángcháng dǎ lánqiǔ de Yuēhàn zài jiānnán de xiě tā gānggāng xuéhuì de hànzì*

The sentence can be translated as 'That tall John who often plays basketball is writing with difficulty the Chinese characters which he has just learnt'. The expansions can be made clearer by breaking the sentence into three parts: subject, verb, and object.

> Subject: *nèi gè* (that M) *gāogāo de* (tall **adjectival-particle**) *chángcháng dǎ lánqiú de* (often plays basketball **relative clause-particle**) *Yuēhàn* (John)

> Verb: *zài* (**progressive particle**) *jiānnán de* (difficult **adverbial-particle**) *xiě* (write)

> Object: *tā gānggāng xuéhuì de* (he just learned **relative clause-particle**) *hànzì* (Chinese character)

The three basic elements of a sentence, i.e. the subject, the verb, and the object are underlined. The subject *Yuēhàn* is expanded by a demonstrative pronoun, an adjective, and a relative clause; the verb *xiě* is expanded by an adverbial phrase; and the object *hànzì* is expanded by a relative clause. Note that all the modifiers appear before the elements they modify. Also note that there are no relative pronouns in Chinese, and the functions of relative clause pronouns are carried out by *de*, a point that has been discussed previously.

Finally, note that the so-called relative clauses are actually sentences which have their own subject, verb, and object. They are not called sentences because they are part of a sentence, the point of which will be discussed when we deal with complex sentences.

Stative verb sentences

When the predicate of a sentence does not contain an action verb, but a stative verb, we may call it a stative verb sentence. The following are all stative verb sentences:

1 *Yuēhàn hěn kèqi* (John very polite) meaning 'John is very polite'.
2 *Xiānggǎng de fángzi yòu gāo yòu jǐ* (Hong Kong **genitive-particle** house as tall as crowded) meaning 'Houses in Hong Kong are tall as well as crowded'.

In this type of sentence the copula, that is, the verb 'to be', which is inflected as *is* and *are* in the English version of the two sentences, is absent in Chinese. As discussed previously, this is one of the reasons why words like *kèqi* (polite) and *gāogāo* (tall) are called stative verbs.

The verb 'to be' (or the copula) revisited

The Chinese equivalent of the English verb 'to be' is *shì* which is very different in that it does not inflect in person, number, or tense. Consider some examples. In:

zhè shì yì běn shū (this *shi* one M book), meaning 'This is a book.'

shì is the verb 'to be' in a sentence involving single number. Even when the subject is plural the morphological form of *shì* is the same, as in:

zhèxiē shì hànyǔ shū (this **plural-particle** shi Chinese book), meaning 'These are Chinese books'.

The plural particle *xiē* has restricted use and it usually goes with demonstrative pronouns like *zhè, nà,* and indefinite quantifiers such as *mǒu* (certain), and *yī* (one). Thus, *zhèxiē* means 'these'; *nàxiē* means 'those'; while *mǒuxiē shū* means 'certain books'; and *yìxiē shū* means 'some books'. However, *xiē* cannot be suffixed to just any noun, like *s* mostly is in English, to form plural nouns. It is ungrammatical to say, for instance, *shūxiē* to mean 'books'.

It is clear that words like *gāo* and *kèqi* are not like the English 'tall' and 'polite' in sentences (1) and (2) and that they behave like verbs in that they do not require the verb 'to be'. However, these types of words do behave like English adjectives if the particle *de* is used with them. In the following sentences, for instance, *shì* is used with an adjective:

dìqiú shì yuán de (the earth *shi* round *de*) meaning 'The earth is round'.

zhè běn shū shì hóng de (this M book *shi* red *de*) meaning 'This book is red.'

Yīngguó rén shì kèqi de (England person *shi* polite *de*) meaning 'The English are polite.'

The same is the case with *gāo*, in, for example:

xiānggǎng de fángzi shì hěn gāo de (Hong Kong **genitive-particle** house *shi* very tall *de*) meaning 'Houses in Hong Kong are very tall'.

In these sentences, words like *gāo* and *hǒng* are used as adjectives. These examples again show that the grammatical category this type of word belongs to depends on syntactical context.

Complex sentences

A complex sentence has a main clause and at least one subordinate clause. A subordinate clause can actually be a sentence in its own right because it usually has a subject, a verb and/or an object. It is subordinate because its function is to assist the formation of a larger sentence. Consider the following two sentences:

wǒ bù zhīdào Yuēhàn qù bu qù (I not know John go not go) meaning 'I do not know whether John is going or not'.

Yuēhàn shénme shíhòu qù hái méi juédìng (John what time go still not decide), meaning 'It is not yet decided when John is going'.

In the first sentence the clause *Yuēhàn qù bu qù* (whether John is going or not) functions as the object of the main clause. In the second the clause *Yuēhàn shénme shíhòu qù* (when John is going) functions as the subject. Both can be called complement clauses. *Yuēhàn qù bu qù* is a complement clause because it functions as an object to complete a sentence. Equally, *Yuēhàn shénme shíhòu qù* functions as the subject to complete a sentence.

Relative clauses

In English a relative clause is usually headed by a *wh*-word such as 'when', 'where', 'who', 'which', 'what'. An exception is that many clauses may be headed by 'that', for example, in 'This is something that you cannot forget'. In Chinese, however, all relative clauses are headed by what is called the relative clause particle *de*, as the examples in table 6.19 show:

Table 6.19 Relative clauses

Chinese sentence	Literal translation	English translation
Yuēhàn shì xué hànyǔ de xuésheng	John is learn Chinese *de* student	John is a student who learns Chinese.
Yuēhàn xué hànyǔ de shíhòu shì yī jiǔ jiǔ liù nián	John learn Chinese *de* when 1996 year	It was in 1996 when John learned Chinese.
wǒ yào qù néng xué hànyǔ de dìfang	I want go can learn Chinese *de* place	I want to go where I can learn Chinese.
zhè shì wǒ yào zhǎo de nèi běn shū	this is I want look *de* that M book	This is the book which I am looking for.
zhè shì nǐ bù néng wàngjì de shì	this is you not can forget *de* thing	This is something that you cannot forget.

Note that in the Chinese sentences relative clauses are always followed by *de* and the clause always appears before the element it modifies.

Compound sentences

A compound sentence is also formed by two or more clauses. The difference between a compound and a complex sentence is that in a compound sentence the clauses are structurally more independent and usually connected by conjunctions such as 'and', or coordinates such as 'but', 'if … then', and so on.

One main feature of compound sentences in Chinese using coordinates is that coordinates go with the preceding clause rather than with the following clause as is the case in English. The Chinese equivalent of 'I will be there if you go' is:

rúguǒ nǐ qù wǒ huì zài nàr (if you go I will be there)

To reverse the order as in:

wǒ huì zài nàr rúguǒ nǐ qù

is an unacceptable sentence. The same is true with a 'because' clause. In English the 'because' clause may precede or may follow the main clause as in 'You had better take more clothes with you because it is going to be cold', or 'Because it is going to be cold you had better take more clothes with you'. In Chinese the 'because' clause has to come first:

yīnwèi tiānqì huì lěng nǐ zuì hǎo duō dài yīfu (because weather will cold you most good more take clothes)

Another feature of compound sentences in Chinese is that conjunction words such as 'and' are not used as much as they are in English. For instance, there is no conjunction in sentences like

wǒ shì hēi rén nǐ shì bái rén (I am black person you are white person)

In English 'and' has to be used to connect the two clauses: 'I am a Black person and you are a White person'. Although coordinates and conjunctions are not used the context makes it clear that they are there for the interpretation. This is particularly true in spoken Chinese:

nǐ bú qù wǒ yě bú qù (you not go I too not go)

can be translated as 'Since you are not going I am not going either' in which case 'since' is implied. Similarly, when:

nǐ lái zhèr wǒ qù nàr dōu kěyǐ (you come here I go there dou OK)

is translated as 'It is OK whether you come here or I go there'. Here the interpretation of 'either ... or' is made obvious by the appearance of *dōu* which is not a conjunction in Chinese (see discussion of *dōu* previously in this chapter).

Sometimes, clauses can just be stacked together in Chinese without coordinates. In:

nǐ kàn wǒ, wǒ kàn nǐ, shéi dōu bú rènshi shéi (you look me I look you who dou not recognise who)

there are three separate sentences without any connecting word. To translate the sentence, either 'and' or 'but' has to be added, as in 'We look at each other, but neither recognises the other' or 'We look at each other and nobody recognises anyone'.

I will thus conclude this rather long chapter, in which numerous aspects of Chinese grammar have been discussed, by making two points. One obvious point is that much more can be said about grammar which has not been mentioned in this chapter. The second point is that many aspects of Chinese grammar are contextual and situational. Therefore, there are less formal properties that can be examined in isolation from context. Whether this makes it more difficult or easier for a student may vary from person to person.

STUDY QUESTIONS

1. List three ways in which Chinese differs from European languages.
2. What are the three major features of grammar that are discussed in this chapter?
3. What is a phrase as opposed to, say, a noun, or a verb?
4. What is the word order in a noun phrase in Chinese?

5. How many ways can one make a question sentence in Chinese?
6. How do you make a passive sentence in Chinese?
7. In what ways is a lack of inflection in Chinese compensated by grammatical words such as particles?
8. What are the semantic as well as the syntactic differences between the verbal *le* and sentence-final *le*?
9. How do you make progressive sentences in Chinese?
10. What are the functions of the three *de*s?
11. What is a measure word?
12. What is a complement in Chinese? Can you make a sentence for each type of complement structure discussed in this chapter?
13. What does *dōu* do as a quantifier?
14. How do interrogative words become quantifiers?
15. In what way does *de* function in a relative clause?

REFERENCE READING

Chao, Y. R., *A Grammar of Spoken Chinese*, University of California Press, Berkeley and Los Angeles, 1968.

Hartmann, R. R. K. and F. C. Stork, *Dictionary of Language and Linguistics*, reprint, Applied Science Publishers Ltd, London, 1973.

Li, C. & Thompson, S., *Mandarin Chinese: A Functional Reference Grammar*, University of California Press, Berkeley, 1981.

Li Chi, *A Provisional System of Grammar for Teaching Chinese* with Introduction and Commentary, Studies in Chinese Communist Terminology no. 6–7, Center for Chinese Studies, Institute of International Studies, University of California, Berkeley, California, June 1960.

——, February 1962, *New Features in Chinese Grammatical Usage*, Studies in Chinese Communist Terminology no. 9, Center for Chinese Studies, Institute of International Studies, University of California, Berkeley, California.

Li Dejin and Cheng Meihua, *A Practical Chinese Grammar for Foreigners*, Beijing, Sinolingua, 1988.

Li Xingjian (ed.), *zhongguo yuyanxue nianjian* (Chinese Linguistics Yearbook), Yuwen chubanshe, Beijing, 1993.

Li Y. C., Robert L. Cheng, Larry Foster, Shang H. Ho, John Y. Hou, and Moira Yip, *Mandarin Chinese: A Practical Reference Grammar for Students and Teachers*, Taipei, The Crane Publishing Co., Chinese Materials Centre Publications, vol. I, 1984 and vol. II 1989.

Liu Jian, Jiang Lansheng et al., *jindai hanyu xuci yanjiu* (A Study of Empty Words in Modern Chinese), Yuwen chubanshe, Beijing, 1992.

Lu, Shuxiang, *yuwen changtan* (Talk about Language), Sanlian shudian, Beijing, 1980.

Marney, John, *A Handbook of Mandarin Chinese Grammar*, Chinese Materials Centre Inc., San Francisco, 1972.

McDonald, Edward, *Clause and Verbal Group Systems in Chinese: A Text-Based Functional Approach*, unpublished PhD thesis, School of English, Linguistics & Media, Macquarie University, 1998.

Nankai hanyuyan wenhua xueyuan, *hanyuyan wenhua yanjiu* (Study on Cultural Aspects of the Chinese Language), Tianjin renmin chubanshe, Tianjin, 1994.

Pulleyblank, Edwin, G., *Outline of Classical Chinese Grammar*, University of British Columbia Press, Vancouver, 1996.

Qian, Nairong (ed.), *hanyu yuyanxue* (Chinese Linguistics), Beijing yuyan xueyuan chubanshe, Beijing, 1995.

Ramsey, Robert, *The Languages of China*, Princeton University Press, Princeton, New Jersey, 1987.

Syrokomla-Stefanowska, A. D. and Mabel Lee, *Basic Chinese Grammar & Sentence Patterns*, Wild Peony, Broadway, NSW, 1986.

Tiee, Henry Hung-Yeh and Donald M. Lance, *A Reference Grammar of Chinese Sentences with Exercises*, The University of Arizona Press. Tucson, 1986.

Tien, Teresa, *A Practical Handbook of Modern Chinese Grammar*, Chinese Materials Centre, Taiwan, 1986.

Xing, Gongwan et al. (eds), *hanyu yanjiu* (Research on Chinese), vol. 3, Nankai daxue chubanshe, Tianjin, 1993.

Yip, Po-ching and Don Rimmington, *Chinese, An Essential Grammar*, Routledge, 1997.

—— , 1998a, *Basic Chinese, A Grammar and Workbook*, Routledge.

—— , 1998b, *Intermediate Chinese, A Grammar and Workbook*, Routledge.

Zhao, Yongxin, *Essentials of Chinese Grammar for Foreigners*, Beijing yuyan xueyuan chubanshe, 2nd printing, 1994.

ENDNOTES

1   Robert Ramsey, *The Languages of China*, Princeton, New Jersey, Princeton University Press, 1987. The following material is based on his enlightening discussion on the subject in chapter 5 of his book. In this chapter, Ramsey also points out how absurd it is for scholars such as Alfred Bloom who tried, as recently as 1981, to prove that the reason the Chinese failed to develop modern sciences was logical defects in the Chinese language.

2   Li Chi, *A Provisional System of Grammar for Teaching Chinese* with Introduction and Commentary, Studies in Chinese Communist Terminology no 6–7, Center for Chinese Studies, Institute of International Studies, University of California, Berkeley, California, June 1960.

3   M hereafter in the text stands for measure word.

4   Although, according to Chao, in some dialects, *men* may be used to make an inanimate noun plural. See Y. R. Chao, *A Grammar of Spoken Chinese*, Berkeley and Los Angeles, University of California, 1969, p. 245, footnote 30.

5   As pointed out in chapter 5, some of what are considered to be particles here
    are thought to be suffixes by some scholars. For a very comprehensive study
    of these words which are called *xuci* ('empty words' meaning functional or
    grammatical words as opposed to content words), see Liu Jian, Jiang Lansh-
    eng, et al., *jindai hanyu xuci yanjiu* (A Study of Empty Words in Modern Chi-
    nese), Yuwen chubanshe, Beijing, 1992.
6   *Zai* is a progressive particle which is discussed further later.
7   Li, C. & S. Thompson, *Mandarin Chinese: A Functional Reference Grammar*,
    University of California Press, Berkeley, 1981.
8   *De* is what is usually called a complement particle which will be dealt with
    later in the chapter.
9   Y. R. Chao, *A Grammar of Spoken Chinese*, pp. 584–6.
10 In some cases, the tone of *qù* is dropped and therefore it becomes neutral.

CHAPTER 7

Discourse

CLASSROOM VERSUS REAL SITUATION CHINESE

Students learning a second language in a classroom situation often feel disconcerted and even disheartened initially when they find themselves in a native speaking environment. They may be struck by the impression that native speakers talk in a different way from what they have been taught in the classroom. Sometimes students may find that the sentence patterns and vocabulary combinations they have learnt from textbooks are not sufficient to cope with real situation conversations.

Students are taught that *nǐ hǎo* is one of the most common greetings, like 'Hello' in English. However, a native speaker may not use *nǐ hǎo* very often. Friends or people familiar with each other frequently just say something like:

Hei! zěnmeyàng?
Ei! zěnmeyàng?
Aiya, shì nǐ ya!

While *zěnmeyàng* can mean 'How are you?', 'How are things?', or 'How are you doing?' and *shì nǐ ya* can mean 'So its you', the utterances *hei, ei, aiya,* and *ya* do not have any out of context English translations. They are just ways of being informal or bringing intimacy to the encounter.

Even part of speech may change in a real situation. For example, the Chinese word for 'humour' or 'humorous' is *yōumò*, which can either be a noun or an adjective, as the following examples show:

1 *nǐ shuō de huà hěn <u>yōumò</u>* (What you said was very humorous.)

2 *nǐ de* <u>*yōumò*</u> *wǒ bù dǒng* (I do not understand your humour.)

Yōumò in (2) is an adjective and a noun in (3). This may be what the student is told in the classroom and in textbooks; however, a native speaker may well use *yōumò* as a verb:

3 wō yào yōumò tā yīxià

which may either mean 'I want to humour him' or 'I want to make fun of him'. Such instances of language usage cannot all be taught in the classroom or through textbooks.

There are other kinds of expressions and formulas which have not been included in previous discussions. These instances of language usage are what we want to discuss in this chapter.

REGIONAL ACCENTS AND DIALECTS

As mentioned previously, in contemporary China class difference is not transparently reflected linguistically. For instance, there is no such thing as a posh accent in China. Mandarin used to and still enjoys prestige not because there is an upper or middle class that speaks it; in fact, very few of the first generation of Communist powerholders spoke standard Mandarin. It is prestigious because it is the dialect designated by the government as the official language for all official media. Because it is used as the official language, urban residents speak better Mandarin than rural residents and the formally educated tend to speak better Mandarin than the uneducated.

In many rural areas of China, Mandarin is considered to be *guānqiāng* (the language of officialdom), sometimes referred to with envy, but very often with resentment. In these countryside regions the majority can barely speak it. Even in urban areas many members of the older generations can only speak Mandarin with strong accents or hardly at all. Therefore, whether one speaks Mandarin or speaks it with an accent is not a matter of class but a matter of formal education.

Regional differences, on the other hand, are more prominent. People around Beijing or in some northern areas speak Mandarin because it is the language based on the northern dialect.

In recent years, as a result of economic reform, Cantonese has gained increasing prestige. In the north, for example, an area where people traditionally used to look down upon the southern dialects, many are now beginning to learn Cantonese. This is because Cantonese is spoken in areas where there is money: Hong Kong and the Pearl River Delta regions. This is another example of how sociolinguistic behaviour in China is more regionally driven than class orientated.

GENDER

We have discussed in chapter 1 that in Chinese writing there is evidence of sexual discrimination against women. Discriminatory expressions, sayings, and vocabulary can also be found widely in the spoken language. However, there is very little gender difference in terms of grammatical structure. There is no masculine or feminine gender difference either in phonology or syntax. Nor is there any article or particle used to differentiate gender. *Tā* is the third-person singular pronoun for both sexes and *tāmen* is the third-person plural for both sexes. There is no inflection in any word to denote gender difference.

FORMAL VERSUS INFORMAL STYLE

Vocabulary

Written Mandarin is usually more formal than its spoken form, and this is reflected in the choice of vocabulary.

There are many pairs of synonyms, one of which is more suitable for writing and the other for speaking. Thus, the colloquial words in Table 7.1 have their respective written counterparts in the right-hand column.

Table 7.1 Formal versus informal words

Colloquial	English translation	Written
lǎojiā	hometown	*gùxiāng*
niànshū	study	*dúshū*
bàba	father	*fùqin*
zěnme	how	*rúhé*
yígòng	total	*zǒngjì*

There are set formulas and expressions used on formal occasions, but with rapid political and social changes occurring, some of the differences due to formality are disappearing while others have arrived just as quickly. There are very few grammatical features which reflect structurally the difference between formal and informal styles.

One grammatical feature that does reflect the difference is the two forms of the second-person pronoun: *nǐ* and *nín*, with the former being informal and the latter indicating either politeness or distance. Even in this case *nín* is not universally used, for example in the south it is hardly used by Mandarin speakers.

Addressee honorifics and other formulas

In contemporary Chinese speaking communities, and particularly in mainland China, there are very few rigid formulas or expressions of the type known as addressee honorifics. That does not mean, however, that the Chinese do not care about how to address one other. In fact, they are very particular about it.

Relation Terms

As we discussed previously, the Chinese do not address each other using personal names except when with colleagues and friends of more or less the same age. Even among family members one has to refer to *bàba, māma, gēge, dìdi, jiějie, mèimei,* and so on (father, mother, elder brother, younger brother, elder sister, and younger sister respectively). Children are always taught to address people in terms of family relationships. This applies even to members outside the family.

The Chinese are so particular about addressing relatives and family members that there is an elaborate system of addressing relatives according to paternal hierarchy. Thus, maternal grandparents are addressed differently to paternal grandparents. The prominent linguist Y. R. Chao, in his *Aspects of Chinese Socio-linguistics*, listed 114 ways of addressing different relatives.

Person in authority

The other prominent feature of address in relational terms (reflecting an orientation towards hierarchy) is to address a person in authority in terms of official position. A communist party secretary has to be addressed as *shūjì*, the head of an office is called *zhǔrèn*, the principal of a school is *xiàozhǎng*, that of a hospital is *yuànzhǎng*, the head of a county is *xiànzhǎng*, and province is *shěngzhǎng*, and so on (the syllable *zhǎng* means 'head').

Everyone called Mao Zedong *Máo zhǔxí* (Chairman Mao). If one does not address his or her senior in these terms they will be considered disrespectful to authority and in some cases this can have grave consequences.[1]

Familiarity and politeness

Friends and colleagues can address each other by either first or full names if they are of the same age, by adding the prefix *lǎo* (old) or *xiǎo* (young) to surnames, or by professional positions. The degree of closeness or intimacy corresponds to this order.[2] The usage of *lǎo* or *xiǎo* depends on the relative ages of the two people involved. A younger person may address an older person with *lǎo* followed by the person's surname, although the addressor in terms of real age may not be so young, and the addressee may not be so old either.

While the Chinese are very particular about hierarchical positions when addressing each other, they are not particularly concerned about polite terms. Expressions such as *xièxie* (thanks) and *qǐng* (please) are hardly used among friends. The general rule seems to be that the closer the relationship the less need there is to use these terms. Among family members these polite terms are used to express distance. To be courteous is to be *kèqi* (air of a guest) or *lǐmào* (ceremonious) and therefore standing on ceremony, and being official is something you should not be with your relatives or close confidants.

Political difference

In the Mao era of contemporary China, everyone was supposed to be addressed as *tóngzhì* (comrade) in public. In practice, however, those in authority always saw being addressed by their official position as a sign of respect. In places where a stranger is was addressed, the term *tóngzhì* was used extensively.

In post-Mao China, however, the term has been fading rapidly. There is no universal term which is suitable for all occasions anymore. Titles such as *xiānsheng* (Mr), *xiǎojie* (Ms), and *tàitai* (Mrs or Madam) have become more and more fashionable. Some people, however, find these terms either too formal or too pre-1949.

The nearest equivalent to *tóngzhì* currently is *shīfu* (master). According to Hu, *shīfu* originated during the Cultural Revolution when workers from factories, who were usually referred to as *shīfu*, were instructed by Mao to activate the government organisations and bureaucratic organs which had been paralysed by Red Guards and 'rebel' revolutionary activities.[3]

Regional difference

While speakers of Mandarin outside mainland China refer to a husband as *xiānsheng* and a wife as *tàitai* or *fūren*, rural residents refer to the former as *lǎogōng*, and to the latter as *lǎopó*. The formally educated, however, think *lǎogōng* and *lǎopó* are too vulgar and instead refer to spouses as *àiren*, which literally means 'love person' or 'lover', a term derived from the Communist ideology of equality and opposition to arranged marriages. When people get older, some feel embarrassed using *àiren*; so they use *lǎobàn* (old partner) to refer to each other.

Words of respect

Some words which are the residues of classical Chinese are still used today as honorifics. One of these is *gōng* which is added to the surname. For instance, Zhou Enlai is often referred to as *Zhōu gōng* and Deng Xiaoping is sometimes referred to as *Dèng gōng*. Another one used in the same way is *jūn*. While *gōng* is used normally to refer to public figures for public purposes, *jūn* is more often used in private reference.

WRITTEN VERSUS SPOKEN

As discussed in the section on vocabulary in this chapter, there are items of vocabulary which can be used on formal occasions but not on informal ones. Formal vocabulary is usually used in written discourse whereas informal vocabulary is used in spoken discourse.

There are many pairs of words which have similar meanings but are used in different discourses. Usually one of the pair is used in written texts while the other is used in speech. For example, *yóu* and *cóng* both mean 'from' and *dào* and *zhì* both mean 'to'. On a signboard, we are likely to see *yóu Běijīng zhì Shànghǎi*, whereas in speech it is more likely to be *cóng Běijīng dào Shànghǎi*. To mean 'yes or no' one may use *shìfǒu* in writing while one is likely to use *shìbushì* in speaking. Finally, the classical word *yǔ* to mean 'with' is used more in writing whereas in speech one is more likely to hear *hé*.

ELLIPSIS AND PRONOUN DROPPING

Situational grammar

We have already talked about the lack of inflection in Chinese in chapters 5 and 6. In many ways Chinese grammar can be said to be very contextual or situational in that many elements of meaning are not explicitly expressed by formal structure but are understood in situational context. In what follows, the discussion on certain aspects of what I call situational grammar will involve some repetition of our previous discussion about the lack of inflection in Chinese.

Tense

We are now familiar with the fact that tense is not expressed by inflection of verbs but understood either through adverbials or by context. The following serves as further illustration:

Table 7.2   Expression of tense

Chinese sentence	Literal translation	English translation
wǒ chī hěn duō dàmǐ	I eat very much rice	I eat a lot of rice.
wǒ yuánlái chī hěn duō dàmǐ	I originally eat very much rice	I used to eat a lot of rice.
wǒ qùnián chī hěn duō dàmǐ	I last year eat very much rice	I ate a lot of rice last year.
wǒ míngtiān chī hěn duō dàmǐ	I tomorrow eat very much rice	I will eat a lot of rice tomorrow.

The present, past, and future tenses are either expressed by context or by adverbs.

Person
The verb is not inflected in any way to express whether the subject is the first, second, or third-person. In the following the verb *chī* remains the same:

> *wǒ chī hěn duō dàmǐ* (I eat a lot of rice.)
> *nǐ chī hěn duō dàmǐ* (You eat a lot of rice.)
> *tā chī hěn duō dàmǐ* (She/He eats a lot of rice.)
> *tāmen chī hěn duō dàmǐ* (They eat a lot of rice.)

Number
The same is the case with numbers. In:

> *wǒ qù shūdiàn mǎi shū* (I go bookshop buy book)

it is not clear whether the speaker is going to buy one or more books. If the exact number or the question of number is a necessary requirement of communication, a figure will have to be included in the sentence. Otherwise, the number is unexpressed. This reliance on context leads to a large scale of ellipsis in Chinese. Or to put it another way, what is clearly understood is omitted in a sentence.

Pronoun dropping
Here we will focus on what is called pronoun dropping. In English, this also occurs, but in a limited way. For instance, in the command sentence 'Sit down!' the logical subject 'you' is dropped or omitted. In most other cases, however, the pronouns have to be said in English, but this is not the case in Chinese:

Table 7.3 Pronoun dropping

Chinese sentence	Literal translation	English translation
fángzi lǐtou yǒu hěn duō dōngxi, kěshì nǐ méiyǒu liú gěi wǒ, dōu ná zǒu le	house in have very many things but you did not leave for me all take away *le*	There were many things in the house, but you did not leave (them) for me, (you) took (them) all.

The words in brackets are the pronouns which have to be expressed in English. The context makes it clear what these pronouns are, but they are not explicitly expressed in Chinese. To express them explicitly in Chinese either the sentence has to be restructured or it sounds wrong or unnatural.

When saying 'I ate it', Chinese do not say (1). Instead, they will either say (2) or (3):

1 *Wǒ chī le tā* (I eat *le* it)
2 *Wǒ bǎ tā chī le* (I *ba* it eat *le*)
3 *Wǒ chī le* (I eat *le*)

In (2) the pronoun is placed before the verb and the particle *bǎ*, which does not have any meaning other than its grammatical function, has to be used. In (3) the pronoun 'it' is not expressed. Because of this feature of dropping pronouns a sentence can be ambiguous if the context is not taken into consideration, as the following example shows:

Yīnwèi bù xiǎoxīn tā diū le (because not careful he/she lose *le*)

Without a context this sentence can be translated into the following in English:

1 Because I was not careful she/he was lost.
2 Because somebody was not careful she/he was lost.
3 Because I was not careful I lost it (something).
4 Because somebody was not careful I lost it (something).

The above four sentences do not exhaust all the possible translations of the original Chinese sentence. The subject who was not careful could be *I*, *you*, *he*, *she*, or *they*, and the person or object that was lost could be *she*, *he*, or *it*. When the sentence is spoken within a particular situation, the context will clarify which pronoun is being referred to.

CONVERSATIONAL FILLERS

Just as there are conversational devices such as 'well', 'er', 'um', and 'and' in English there are fillers and responders in Chinese to fill in the gaps in conversation. One of these is *zhège* (this one) which is used by mainland Chinese as a filler. Other examples include *nàge* (that one), *nàme* (in that case), *shénme de* (whatever), *nǐ zhīdao ma* (Do you know?), and *duì bu duì* (correct?).[4]

The Chinese may find that being silent while listening to somebody speaking indicates a lack of interest on the part of the listener. They will say *duì* (correct), *shì* (yes), *hǎo* (good), or *xíng* (OK) while listening to a speaker. Also in order to show that one is a responsive and keen listener, a person will repeat a word two or three times like *duì duì duì, shì shì shì,* and *hǎo hǎo hǎo*.

PHRASEOLOGY

Common phrases in conversations

Some phrases are used as common responses in conversations. To respond to greetings such as *zěnmeyàng* (How are you? How are things?) the response can be any of these fixed phrases:

hái xíng (OK.)
hái kěyǐ (OK.)
bù zěnmeyàng (Not so fantastic.)
mǎmahūhu (So-so.)
bú cuò (Not bad.)
chàbuduō (So-so.)
hái néng zěnmeyàng (What else could it be?)

To respond to an expression of gratitude or thanks, the usual phrase is:

méi shì (It doesnt matter.)
méi shénme (It's nothing.)
méi guānxi (It's nothing.)
bú yòng xiè (No need to say thanks.)
bié kèqi (Do not be so polite.)
nǐ tài kèqi le (You are too polite.)
nà nǐ jiù jiàn wài le (You take me as an outsider by saying that.)

Greetings to customers

The open door and economic reform polices since the 1980s have led to a great leap forward in commercialism in mainland China. Many private and foreign-owned service enterprises now make great efforts to be polite to customers. In many shops in Shanghai, for instance, the staff are told to say:

huānyíng guānglíng (welcome your bright presence)

as soon as a customer enters the door.

Words of good luck

The Chinese have always believed that certain words can bring them good luck. This is particularly reflected in Spring Festival messages when the Chinese pay obeisance in the New Year (*bàinián*). There are therefore some set phrases that people say to each other during this time. The most common ones are:

xīnnián hǎo (New Year good)
gōngxǐ fācái (Wishing you prosperity.)

Expressions of modesty

To say that the Chinese are very modest is to participate in the perpetuation of a myth. The Chinese are probably no more or less modest than any other people. For instance, the official Chinese newspapers show no sign at all of modesty. They always boast about great achievements.

On the other hand, it is socially expected that one should be modest on certain occasions. For instance, when presenting a gift the giver may say something like:

xiǎo lǐwù, bù chéng yìsi (Only a small gift, not that much significance.)

Also, do not be baffled when you are sitting down to a lavish dinner of more than ten delicious courses and the host who has cooked the meal says:

wǒ cài zuò de bù hǎo, qǐng yuánliàng (I don't cook good food, please forgive me.)

or when a very knowledgeable professor starts his or her lecture by saying:

wǒ shuǐpíng yǒu xiàn, cuòwù quēdiǎn yídìng bù shǎo (As my knowledge is limited, there will be many errors and shortcomings in what I say.)

do not stand up and leave because you think it will be a waste of time.

Conversational greetings

Other socially accepted formulas may puzzle the uninitiated as well. When a Chinese person bumps into a friend, they may greet each other by saying:

> *nǐ qù nǎr?* (Where are you going?)
> *nǐ mǎi le shénme?* (What have you bought?)

While these may sound very intrusive and nosy to a Westerner, in fact they are ceremonial greetings for the Chinese—not real questions that require a specific answer.

Sometimes Chinese may ask the most obvious question as a means of greeting. Say two friends bump into each as they are walking into the cinema; one may ask:

> *nǐ yě lái kàn diànyǐng ma?* (Are you coming to the movie as well?)

It is obvious to both of them that they have come to see the movie. The speaker is not really asking a question. He or she is simply offering a greeting and trying to strike up a conversation.

There used to be one very common way for people to greet each other; that is:

> *chī le ma?* (eat completion-particle question-particle)

meaning 'Have you eaten?' This is still used a lot in China. One might think that this is used as a common greeting phrase because the Chinese are obsessed with food. There may be a sociological element of truth in this if we think about the fact that the Chinese have always had the problem finding enough resources to feed themselves. As conversations tend to reflect what people in a given society are most concerned about, greetings may reveal sociological change in a society. According to some writers, the phrase *chī le ma* is used less frequently in the late 1990s, at least among urban residents.

Increasingly, more and more urban residents greet each other by saying:

1 *qù nǎr wán le* (go where play completion-particle) meaning 'Where did you go for your holidays?'
2 *mǎi chē le ma?* (buy vehicle completion-particle question-particle) meaning 'Have you bought a car?'
3 *shàng wǎng le ma* (on net completion-particle question-particle) meaning 'Are you connected?'—to the internet

These phrases of greeting show, on the one hand, that these are the topics which concern them most and, on the other, that they have become affluent enough to afford travel, a car, and computer technology.[5]

WORD ORDER

As we have discussed previously, the word order in modern Chinese is that of subject followed by verb and then object. However, there are instances in which the word order changes into subject followed by object and then verb. This is particularly so in informal and spoken Chinese when the *bǎ*-structure is used.

WRITING: CHARACTERS

It may be difficult for those who are brought up with alphabetic languages like English to imagine how important Chinese characters are for Chinese people. Calligraphy is considered to be an art form of great poetic beauty practised by professional artists. It not only has aesthetic value and ornamental function, but also implies personal attainment and quality. The Chinese still judge whether a person is educated by his or her writing of characters. They are marks of power and knowledge. For instance, while traditional seals in the West or the Balkan states usually have a drawing on them, Chinese seals, or chops as they are sometimes called, comprise characters.

Even today in some areas of rural China the five characters:

天地君亲师

are still displayed on a signboard on the altar in the family's lounge room. The five characters represent, respectively, 'heaven', 'earth', 'emperor', 'relatives', and 'teacher'; the relative importance of each is reflected in that order.

Characters can serve as representations for wishes of all kinds: desire for happiness, long life, success in career, or wealth.[6] Let us look at one example: 福 is the character for happiness and luck. Many Chinese have it written and hang it up in their homes, but upside down. Because the pronunciation of the word for 'upside down' is *dào*, which is also the sound of the word meaning 'arrive', it is therefore believed that by putting 福 upside down happiness and luck have already arrived.

STUDY QUESTIONS

1. Why do you think one cannot learn everything about a language in the classroom?
2. Chinese people tend to address each other in relational terms instead of using personal names. Why do you think this is?
3. How are political differences reflected in terms of address?
4. In what way is Chinese grammar situational or contextual?
5. Why do you think the omission of pronouns in Chinese does not cause ambiguity in everyday communication?
6. Do conversational fillers and phraseology reflect cultural values of a society?
7. Would you address Mr Lee who is a teacher in the same way as a student in China does as 'Teacher Lee?' Why not?
8. Can you think of an example in Chinese which shows that greetings reflect everyday concerns of the speakers?
9. Why do you think character writing has such a spell on the Chinese?

REFERENCE READING

Chen, Ping, *Modern Chinese, History and Sociolinguistics*, Cambridge University Press, Melbourne, 1999.

Cui, Jianxin, 'hanyu kouyu zhong de rongyu xianxiang', (The Phenomenon of Redundancy in Colloquial Chinese), in Xing Gongwan et al. (eds), *hanyu yanjiu* (Research on Chinese), vol. 3, Nankai daxue chubanshe, Tianjin, 1993.

Georges, Jean, *Writing the Story of Alphabets and Scripts*, English translation, Thames and Hudson Ltd, London, and Harry N. Abrams, Inc., New York, 1992.

Hodge, Robert and Kam Louie, *The Politics of the Chinese Language: The Art of Reading the Dragon*, Routledge, London, 1998.

Hu, Mingyang, 'Beijing hua de chengwei xitong', (The Format of Addressing in Beijing Dialect), in Xing Gongwan et al. (eds), *hanyu yanjiu* (Research on Chinese), vol. 3, Nankai daxue chubanshe, Tianjin, 1993.

Li, Rui, *Li Rui wangshi zayi* (Memoirs of Li Rui), Jiangsu renmin chubanshe, Nanjing, 1995.

ENDNOTES

1   Even prominent figures such Zhou Enlai addressed Mao as **zhǔxí**. One of the errors the Defence Minister Peng Dehuai was accused of in 1959 was that he called Mao *Lao Mao* (Old Mao), which was and still is an intimate term of address among close colleagues, instead of **zhǔxí**. He was considered to be disrespectful and rebellious. See Li Rui, *Li Rui wangshi zayi* (Memoirs of Li Rui), Jiangsu renmin chubanshe, Nanjing, 1995, p. 348.

2   Hu Mingyang, 'Beijing hua de chengwei xitong', (The Format of Addressing in Beijing Dialect), in Xing Gongwan et al. (eds), *hanyu yanjiu* (Research on Chinese), vol. 3, Nankai daxue chubanshe, Tianjin, 1993, pp. 114–25.

3   Ibid., p. 124.

4   Cui Jianxin, 'hanyu kouyu zhong de rongyu xianxiang', (The Phenomenon of Redundancy in Colloquial Chinese), in Xing Gongwan et al. (eds), *hanyu yanjiu* (Research on Chinese), vol. 3, pp. 139–53.

5   Tang Shubiao, 'cong chi le ma shuo kai qu', (From Have you eaten), *China Today*, vol. 48, no. 1, Beijing, p. 7.

6   Jean Georges, *Writing the Story of Alphabets and Scripts*, English (translated from French by Jenny Oates), Thames and Hudson Ltd, London and Harry N. Abrams, Inc., New York, 1992, p. 184.

Appendix I

In this appendix, there are eight syllable tables, four in *pinyin* and four in the Wade-Giles system for the reader to use as a comparison tool.

By comparing the first four tables with tables five to eight the interested reader can see the similarities and differences between the *pinyin* system and the Wade-Giles system. The *pinyin* system is used in mainland China and has become increasingly popular; many authors have adopted the system in their writings. On the other hand, the Wade-Giles system is still used by some authors. Moreover, many materials were written in the Wade-Giles system before *pinyin* became widely accepted. In libraries all over the world, the Wade-Giles system has been used for cataloguing sources in the Chinese language. However, some libraries have adopted or are beginning to adopt the *pinyin* system. As a result, many libraries have the two systems in place, one for those who are familiar with the older Wade-Giles system and one for those who are familiar with the newer *pinyin* system.

Here we present first the four tables in *pinyin*.[1]

Table I.1   Syllables consisting of finals other than *i*, *u*, and *ü*, in *pīnyīn*

	a	o	e	-i	er	ai	ei	ao	ou	an	en	ang	eng	ong
b	ba	bo				bai	bei	bao		ban	ben	bang	beng	
p	pa	po				pai	pei	pao	pou	pan	pen	pang	peng	
m	ma	mo	me			mai	mei	mao	mou	man	men	mang	meng	
f	fa	fo					fei		fou	fan	fen	fang	feng	
d	da		de			dai	dei	dao	dou	dan	den	dang	deng	dong
t	ta		te			tai		tao	tou	tan		tang	teng	tong
n	na		ne			nai	nei	nao	nou	nan		nang	neng	nong
l	la		le			lai	lei	lao	lou	lan		lang	leng	long
z	za		ze	zi		zai	zei	zao	zou	zan	zen	zang	zeng	zong
c	ca		ce	ci		cai		cao	cou	can	cen	cang	ceng	cong
s	sa		se	si		sai		sao	sou	san	sen	sang	seng	song
zh	zha		zhe	zhi		zhai	zhei	zhao	zhou	zhan	zhen	zhang	zheng	zhong
ch	cha		che	chi		chai		chao	chou	chan	chen	chang	cheng	chong
sh	sha		she	shi		shai	shei	shao	shou	shan	shen	shang	sheng	
r			re	ri				rao	rou	ran	ren	rang	reng	rong
j														
q														
x														
g	ga		ge			gai	gei	gao	gou	gan	gen	gang	geng	gong
k	ka		ke			kai	kei	kao	kou	kan	ken	kang	keng	kong
h	ha		he		er	hai	hei	hao	hou	han	hen	hang	heng	hong

Table I.2 Syllables consisting of finals starting with *i* in *pīnyīn*

	i	ia	iao	ie	iou[a]	ian	in	iang	ing	iong
b	bi		biao	bie		bian	bin		bing	
p	pi		piao	pie		pian	pin		ping	
m	mi		miao	mie	miu	mian	min		ming	
f										
d	di		diao	die	diu	dian			ding	
t	ti		tiao	tie		tian			ting	
n	ni		niao	nie	niu	nian	nin	niang	ning	
l	li	lia	liao	lie	liu	lian	lin	liang	ling	
z										
c										
s										
zh										
ch										
sh										
r										
j	ji	jia	jiao	jie	jiu	jian	jin	jiang	jing	jiong
q	qi	qia	qiao	qie	qiu	qian	qin	qiang	qing	qiong
x	xi	xia	xiao	xie	xiu	xian	xin	xiang	xing	xiong
g										
k										
h										
y[b]	yi	ya	yao	ye	you	yan	yin	yang	ying	yong

a   This is pronounced 'iou' but normally spelt 'iu'.
b   As a convention, when a syllable starts with 'i' a 'y' is either added in front, or replaces 'i' to spell the syllable.

Table I.3   Syllables consisting of finals starting with *u* in *pīnyīn*

	u	ua	uo	uai	uei[a]	uan	uen[b]	uang	ueng
b	bu								
p	pu								
m	mu								
f	fu								
d	du		duo		dui	duan	dun		
t	tu		tuo		tui	tuan	tun		
n	nu		nuo			nuan			
l	lu		luo			luan	lun		
z	zu		zuo		zui	zuan	zun		
c	cu		cuo		cui	cuan	cun		
s	su		suo		sui	suan	sun		
zh	zhu	zhua	zhuo	zhuai	zhui	zhuan	zhun	zhuang	
ch	chu	chua	chuo	chuai	chui	chuan	chun	chuang	
sh	shu	shua	shuo	shuai	shui	shuan	shun	shuang	
r	ru	rua	ruo		rui	ruan	run		
j									
q									
x									
g	gu	gua	guo	guai	gui	guan	gun	guang	
k	ku	kua	kuo	kuai	kui	huan	kun	kuang	
h	hu	hua	huo	huai	hui	huan	hun	huang	
w[c]	wu	wa	wo	wai	wei	wan	wen	wang	weng

a   This is pronounced 'uei' but normally spelt 'ui'
b   This is pronounced 'uen' but normally spelt 'un'
c   As a convention, when a syllable starts with 'u', a 'w' is either added in front, or replaces 'u' to spell the syllable.

Table I.4   Syllables consisting of finals starting with *ü* in *pīnyīn*

	ü	üe	üan	ün
b				
p				
m				
f				
d				
t				
n	nü	nüe		
l	lü	lüe		
z				
c				
s				
zh				
ch				
sh				
r				
j[a]	ju	jue	juan	jun
q	qu	que	quan	qun
x	xu	xue	xuan	xun
g				
k				
h				
y	yu	yue	yuan	yun

a   Notice that the 'u' in all the syllables starting with 'j', 'q', and 'x' should be pronounced as 'ü', however as a convention, the sound is spelt not as 'ü' but as 'u'. This is the case because of the complementary distribution of 'u' and 'ü' discussed in chapter 3.

Table I.5   Syllables consisting of finals other than *i*, *u*, and *ü* in the Wade-Giles system

	a	o	e[a]	-i	er	ai	ei	ao	ou	an	en	ang	eng	ung
p	pa	po				pai	pei	pao		pan	pen	pang	peng	
p'	p'a	p'o				p'ai	p'ei	p'ao	p'ou	p'an	p'en	p'ang	p'eng	
m	ma	mo	me			mai	mei	mao	mou	man	men	mang	meng	
f	fa	fo					fei		fou	fan	fen	fang	feng	
t	ta		te			tai	dei	tao	tou	tan	ten	tang	teng	tung
t'	t'a		t'e			t'ai		t'ao	t'ou	t'an		t'ang	t'eng	t'ung
n	na		ne			nai	nei	nao	nou	nan	nen	nang	neng	nung
l	la		le			lai	lei	lao	lou	lan		lang	leng	lung
ts	tsa		tse	tzu[b]		tsai	tsei	tsao	tsou	tsan	tsen	tsang	tseng	tsung
ts'	ts'a		ts'e	tz'u		ts'ai		ts'ao	ts'ou	ts'an	ts'en	ts'ang	ts'eng	ts'ung
s	sa		se	szu		sai		sao	sou	san	sen	sang	seng	sung
ch	cha		che	chih		chai	chei	chao	chou	chan	chen	chang	cheng	chung
ch'	ch'a		ch'e	ch'ih		ch'ai		ch'ao	ch'ou	ch'an	ch'en	ch'ang	ch'eng	ch'ung
sh	sha		she	shih		shai	shei	shao	shou	shan	shen	shang	sheng	
j			je	jih				jao	jou	jan	jen	jang	jeng	jung
ch														
ch'														
hs														
k	ka		ke			kai	kei	kao	kou	kan	ken	kang	geng	kung
k'	k'a		k'e			k'ai	k'ei	k'ao	k'ou	k'an	k'en	k'ang	k'eng	k'ung
h	ha		he		erh	hai	hei	hao	hou	han	hen	hang	heng	hung

a   There is some complication for the vowel e. Some authors use a circumflex (ˆ) over the vowel to distinguish the vowel quality of 'uh' in syllables such as 'men' from the 'eh' quality in syllables such as 'mei'. Some other authors use *o* instead of *e* as a final after velar initials such as 'g', 'k' and 'h', or as a initial-less final.

b   Variations of spelling for this group of three syllables which have sibilant initials are ignored here.

Table I.6   Syllables consisting of finals starting with *i* in the Wade-Giles system

	i	ia	iao	ieh	iu	ien	in	iang	ing	iung
p	pi		piao	pieh		pien	bin		ping	
p'	p'i		p'iao	p'ieh		p'ien	p'in		p'ing	
m	mi		miao	mieh	miu	mien	min		ming	
f										
t	ti		tiao	tieh	tiu	tien			ting	
t'	t'i		t'iao	t'ieh		t'ien			t'ing	
n	ni		niao	nieh	niu	nien	nin	niang	ning	
l	li	lia	liao	lieh	liu	lien	lin	liang	ling	
ts										
ts'										
s										
ch										
ch'										
sh										
j										
ch	chi	chia	chiao	chieh	chiu	chien	chin	chiang	ching	chiung
ch'	ch'i	ch'ia	ch'iao	ch'ieh	ch'iu	ch'ien	ch'in	ch'iang	ch'ing	ch'iung
hs	hsi	hsia	hsiao	hsieh	hsiu	hsien	hsin	hsiang	hsing	hsiung
k										
k'										
h										
y[a]	i	ya	yao	yeh	yu	yen	yin	yang	ying	yung

a   As a convention, when a syllable starts with 'i' a 'y' is either added in front, or replaces 'i' to spell the syllable.

Table I.7   Syllables consisting of finals starting with *u* in the Wade-Giles system

	u	ua	uo	uai	ui	uan	un	uang	ueng
p	pu								
p′	p′u								
m	mu								
f	fu								
t	tu		to		tui	tuan	tun		
t′	t′u		t′o		t′ui	t′uan	t′un		
n	nu		no			nuan			
l	lu		lo			luan	lun		
ts	tsu		tso		tsui	tsuan	tsun		
ts′	ts′u		ts′o		ts′ui	ts′uan	ts′un		
s	su		so		sui	suan	sun		
ch	chu	chua	cho	chuai	chui	chuan	chun	chuang	
ch′	ch′u	ch′ua	ch′o	ch′uai	ch′ui	ch′uan	ch′un	ch′uang	
sh	shu	shua	shuo	shuai	shui	shuan	shun	shuang	
j	ju	jua	jo		jui	juan	jun		
ch									
ch′									
hs									
k	ku	kua	kuo	kuai	kuei	kuan	kun	kuang	
k′	k′u	k′ua	k′uo	k′uai	k′uei	k′uan	k′un	k′uang	
h	hu	hua	huo	huai	hui	huan	hun	huang	
w[a]	wu	wa	wo	wai	wei	wan	wen	wang	weng

a   As a convention, when a syallable starts with 'u', a 'w' is either added in front, or replaces 'u' to spell the syllable.

Table I.8 Syllables consisting of vowels starting with *ü* in the Wade-Giles system

	ü	üeh	üan	ün
p				
p′				
m				
f				
t				
t′				
n	nü	nüeh		
l	lü	lüeh		
ts				
ts′				
s				
ch				
ch′				
sh				
j				
ch	chü	chüeh	chüan	chün
ch′	ch′ü	ch′üeh	ch′üan	ch′ün
hs	hsü	hsüeh	hsüan	hsün
k				
k′				
h				
y	yü	yüeh	yüan	yün

Appendix II[2]

SOME BASIC GRAMMATICAL TERMS

This appendix contains working definitions for some very basic grammatical terms. Since our purpose is not to summarise English grammar but to help the student become familiar with Chinese grammar, the number of terms explained and the extent of the explanations are very limited. Lengthy theoretical discussions are avoided whenever possible.

SENTENCE

A sentence is a complete linguistic unit and its end is usually indicated by a full stop. A sentence with a question mark is an interrogative or question sentence. Sentences such as command and exclamation sentences may end with an exclamation mark.

SUBJECT AND PREDICATE

Traditionally, there is a primary distinction between subject and predicate in a sentence. According to this division, the subject is the theme of the sentence and has a close general relation to what is being discussed.

  1 John has studied Chinese very hard for two years.

In (1) 'John' is the subject and 'has studied Chinese very hard for two years' is the predicate. When we form an interrogative sentence in English the subject changes its position, as in (2):

  2 Has John studied Chinese very hard for two years?

Auxiliary and predication

Within a predicate, a further distinction can be made between an auxiliary or auxiliary operator, and predication. In (1) 'has' is the auxiliary and 'studied Chinese very hard for two years' is the predication. This distinction is important because when we form an interrogative sentence, it is the auxiliary that moves to the front of the sentence, as in (2). This distinction is important in English for that reason, but not for Chinese.

Clauses

A clause can also be a sentence, but acts as a part of a larger sentence. What a sentence and a clause have in common is that they both have subjects and predicates. A sentence can consist of two or more clauses:

3 John is the husband and Mary is the wife.
4 Because the Chinese have never been far away from starvation they have formed the habit of greeting each other by saying 'have you eaten?'

(3) is a sentence of two clauses connected by 'and'. (4) is also one sentence of two clauses, the sentence led by 'because' is called the subordinate clause and the clause starting with 'they' is called the main clause.

Subject

Within a sentence, a subject may denote an agent or doer of an action, or a person or a thing or a concept about which a statement is made. The subject in an interrogative sentence is what the question is about. Consider the following examples:

John is English.
I speak Chinese.
Is a *swan* white?
Here comes *the bus*.
Working is a necessary part of life.

The italicised word in each of the above sentences is the subject of that sentence.

PARTS OF A SENTENCE: FURTHER DIVISION

We may want to divide a predicate into even smaller units, such as verb, object, adverb phrase, and complement. Thus in (1) 'studied' is a verb, 'Chinese' an object, 'very hard' an adverb phrase, and 'for two years' a preposition complement (the concept of phrase and complement will be discussed below).

Categories of verb

Verbs can be further classified into categories according to different grammatical functions, as the following brief discussion shows.

Action verbs

Verbs like 'go', 'work', and 'sleep' which indicate actions.

Stative verbs

Some verbs such as 'know' and 'see' are sometimes called stative verbs. The primary reason for this distinction in English is that these verbs cannot permit the progressive aspect, as the contrast in (6) shows (the convention of an asterisk is used here to indicate an ungrammatical or unacceptable sentence).

6 I knew the answer.
   *I know*ing* the answer
7 I saw that it rained.
   *I see*ing* that it rained

Auxiliary verbs

Auxiliary operators such as 'will', 'shall', and 'have' are sometimes called auxiliary verbs. They are referred to as auxiliaries because their function is to appear with a main verb.

The verb 'to be' (the copula)

The verb 'to be', sometimes called a copula, can be in the form of 'be' when it is used with an auxiliary, as in 'shall be', 'will be', or 'would be'; or 'been' as in 'have been'. It can also be 'are', 'were', or 'is' depending on the number and person of the subject or the tense of the verb.

Transitive versus intransitive verbs

8 I will *go*. (intransitive)
9 *I will *go* China.
10 John *drinks*. (intransitive)
11 John *drinks* milk. (transitive)

Transitive verbs take a direct object to complete a sentence. 'Go' can only be intransitive and (9) is ungrammatical because 'go' cannot take a direct object. On the other hand 'drink' can be both transitive and intransitive.

Object
Within a sentence, the part which is taken by a verb or preposition is the object.

Adverb
An adverb modifies a verb and expresses degree, extent, or manner of an action. But in English some adverbs can modify a whole sentence.

12 He works *hard*.
John swims *beautifully*.
I *seldom* go.
He is *probably* right.

'Probably' in (12) modifies a whole sentence, not just a verb. In English an adverb is typically marked by 'ly'. Of course, there are adverbs without 'ly', for example 'hard'.

Parts of speech
It will have become clear from the preceding discussion that a sentence is composed of units which are referred to as subject and predicate which include auxiliary, verb, adverb, object, and complement. These terms are so referred to because of their functions in a sentence. However, the smallest unit in a sentence is what is usually called a word.

According to its grammatical function in a sentence a word can be referred to as a part of speech. Different parts of speech have their own function in a sentence. For instance, a noun can function either as a subject or an object in a sentence, and a preposition can be part of a complement. Since classical times traditional terms for parts of speech have been used to analyse members of Indo-European language groups. The following are examples of how words are commonly classified as parts of speech:

Table II.1   Words as parts of speech

noun	John, room, reply, play, tree
adjective	beautiful, happy, new, tall
adverb	probably, very, really, hard
verb	work, sleep, drink, play
article	the, a, an
demonstrative	this, that, those, these
pronoun	he, they, anybody, one
preposition	of, at, in, on, without
conjunction	and, that, when, although
interjection	oh, ah, phew
interrogative	when, where, who, what, which
numeral	one, two, first, second
modal auxiliary	can, could, would, will

Some words may function as more than one part of speech. For instance, 'play' is both a noun and a verb.

PHRASE

A phrase is a group of words put together to function as a noun, an adjective, or an adverb, and so on. Hence we have what are called noun phrases, adjective phrases, and adverb phrases, for example.

Noun phrase

A noun phrase consists of a noun as its head and any other elements such as a pronoun, a nominal adjective (a noun functioning as an adjective), or a numeral as modifiers. The following examples will make the definition clear:

13
(a) language
(b) the English language
(c) the English language spoken by Americans
(d) the English language which Americans, Britons, Canadians, Australians, and New Zealanders all speak

(13a) is a noun whereas the rest of the constructions in (13) are noun phrases. (13b) consists of a head noun, i.e. 'language' and 'the English' in which the latter modifies the former. (13c) is a noun phrase in which the head noun 'language' is modified by both 'the English' and 'spoken by Americans'. (13d) is a noun phrase as well in which the head noun 'language' is modified by even a larger unit.

Adjective phrase
An adjective phrase has as its head an adjective, which may be preceded by modifiers and followed by modifiers.

14
(a) beautiful
(b) extremely beautiful
(c) hard pressed

(14a) is an adjective, (14b) is an adjective phrase in which an adjective, i.e. 'beautiful', is modified by an adverb 'extremely', and (14c) is an adjective followed by a modifier.

Adverb phrase
An adverb phrase has as its head an adverb, which may preceded by modifiers or followed by modifiers.

15
(a) hard
(b) very hard
(c) very hard indeed

(15a) is an adverb and the other two constructions in (15) are adverb phrases.

Preposition phrase

A preposition phrase consists of a preposition and the complement of the preposition. The complement may be a noun or a
clause.

16
(a) in
(b) in a country
(c) in a country where Chinese is spoken

'In' in (16a) is expanded into two preposition phrases, i.e.
(16b) and (16c). Sometimes a preposition phrase functions as an
adverb in a sentence.

17
(a) I would like to work *there*.
(b) I would like to work *in a country where Chinese is
     spoken*.

'There' is a place adverb and the function of the preposition
phrase 'in a country where Chinese is spoken' is the same as that
of 'there'. Therefore 'in a country where Chinese is spoken' is
sometimes called a place adverbial phrase.

Verb phrase

A verb phrase has as its head a main verb and may be preceded by up to four auxiliaries. The italicised part in (18) is a
verb phrase.

(18) I *have been wrong* on this.

TENSE AND ASPECT

Tense is a grammatical category referring to the location of a situation in time. If tense is defined as being shown by verb inflection, English has only two tenses: past and present.

However, there are many ways of referring to past, present,
and future time in English. A number of auxiliary verbs are used
in combination with main verbs to refer to time. Distinctions in

tense are shown by the inflections of the first or only verb in the verb phrase. Apart from some irregular verbs, the present tense of a verb (except the modal auxiliaries) distinguishes between the *-s* form (e.g. 'work*s*') for the third person singular and the uninflected form for the rest. For the regular and many irregular verbs, the past tense has the *-ed* inflection (e.g. 'work*ed*').

The aspect of the verb refers to the way the time of the situation is regarded rather than its location in time in absolute terms. There are two aspects in English: perfect, as the italicised part denotes in (19); and progressive, as marked by the italicised segment in (20):

19   I *have written* the letter already.
20   I *am writing* a letter.

Aspect is always combined with tense in a sentence. Thus *have worked* and *has worked* are present (tense) perfect (aspect) and *had worked* is past (tense) perfect (aspect). Similarly, *am working* and *are working* are present (tense) progressive (aspect), and *was working* and *were working* are past (tense) progressive (aspect). Of course we may have a sentence in which two aspects are combined as in (21):

21   I have been writing for an hour.

Tense: Present, past, and future

Except for the third person singular, the simple present tense of a verb in English is uninflected, i.e. the form of a verb is the same as it is in a dictionary entry, like, for example, 'go'. For the simple past tense, the inflection of a verb is shown by the addition of *-ed* to the verb except for irregular verbs. The most common ways of expressing future time in the verb phrase are with the modal *will* and its contraction *'ll* and by using various forms of *be going*. Some speakers use *shall* instead of *will* for future time when the subject is *I* or *we*.

Aspect

The perfect aspect is used to locate the time of a situation as preceding that of another situation, as in:

22 She *had travelled* to many countries before she eventually settled down in one.

The progressive aspect is used mainly to focus on the duration of a situation, as in:

23 John *was calling* for help.

The two aspects may be used together in one sentence, with the perfect followed by the progressive, as in:

24 The group *had been calling* for help.

ACTIVE AND PASSIVE VOICE

A difference can be made in terms of active versus passive voice. In an active sentence the sense of some agent (be it a human agent or the cause of an event) doing something is expressed, whereas in a passive sentence the sense of something being done by some agent is expressed.

An active sentence usually has a verb which is transitive, i.e. takes an object, and the order of the sentence is subject+verb+object. The verb may take two objects, the indirect followed by the direct, as in 'I gave him the book'.

An active sentence can generally be made into a passive sentence by moving the direct object to the subject position, whereas the active subject can either appear after the verb in a *by* phrase or is omitted, shown in respective order:

25 The book was given by me.
26 The book was given.

In this process of change, the active verb is turned into the passive by the introduction of the auxiliary *be* followed by what is called the *-ed* participle of the main verb. Note that *-ed* participle is added for regular verbs whereas the participle of the verb 'give' is irregular. For all regular and for many irregular verbs the *-ed* participle is identical with that of the simple past, as in 'I *invited* all the students' (simple past) and 'All the students *were invited*' (*-ed* participle in a passive sentence).

PARTICLES

A particle in English usually refers to a word which does not take inflections and does not fit into the traditional word classes. A particle is the smallest grammatical unit, for example the *-ed* particle discussed above. The negative *not* and the infinitive *to* are considered to be particles in English. Other particles include *in, at, on, up*, and so on. In Chinese there are a dozen or so particles which have important grammatical functions.

MEASURE WORDS

Measure expressions are used in English to express quantity of mass nouns, like 'an *acre* of land' and 'a *sheet* of paper'.

Words like 'sheet', 'piece', 'heap', and 'acre' are sometimes called partitives. With many nouns, there is a typical partitive appropriate to each specific case. In English only mass nouns require a partitive word. For instance, it is incorrect to say 'a paper' to refer to a piece of the physical object for writing. One has to say 'a sheet of paper' or 'a piece of paper'. Countable nouns (nouns can have both singular and plural forms) in English do not require partitive words. For instance, we just say 'a table', 'a house', or 'tables' and 'houses'.

In Chinese there is no syntactic difference between a countable and a non-countable (or mass) noun. In other words, whether a noun is counted as singular or plural does not show in forms.

On the other hand, every noun requires a partitive word when used with a numeral. It is to explain this phenomenon that the term 'measure word' is used in Chinese grammar. Measure words are also referred to as 'classifiers'. The order of a noun phrase with a numeral is numeral+measure word+noun, as shown in table 2:

Table II.2 Measure words

Chinese	Literal meaning	English translation
一张桌子	one measure-word table	a table
一栋房子	one measure-word house	a house

COMPLEMENTS

A complement in English is a phrase or a clause which is added to a word, a phrase, or a clause to make the expression a complete whole and whose form is determined by what it complements.

For instance in the sentence 'She *asked* three questions', 'three questions' may be called a verbal complement. The phrase 'of orange juice' in 'He is *fond* of orange juice' is an adjective complement. The phrase 'for your sake' in 'I am doing this *for* your sake' is a preposition complement. As we can see in the main body of this book, complement structures in Chinese have their own specific definitions and usages.

REFERENCE READING

Greenbaum, Sydney, *The Oxford English Grammar*, Oxford University Press, London, 1996.

Hartmann, R. R. K. and F. C. Stork, *Dictionary of Language and Linguistics*, Applied Science Publishers Ltd, London, reprint, 1973.

Huddleston, Rodney, *Introduction to the Grammar of English*, Cambridge University Press, Cambridge, 1984.

Pei, Mario and Frank Gaynor, *Dictionary of Linguistics*, Littlefield, Adams & Co., New Jersey, 1975.

Quirk, Randolph, Sydney Greenbaum, Geoffrey Leech, and Jan Svartvik, *A Grammar of Contemporary English*, Longman, London, 1972.

——, 1985, indexed by David Crystal, *A Comprehensive Grammar of The English Language*, Longman, London.

Quirk Randolph, Sydney Greenbaum, *A University Grammar of English*, Longman, London, 1974.

——, 1985, *A Student's Grammar of the English Language*, Longman, Harlow.

ENDNOTES

1   To organise syllables into tables according to vowel quality is widely used in teaching in China. For instance, *Introductory Chinese* published in 1988 by Sinolingua and *Elementary Chinese Reader* also published by Sinolingua in 1994 both use these tables to illustrate the structures of syllables of Mandarin. Here I have made use of their principles and format them differently to make a comparison between *pinyin* and the Wade-Giles system

2   This chapter is a revised version based on the appendix in Mobo C. F. Gao, *A Reference Book of Mandarin Chinese*, XACT Publications, Queensland, 2000.

Bibliography

Alleton, Viviane, *Les Chinois et la Passion des Noms* (The Chinese Passion for Names), Paris, Aubier, 1993.

Ann, T. K., *Cracking the Chinese Puzzles*, vol. 1, Stockflows Co., Ltd, Hong Kong, 1982.

Aria, Barbara, *The Nature of the Chinese Characters*, Australia: Simon Schuster, 1991.

Backhouse, A. E., *The Japanese Language: An Introduction*, Melbourne, Oxford University Press, 1993, p. 65.

Barnes, Dayle, 'Language Planning in Mainland China: Standardisation', in Joshua A. Fishman (ed.), *Advances in Language Planning*, The Hague, Mouton, 1974.

Befu, Harumi (ed.), *Cultural Nationalism in East Asia, Representation and Identity*, Institute of East Asian Studies, University of California, Berkeley, California, Summer 1964.

Benedict, Paul K., *Sino-Tibetan: a Conspectus*, Cambridge University Press, Cambridge, 1972.

Bodman, Nicholas C., 'Proto-Chinese and Proto-Tibetan: Data towards Establishing the Nature of the Relationship', in Frans Van Coetsam and Linda R. Waugh (eds), *Contributions to Historical Linguistics, Issues and Materials*, E. J. Brill, Leiden, 1980.

Bolts, William G., 'Early Chinese Writing', *World Archaeology*, no. 17, 1986, pp. 420–36.

Buoye, Thomas M. A., *Study Guide for the Chinese Adopting the Past Facing the Future*, Center for Chinese Studies, University of Michigan, Ann Arbor, Michigan, 1992.

Carroll, Lewis, illustrated by John Tenniel, *The Annotated Alice, Alice's Adventures in Wonderland and Through the Looking Glass*, New York, Bramhall House, 1960.

Carroll, Lewis, illustrated by John Tenniel, The Annotated Alice, Alice's Adventures in Wonderland and Through the Looking Glass, New York, Bramhall House, 1960.

Chao, Y. R. et al., 'A system of Tone Letters', *Le Maitre phonetique*, 45, 1930, pp. 24–7.

Chao, Y. R. et al., 'yuyan quyu tu' (Language Distribution Map), *zhonghua minguo xin ditu* (the New Atlas of China), map 5-b, Shenbaoguan, Shanghai, 1934.

Chao, Y. R., *A Grammar of Spoken Chinese*, University of California Press, Berkeley and Los Angeles, 1968.

Chao, Y. R., *A Grammar of Spoken Chinese*, University of California Press, Berkeley and Los Angeles, 1968.

Chao, Y. R., *Mandarin Primer*, Harvard University Press, Cambridge, Mass. 1948.

Chao, Y.R., *Aspects of Chinese Linguistics*, Stanford University Press, Stanford, 1976.

Chen, Ping, 'Modern Written Chinese in Development', *Language and Society*, 22 (4) Dec. 1993, pp. 505–37.

——, 1999, *Modern Chinese*, Cambridge University Press.

Chen Ping, *Modern Chinese, History and Sociolinguistics*, Cambridge University Press, Melbourne, 1999.

Chen Yulong, Yang Tongfang et al., *han wenhua lungang-jian shu zhongchao zhongri zhongyue wenhua jiaoliu* (An Outline of Chinese Culture and Sino-Korean, Sino-Japanese and Sino-Vietnamese Cultural Exchange), Beijing daxue chubanshe, Beijing, 1993.

China Statistical Publishing House, *China Statistical Yearbook*, Beijing, 1995, p.59, table 3–1.

Chuang, H. C., *The Great Proletarian Cultural Revolution A Terminological Study*, Studies in Chinese Communist Terminology, no 12, Center for Chinese Studies, Institute of International Studies, University of California, Berkeley, California, August 1967.

——, August 1968, *The Little Red Book and Current Chinese Language*, Studies in Chinese Communist Terminology, no 13, Center for Chinese Studies, Institute of International Studies, University of California, Berkeley, California.

Cui, Jianxin, 'hanyu kouyu zhong de rongyu xianxiang', (The Phenomenon of Redundancy in Colloquial Chinese), in Xing Gongwan et al. (eds), *hanyu yanjiu* (Research on Chinese), vol. 3, Nankai daxue chubanshe, Tianjin, 1993.

Defrancis, John, *Nationalism and Language Reform in China*, Princeton University Press, Princeton, 1953.

DeFrancis, John, *The Chinese Language, Fact and Fantasy*, University of Hawaii Press, Honolulu, 1984

Dittmer, Lowell and Chen Ruoxi, *Ethics and Rhetoric of the Chinese Cultural Revolution*, Studies in Chinese Terminology, no, 9, The Centre for Chinese Studies, Institute of East Asian Studies, University of California, 1981.

Driscoli, Lucy and Kenji Toda, *Chinese Calligraphy*, Paragon Book Reprint Corp., New York, 1964.

Ebrey, Patricia Buckley (ed.), *Chinese Civilisation: A Sourcebook*, second edition, the Free Press, New York, 1993.

Elvin, Mark, *The Patterns of Chinese Past*, University of California Press, Stanford, 1973.

Erbaugh, M. S., 'Southern Chinese Dialects as a Medium for Reconciliation within Greater China', *Language and Society* 24, (1) March 1995, pp. 79–94.

Fairbank, John King and Edwin Reischauer, *Tradition and Transformation*, Allen & Unwin, Sydney, 1989.

Fairbank, John King, *China—A New History*, Harvard University Press, Cambridge, Mass., and London, 1992.

Fazzioli, Edoardo, *Understanding Chinese Characters, A Beginner's Guide to the Chinese Language*, William Collins Sons & Co. Ltd, London, English Translation 1987.

Fitzgerald, C. P., *China, A Shorter Cultural History*, Century Hutchison Publishing Group, Melbourne, first published in 1935, revised edition, 1987.

Forrest, R. A. D., *The Chinese Language*, 2nd edition, Faber and Faber Ltd, London, 1965.

Georges, Jean, *Writing the Story of Alphabets and Scripts*, English translation, Thames and Hudson Ltd, London and Harry N. Abrams, Inc., New York, 1992.

Georges, Jean, *Writing the Story of Alphabets and Scripts*, English translation, Thames and Hudson Ltd, London and Harry N. Abrams, Inc., New York, 1992.

Gray, Jack, 'Rebellions and Revolutions, China from the 1800s to the 1980s', in J.M. Roberts (ed.)*The Short Oxford History of the Modern World Series*, Oxford University Press, Oxford, New York, Toronto, 1990.

Greenbaum, Sydney, *The Oxford English Grammar*, Oxford University Press, 1996.

Guan Erjin and Tian Lin, 'ruhe shixian hanzi biaozhunhua', (How to standardise the use of characters), *zhongguo yuwen*, 2, Yuwen chubanshe, Beijing, 1981.

Hansen, Chad, *Language and Logic in Ancient China*, University of Michigan Press, Ann Arbor, 1983.

Harrell S. and Ayi, B., Combining Ethnic Heritage and National Unity: A Paradox of Nuosu (Yi) Language Textbooks in China, *Bulletin of Concerned Asian Scholars*, vol. 30 no. 2, 1998, pp. 62–71.

Hartmann, R. R. K. and F. C. Stork, *Dictionary of Language and Linguistics*, London, Applied Sciences Publishers Ltd, reprint, 1973. (Chinese version translated by Changzhu H. et al., Shanghai cishu chubanshe, Shanghai, 1981, pp. 169, 379.)

Hartmann, R. R. K. and F. C. Stork, *Dictionary of Language and Linguistics*, reprint, Applied Science Publishers Ltd, London, 1973.

Hartmann, R. R. K. and F. C. Stork, *Dictionary of Language and Linguistics*, Applied Science Publishers Ltd, London, reprint, 1973

He Jiu Ying, Hu Shuangbao and Zhang Meng et al. (eds.), *zhong guo han zi wen hua da guan* (Aspects of Chinese Character Culture), Beijing daxue chubanshe, 1995.

Hirth, Friederick and Rockhill, W. W,. *Chau Ju-hua: His work on the Chinese and Arab Trade in the Twelfth and Thirteenth Centuries, Entitled Chu-fan-chi*, 1911, Printing Office of the Imperial Academy of Sciences, St Petersburg, reprinted by Cheng-wen Publishing Co., Taipei, 1970.

Hisa, T. A., *A Terminological Study of the Hia-Fang Movement*, Studies in Chinese Communist Terminology, no. 10, Center for Chinese Studies, Institute of International Studies, University of California, Berkeley, California, February 1962.

——, *The Commune in Retreat as Evidenced in Terminology and Semantics*, Studies in Chinese Communist Terminology, no. 11, Center for Chinese Studies, Institute of International Studies, University of California, Berkeley.

Hodge, Robert and Kam Louie, *The Politics of the Chinese Language: The Art of Reading the Dragon*, Routledge, London, 1998.

Hodge, Robert and Kam Louie, *The Politics of the Chinese Language: The Art of Reading the Dragon*, Routledge, London, 1998.

Hu Mingyang, 'Beijing hu de chengwei xitong', (The Format of Addressing in Beijing Dialect), in Xing Gongwan et al. (eds), *hanyu yanjiu* (Research on Chinese), vol. 3, Nankai daxue chubanshe, Tianjin, 1993.

Hu, Jerome, P. and Stephen C. Lee, *A Basic Chinese Vocabulary*, Longman Cheshire, Melbourne, 1989.

Huddleston, Rodney, *Introduction to the Grammar of English*, Cambridge University Press, 1984.

Kennedy, George A., 'Word-Class in Classical Chinese', in Tien-yi Li (ed.), *Selected Works of George A. Kennedy*, Far Eastern Publications, New Haven, 1964, pp. 423–33.

Kratochril, Paul, *The Chinese Language Today: Features of an Emerging Standard*, Hutchinson University Library, London, 1968.

Laufer, Berthold, 'Sino-Iranica: Chinese Contributions to the History of Civilisation in Ancient Iran', *Anthropological Series*, vol. 15, no. 3, 1919, Field Museum of Natural History, Publication 201, Chicago.

Li, C. & S. Thompson, *Mandarin Chinese: A Functional Reference Grammar*, University of California Press, Berkeley, 1981.

Li Chi, *A Provisional System of Grammar for Teaching Chinese* with Introduction and Commentary, Studies in Chinese Communist Terminology no. 6-7, Center for Chinese Studies, Institute of International Studies, University of California, Berkeley, California, June 1960.

——, February 1962 *New Features in Chinese Grammatical Usage*, Studies in Chinese Communist Terminology no. 9, Center for Chinese Studies, Institute of International Studies, University of California, Berkeley, California.

Li, Chi, *General Trends of Chinese Linguistic Changes under Communist Rule*, Studies in Chinese Communist Terminology, no. 1, East Asia Studies, Institute of International Studies, University of California, Berkeley, California, July 1956.

——, July 1956, *Preliminary Study of Selected Terms*, Studies in Chinese Communist Terminology, no. 2, East Asia Studies, Institute of International Studies, University of California, Berkeley, California.

——, December 1958, *The Use of Figurative Language in Communist China*, Studies in Chinese Communist Terminology, no. 5, East Asia Studies, Institute of International Studies, University of California, Berkeley, California.

——, April 1957, *Part I, Literary and Colloquial Terms in New Usage, Part II, Terms Topped by Numbers*, Studies in Chinese Communist Terminology, no 3, East Asia Studies, Institute of International Studies, University of California, Berkeley, California.

——, December 1957, *Part I, The Communist Term 'The Common Language' and Related Terms, Part II, Dialectal Terms in Common Usage, Part III, Literary and Colloquial Terms in New Usage*, Studies in Chinese Communist Terminology no. 4, East Asia Studies, Institute of International Studies, University of California, Berkeley, California.

——, June 1960, *A Provisional System of Grammar for Teaching Chinese* with Introduction and Commentary, Studies in Chinese Communist Terminology, no. 6-7, Center for Chinese Studies, Institute of International Studies University of California, Berkeley, California.

Li, Dejin and Cheng Meihua, *A Practical Chinese Grammar for Foreigners*, Beijing: Sinolingua, 1988.

Li Leyi, *hanzi yanbian wu bai li* (Tracing the Roots of Chinese Characters: 500 Cases), Beijing, Beijing Language and Culture University Press, 1993.

Li, Lincoln, *Student Nationalism in China, 1924-1949*, State University of New York Press, Albany, 1994.

Li, Rui, *Li Rui wangshi zayi* (Memoirs of Li Rui), Jiangsu renmin chubanshe, Nanjing, 1995.

Li, Sijing, *hanyu r yinshi yanjiu* (A Study on the History of r in Chinese), revised edition, Shangwu yinshuguan, Beijing, 1994.

Li, Sijing, *hanyu r yinshi yanjiu* (A Study on the History of r in Chinese), revised edition, Shangwu yinshuguan, Beijing, 1994.

Li, W. and Guzhang, W. et al., *xiandai hanyu jiangzuo* (lectures on Modern Chinese), Zhishi chubanshe, Beijing, 1983, pp. 49, 52.

Li Xiaoding, *hanzi shihua* (On the History of Chinese Characters), Taipei, Lianjing, 1977.

Li, Xingjian (ed.), *zhongguo yuyanxue nianjian* (Chinese Linguistics Yearbook), Yuwen chubanshe, Beijing, 1993.

Li, Xingjian (ed.), *zhongguo yuyanxue nianjian* (Chinese Linguistics Yearbook), Yuwen chubanshe, Beijing, 1993.

Li, Y. C., Robert L. Cheng, Larry Foster, Shang H. Ho, John Y. Hou, and Moira Yip, *Mandarin Chinese: A Practical Reference Grammar for Students and Teachers*, Taipei: The Crane Publishing Co. Chinese Materials Centre Publications, vol. I, 1984 and vol. II 1989.

Light, Timothy, 'Bilingualism and Standard Language in the People's Republic of China', in James E. Alatis (ed.), *Current Issues in Bilingual Education*, Georgetown University Press, Washington DC, 1980.

Lindqvist, Cecilia, *China, Empire of the Written Symbol*, London: Harvill, 1989.

Little, W. and Onions, C.T. et al., *The Shorter English Oxford Dictionary on Historical Principles*, vol. 1, third edition, Guild Publishing, London, 1987, p.1174.

Liu, Jian, Jiang Lansheng et al., *jindai hanyu xuci yanjiu* (A Study of Empty Words in Modern Chinese), Yuwen chubanshe, Beijing, 1992.

Lü, Shuxiang, *yuwen changtan* (Talk about Language), Sanlian shudian, Beijing, 1980.

Lü, Shuxiang, *yuwen changtan* (Talk about Language), Sanlian shudian, Beijing, 1980.

Marney, John, *A Handbook of Mandarin Chinese Grammar*, San Francisco, 1972.

McDonald, Edward, *Clause and Verbal Group Systems in Chinese: a Text-Based Functional Approach*, unpublished PhD thesis, School of English, Linguistics & Media, Macquarie University, 1998.

Meisner, Maurice, *Mao's China and After Mao, A History of the People's Republic*, The Free Press, New York, and Collier MacMillan Publishers, London, revised edition, 1986.

Nairong Q. (ed.), *hanyu yuyanxue* (Chinese Linguistics), Beijing yuyan xueyuan chubanshe, Beijing, 1995, pp. 6, 15.

Nankai Hanyuyan wenhua xueyuan, *hanyuyan wenhua yanjiu* (Study on Cultural Aspects of the Chinese Language), Tianjin renmin chubanshe, Tianjin, 1994.

Needham, Joseph, *Science and Civilisation in China*, Cambridge University Press, 1954 onwards.

——, 1979, *The Grand Titration, Science and Society in East and West*, George Allen & Unwin, London, second impression.

Norman, Jerry, *Chinese*, Cambridge University Press, Cambridge, 1988, p. 58, 78.

Norman, Jerry, *Chinese*, Cambridge University Press, first published in 1988

Pei, Mario and Frank Gaynor, *Dictionary of Linguistics*, Littlefield, Adams & Co., 1975.

Pickowicz, Paul, *Marxist Literary Thought and China: A Conceptual Framework*, Studies in Chinese Communist Terminology no. 18, Center for Chinese Studies, Institute of International Studies, University of California, Berkeley, California, 1980.

Pulleyblank, Edwin G., *Outline of Classical Chinese Grammar*, Vancouver, UBC Press, 1995, reprint 1996.

Pulleyblank, Edwin, G., *Outline of Classical Chinese Grammar*, University of British Columbia Press, Vancouver, 1996.

Putian, J., shilun xiandai hanyu gudigshi de leixing he jiben tedian, (On the Categories and Basic Features of Set Expressions in Modern Chinese), *hanyuyan wenhua yanjiu* (Study on Cultural Aspects of the Chinese Language), Nankai Hanyuyan wenhua xueyuan, Tianjin renmin chubanshe, Tianjin, 1994, pp. 49–64.

Qi, Xigui, *wenzixue gaiyao* (An Outline Study of Characters), Shangwu yinshuguan, Beijing, 1988.

Qian, Nairong (ed.), *hanyu yuyanxue* (Chinese Linguistics), Beijing yuyan xueyuan chubanshe, Beijing, 1995, p. 1.

Qian, Nairong (ed.), *hanyu yuyanxue* (Chinese Linguistics), Beijing yuyan xueyuan chubanshe, Beijing, 1995, p. 107.

Quirk, Randolph & Sydney Greenbaum, *A University Grammar of English*, Longman, 1974.

——, 1985, *A Student's Grammar of the English Language* Longman.

Quirk, Randolph, Sydney Greenbaum, Geoffrey Leech, and Jan Svartvik, *A Grammar of Contemporary English*, Longman, 1972.

——, 1985, indexed by David Crystal, *A Comprehensive Grammar of The English Language*, Longman, 1985.

Ramsey, Robert, S., *The Languages of China*, New Jersey, Princeton University Press, 1987.

Ramsey, Robert, *The Languages of China*, Princeton University Press, Princeton, New Jersey, 1987.

Ramsey, S.R., *The Languages of China*, Princeton University Press, 1989, pp.250–61.

Rodman, Fromkin, *An Introduction to Language*, second edition, Holt, Rinehart and Winston, New York, 1978.

Serbolt, Peter J. and Gregory Kuei-ke Chiang, *Language Reforms in China, Documents and Commentary*, M. E. Sharpe, Inc., University Microfilms International, Michigan, 1978.

Serruys, Paul L. M., *Survey of the Chinese Language Reform and the Anti-Illiteracy Movement in Communist China*, Studies in Chinese Communist Terminology, no. 8, Center for Chinese Studies, Institute of International Studies, University of California, Berkeley, California, February 1962.

Shao Jingmin and Shi Youwei (eds), *wenhua yuyan zhonguo chao* (the Tide of Cultural Linguistics in China), Yuwen chubanshe, Beijing, 1995.

Shao Jingmin and Shi Youwei (eds.), *wenhua yuyan zhonguo chao* (the Tide of Cultural Linguistics in China), Yuwen chubanshe, Beijing, 1995.

Spence, Jonathan D., *The Search for Modern China*, Norton, New York, 1990.

Spence, Jonathan, D., *The Gate of Heavenly Peace: the Chinese and Their Revolution*, Penguin Books, New York, 1982.

Su, Peicheng, *hanzi jianhua yu fanti zi dui zhao zidian* (A Dictionary of Traditional and Simplified Characters in Contrast), Beijing, Zhongxin Chubanshe, 1992.

Syrokomla-Stefanowska, A. D. and Mabel Lee, *Basic Chinese Grammar & Sentence Patterns*, Wild Peony, Broadway, NSW, 1986.

Tiee, Henry Hung-Yeh and Donald M. Lance, *A Reference Grammar of Chinese Sentences with Exercises*, The University of Arizona Press, 1986.

Tien, Teresa, *A Practical Handbook of Modern Chinese Grammar*, Chinese Materials Centre, Taiwan, 1986.

Wang, Gungwu, *The Chineseness of China, Selected Essays*, Oxford University Press, Hong Kong, 1991.

Wang, Li, Wang Guzhang et al., *xiandai hanyu jiangzuo* (Lectures on Modern Chinese), Zhishi chubanshe, Beijing, 1983.

Wang, Li, Wang Guzhang et al., *xiandai hanyu jiangzuo* (Lectures on Modern Chinese), Zhishi chubanshe, Beijing, 1983, p. 98.

Wang Tiekun et al., *hanzi guifan tongsu jianhua* (Lectures on Standardisation of Common Characters), Renmin ribao chubanshe, Beijing, 1994.

Wang, Zhigang and Michael Micklin, 'The Transformation of Naming Practices in Chinese Families: Some Linguistic Clues to Social Change', *International Sociology*, June 1996, vol. 11 (2) pp. 187–212.

Wurm, S. A., Li Rong et al. (eds), *Language Atlas of China*, Longman, Hong Kong, 1987.

Xiao, Shiling et al. (eds), *China's Cultural Heritage: Rediscovering a Past of 7~000 Years*, Beijing: Morning Glory Publishers, 1995.

Xiaolin, Y., *han yu shu mu ci cidian* (A Dictionary of Words Starting with a Numeral), Beijing, Zhong hua shu ju, 1993.

Xie, Wenqing, 'erhua xianxiang de gongneng fenxi', (An analysis of the Function of the Phenomenon of r), in *hanyuyan wenhua yanjiu* (Study on the Cultural Aspects of the Chinese Language), Nankai daxue hanyuyan wenhua xueyuan (ed.), vol. 4, Tianjin Renmin Chubanshe, Tianjin, 1994.

Xing Gongwan et al. (eds), *hanyu yanjiu* (Research on Chinese), vol. 3, Nankai daxue chubanshe, Tianjin, 1993.

Xing, Gongwan et al. (eds), *hanyu yanjiu* (Research on Chinese), vol. 3, Nankai daxue chubanshe, Tianjin, 1993.

Yee, Dennis K., *Chinese Romanization Self-Study Guide, Comparison of Yale and Pinyin Romanizations Comparisons of Pinyin and Wade-Giles Romanizations*, Honolulu, The University of Hawaii Press, 1975.

Yip, Po-ching and Don Rimmington, *Chinese, An Essential Grammar*, Routledge, 1997.

——, 1998a, *Basic Chinese, A Grammar and Workbook*, Routledge.

——, 1998b, *Intermediate Chinese, A Grammar and Workbook*, Routledge.

Yuan, C., *shehui yuyanxue* (Sociolinguistics), Xuelin chubanshe, Shanghai, 1983, p. 219.

Zhao, Yongxin, *Essentials of Chinese Grammar for Foreigners*, Beijing yuyan xueyuan chubanshe, 2nd printing, 1994.

Zhou, Fagao, *lun zhonguo yuyanxue* (On Chinese Linguistics), Chinese University Press, Hong Kong 1980.

Index